Voice Enabling Web Applications: VoiceXML and Beyond

KEN ABBOTT

Apress™

Voice Enabling Web Applications: VoiceXML and Beyond
Copyright ©2002 by Ken Abbott

ISBN (pbk): 1-893115-73-9

Printed and bound in the United States of America 12345678910

Trademarked names may appear in this book. Rather than use a trademark symbol with every occurrence of a trademarked name, we use the names only in an editorial fashion and to the benefit of the trademark owner, with no intention of infringement of the trademark.

Editorial Directors: Dan Appleman, Gary Cornell, Jason Gilmore, Karen Watterson
Marketing Manager: Stephanie Rodriguez
Managing Editor: Grace Wong
Technical Reviewer: Dennis McCarthy
Developmental Editor: Marty Minner
Copy Editor: Nicole LeClerc
Production Editor: Laura Cheu
Compositor: Impressions Book and Journal Services, Inc.
Artists: Susan Glinert Stevens, Impressions Book and Journal Services, Inc.
Indexer: Valerie Haynes Perry
Cover Designer: Tom Debolski

Distributed to the book trade in the United States by Springer-Verlag New York, Inc.,175 Fifth Avenue, New York, NY, 10010
and outside the United States by Springer-Verlag GmbH & Co. KG, Tiergartenstr. 17, 69112 Heidelberg, Germany.
In the United States, phone 1-800-SPRINGER, email orders@springer-ny.com, or visit http://www.springer-ny.com.
Outside the United States, fax +49 6221 345229, email orders@springer.de, or visit http://www.springer.de.

For information on translations, please contact Apress directly at 901 Grayson Street, Suite 204, Berkeley, CA 94710.
Phone 510-549-5930, fax: 510-549-5939, email info@apress.com, or visit http://www.apress.com.

Contents

Author's Note on VoiceXML 2.0

THE FIRST VERSION of VoiceXML, VoiceXML 1.0, was officially released in May 2000 by the VoiceXML Forum. Subsequently, the VoiceXML Forum turned over control of the VoiceXML specification to the World Wide Web Consortium (W3C). The next version of VoiceXML, popularly known as VoiceXML 2.0, has been pending throughout the writing and production of this book, but still has not been publicly released as of mid-October 2001.

As anyone who works with software technology knows, one and one half years between releases of a burgeoning technology is an eternity. The delay has been due to internal issues within the W3C regarding intellectual property rights. In the past, the W3C has been a strong of advocate of open-source (public domain) technologies. Modern reality is that many, if not most, new and evolving technologies are being developed by parties who hold some intellectual rights to the technology, so the W3C must adapt. VoiceXML is one such technology under the W3C's purview (but not the only one).

As a result of this turmoil, the anxiously awaited VoiceXML 2.0 specification has been pending release as a W3C Working Draft for over a year. Both the internal deliberations of the W3C and the contents of any unreleased work-in-progress are closed to the public. Therefore, the specification cannot be discussed publicly, and there has been no firm official information from the W3C about when it can be. (And the W3C finds itself in the unique position of being an open standards body fighting fiercely to keep a much-requested standard secret.)

People who buy technical books want information that is up-to-date and timely. This presented a dilemma to authors and publishers. To provide timely information on an infant technology such as VoiceXML, books are often rushed into production. On the other hand, to provide up-to-date information, books are often timed to appear as soon as a particular new technology is released. For books on VoiceXML, the choice was to rush to market with books on VoiceXML 1.0 (already decrepit in Web time and due to be superseded by the imminent VoiceXML 2.0), or wait for VoiceXML 2.0 (which was making little publicly visible progress toward release).

Initially, Apress and I decided that the smart thing to do was write the manuscript, wait for VoiceXML 2.0 publication, and then follow as soon as possible with publication of this book, compatible with VoiceXML 2.0. However, books don't hold well in captivity, and as months passed with no resolution to uncertainty concerning the schedule for release of VoiceXML 2.0, we decided that the book needed to get into people's hands.

So, strictly speaking, this book can only claim that it is compatible with the VoiceXML 1.0 specification and that an online supplement will reconcile any incompatibilities when VoiceXML 2.0 appears. However, due to the long gestation of VoiceXML 2.0, a fair amount of information about VoiceXML 2.0 has become publicly known, whether the W3C likes it or not. So there is some good news:

- Based on publicly known information, I have anticipated VoiceXML 2.0 throughout the book.

- All indications are that VoiceXML 2.0 is an incremental improvement on VoiceXML 1.0. For learning VoiceXML, it doesn't matter which specification you're using.

- This book is not just about VoiceXML. It's about voice enabling Web applications, and there is a lot of valuable information herein about integrating voice with Web technologies and with existing applications that can be found nowhere else.

- When VoiceXML 2.0 becomes available, so will information to update this book—you can find it online at
  `http://www.apress.com/catalog/book/1893115739/`.

So indulge your interest—use this book to start voice enabling your Web applications right now!

Kenneth R. Abbott
October 2001
Holliston, MA
`abbott@acm.org`

Preface

This book is about two topics that I've pretty well mixed together: using voice to access the Web and the VoiceXML language. Of the two, the former topic is the bigger, more conceptual one, and it is the one that will wear the best over time. I believe that VoiceXML will enable the use of voice to access the Web in a big way. VoiceXML is a hot new enabling technology destined to live its meteoric life in Web time: new and brilliant today but commonplace tomorrow. However, in the grand tradition of computer technology, details get the attention and the major trends take care of themselves.

I am a "big picture" person, and for me, the key to mastering the ever-changing details of technology is to keep the details in context. My years in the computer software industry have taught me that not everyone thinks the way I do, and for many technically oriented people, "God is in the details." In this book I have attempted to strike a balance between providing context and explaining the current technical details.

In the admixture of voice, computers, and the Web, I've observed the following overlapping constituencies with strong interest in seeing VoiceXML succeed.

- One constituency is people with backgrounds in telephony and highly customized voice applications. They've been making telephones and automated voice systems work together for years using expensive, special-purpose gateways and expensive, proprietary software.

- Another group is voice technologists, who are grounded in the deep complexities of voice recognition, voice synthesis, and natural language processing. They have been working for decades on a complex and frustrating technology, and they feel it is now getting close to the point where the masses can use it.

- Web enthusiasts are technically oriented people who are deeply involved with the development, care, and feeding of Web applications and the Web itself. To them, voice is a new technology to be quickly mastered and assimilated.

- Finally, there are technology integrators, who occupy the shadowy realm between business and technology. They are interested in finding better ways to do business using technology. Technology integrators tend to be interested in markets, products, architectures, and standards—they are the architects and general contractors of the computer-system building industry.

In terms of my personal background, I am part Web enthusiast and part technology integrator. My background is in computer software, primarily large-scale applications, and my current specialty is helping clients develop and deploy large-scale business applications on the Web. Proving the technical feasibility of an architecture or design is a vital part of what I do, so also I dive in and develop prototypes and pilots.

In this book, I have tried to speak to all constituencies. I introduce and review, but do not labor over, material that may be familiar to some and not to others. I've tried to give you the same mixture of abstract and concrete advice I give my clients. In this book, I have established a context for voice technology in general and VoiceXML in particular; I have architecturally "sited" voice and VoiceXML relative to other major technology landmarks such as XML and application servers; and I have provided a step-by-step tutorial for hands-on beginners and a working prototype for advanced users.

What does this book give you that others don't? Most books you see on the shelf with VoiceXML in the title will have some sort of tutorial, walk-through, or annotated examples of VoiceXML programs—most will have extensive reference material covering all details of the VoiceXML language. This book has those things. However, this book also provides a thorough grounding in what it takes to actually use VoiceXML effectively in the complex, polyglot world of modern Web applications. In terms of enabling voice access to a Web site, VoiceXML is but one specialist niche in a much broader landscape that includes stylesheets, servlets, databases, and so on. In this book, these related technologies are approached as a professional systems designer or architect would approach them: with basic knowledge of the technology, with respect for unseen details, and with a desire to put the technology to work as quickly and painlessly as possible.

Structure of the Book

To achieve the balance between context and detail discussed previously, I have laid the book out into the following parts.

> Part I (Chapters 1–3) takes a retrospective view on two key technologies that VoiceXML brings together: speech and the Web. This part provides valuable context for understanding how these technologies came to be converging now, and it provides a base for extrapolating how the merged technologies will progress together.

> Part II (Chapters 4–9) focuses on the nuts and bolts of the VoiceXML language. Using a Simplified Personal Information Manager as a specimen application, Part II guides you through an initial analysis of the application (Chapter 4), introduces basic VoiceXML concepts (Chapter 5), helps you set up your own VoiceXML development environment using software from the companion CD (Chapter 6), and leads you through a hands-on VoiceXML tutorial (Chapter 7). With the tutorial mastered, Chapters 8–10 examine

advanced, pragmatic issues concerning the effective design and development of voice interfaces using the full power of the VoiceXML language.

Part III (Chapters 11–13) dollies back from the details of the VoiceXML language and explores the issues involved in building a single Web application that incorporates multiple access modes, such as voice and graphical interfaces. Chapter 11 briefly reviews major technologies that are used in enterprise Web applications, including XML, XSL, JavaServer Pages, and application servers. Chapter 12 introduces a transformational approach for putting together the various technologies, including VoiceXML, into a scalable, multiple access mode architecture. Chapter 13 presents a working prototype that demonstrates the transformational architecture. Detailed instructions are provided for installing the prototype from the companion CD, and the various components are dissected. Finally, Chapter 14 explores future directions for VoiceXML.

Appendix A (A Quick Reference to VoiceXML 1.0 Syntax) contains condensed reference material on the VoiceXML language. The reference material is geared toward providing an experienced VoiceXML programmer exactly the information he or she needs while in the throes of a coding frenzy.

Companion CD

The companion CD contains all the software you need to begin developing VoiceXML applications on your PC. The CD includes IBM WebSphere Voice Server SDK 1.5, IBM WebSphere Studio (trial edition), Allaire JRun 3.1 (developer version), Altova XML Spy IDE for XML (30-day evaluation), plus an assortment of goodies, such XML Quick Reference Cards from MulberryTech and a small gallery of computer-synthesized voices to break in your new headset.

Building Up Your Courage

If you're still not sure that you're ready to take the plunge into the world of the voice-enabled Web, I suggest you visit some of the major resource sites on the Web. You'll see that there are a lot of people getting excited about combining voice and the Web, and there are a lot of resources for newbies. I recommend starting with the following sites.

- VoiceXML Forum (`http://www.voicexml.org/`): The VoiceXML Forum is the industry consortium that first standardized VoiceXML. This site has lots of information about VoiceXML, including FAQs, technical resources, and details about important activities such as user group meetings. In addition, there are links to just about every business, individual, and organization active in the VoiceXML area.

- The World Wide Web Consortium (http://www.w3.org/): The W3C is the preeminent standards body for the Web. The W3C is now responsible for VoiceXML as well as related standards for speech markup languages, speech grammar languages, and so on. The W3C is also the authoritative source for information about Web infrastructure technologies such as HTTP, HTML, and MIME. The site offers FAQs and tutorials for newbies and concise technical documents for experts.

- XML.org (http://www.xml.org/): This site is the best jumping-off point for immersing yourself in XML. XML.org is dedicated to promoting the use of XML, and the site provides links to FAQs, books online, online courses, examples, free software tools, and much more.

After you have surfed around a bit, I think you'll discover two things.

- Taken individually, the component technologies involved in a voice-enabled Web application (such as VoiceXML, XSL, server pages, and so on) are fairly accessible and can be tamed by any experienced technical person.

- Quite of number of component technologies must be lashed together to create a working voice-enabled Web application, but there's not much documentation about the architecture and integration required to make all the components work together smoothly. That is why the book in your hands is valuable.

Acknowledgments

Thanks to Dennis McCarthy, both for getting me turned on to this whole "VoiceXML thing" and for providing valuable comments and suggestions as the principal technical reviewer for the manuscript. Thanks to Sue Spielman of Switchback Software, who provided technical feedback from the perspective of an expert Cocoon user and XML developer.

Special thanks to my wife Susan, who has seen more of me around the house than she thought possible or tolerable, and who struggled through the first three pages of the manuscript and concluded, "It's wonderful, dear." Which was exactly the right thing to say.

Ken Abbott
August 2001
Holliston, MA
abbott@acm.org

Part One

Retrospective on Voice
and the Web

THIS PART INTRODUCES and reviews the key concepts that underlie voice technology and the World Wide Web. Voice technology and the Web have very different origins. Understanding the context and trajectory of each technology will help answer many of the questions that will pop up in subsequent parts as you grapple with the technical details: Why do things work this way? Why isn't this obvious feature standardized?

Chapter 1 provides a brief introduction to voice and its significance. Chapter 2 explores how and why voice and the Web are converging. Chapter 3 closes this part with a review of how the Web has evolved technically and draws some parallels to the future evolution of VoiceXML.

CHAPTER 1

The Role of Voice on the Web

PUNDITS OF THE INFORMATION AGE portray the Internet as a tidal wave of innovation that is sweeping human culture. Skeptics, Luddites, and technical curmudgeons point out that if the Internet is a revolution, it is one limited to the elite minority with regular access to computers. Both sides have a point. Those who encounter the Internet often find the experience transforming, but not everyone has that opportunity.

However, very soon the Internet will be accessible to pretty much everyone as a result of technological advances that will enable people to access the Internet from their homes, workplaces, cars, and so on. Access will be through a low-cost, ubiquitous "Internet appliance": the telephone. The enabling technology is voice technology, which will enable people to interact with computers over the telephone using their voices.

The idea of talking to computers has been around as long as computers have. The technology to make computers recognize voices and generate speech in response has been developing for decades, and it is still imperfect. Within a constrained conversational context, however, voice technology has recently become good enough that computers and people can understand each other tolerably well.

VoiceXML is a new, first-cut technology that holds the promise of making voice interfaces as easy to build, deploy, and use as the graphical interfaces that currently dominate the Web. What's significant about VoiceXML is that it reaches an audience much larger than just the digerati who currently populate cyberspace—it has the potential to reach everyone that uses a phone.

Using Sight and Sound Together

There is no doubt that human beings perceive, use, and respond to sight and sound very differently. Sound is the medium of music. Sight is the medium of pictures, of reading, and of art. Perhaps because it's omnidirectional and works day or night, sound is the original form of communication between people. Perhaps because it's immediate and information can be absorbed quickly, sight is the popular medium of communication in our technological age.

Due to its technical history and orientation, the Web has favored the explosion of visual interfaces over auditory interfaces. Much of the thrust of new developments in user interfaces in the Information Age has been to increase the rate at which information can be exchanged and the volume of information available at any given moment. (Think 21" monitors set at high resolution.) This approach has favored the visual over the audible, because visual interfaces are "scalable"—to increase the amount of visual information, you simply increase the transfer rate and the display capacity. On the other hand, speech cannot be significantly speeded up without becoming incomprehensible. To increase the amount of information conveyed through speech, you increase the length of the conversation.

As Table 1-1 shows, the different characteristics of sight and speech make them useful in different situations.

Table 1-1. Characteristics of Sight and Speech

CHARACTERISTIC	SIGHT		SPEECH	
	STRENGTH	**WEAKNESS**	**STRENGTH**	**WEAKNESS**
Conveying information	Immediate and excellent for conveying relationships between things.	May require knowledge of symbol vocabularies.	Good for concisely conveying emotions and imprecise/ ambiguous information.	More information requires more time.
Robustness	Pictures can be understood by people with different levels of knowledge and experience.	Degraded by poor viewing conditions (poor lighting, no moni-tor available, and so on).	Highly robust and error tolerant. Conversations can occur in a wide variety of situations.	Doesn't work between people speaking different languages.

Now that both sight and speech are viable modes for accessing the Web, there are some interesting questions to be answered.

- What types of interactions are more appropriate for speech, and what types are more appropriate for sight?

- If the same information can be accessed by either speech or sight, then how is the information structured so that it can be effectively rendered into the different media?

- Can and should the interfaces be merged?

For example, consider the adage "A picture is worth a thousand words." A picture that can be perceived instantaneously by the eyes may require a long description to convey similar information through speech. On the other hand, audible speech can rapidly convey emotions and shades of meaning that are lost in sight-mediated representations (think of sending e-mail versus talking on a phone). Entering names and addresses through a graphical interface requires manipulating mice and keyboards, as opposed to simply saying the names and addresses.

At this time, we are just becoming able to use speech as a means of (limited) communication between people and machines. This book is about a key enabler of this limited capability: VoiceXML. VoiceXML, in its current form, is strictly concerned with speech interaction. However, it is important to bear in mind that sight and speech are complementary, each with its own set of strengths and weaknesses.

The Convergence of Speech and the Web

What Is VoiceXML?

VOICEXML IS A PROGRAMMING LANGUAGE for scripting voice interactions between a computer and a person. The basic element of interaction is a spoken dialog in which the computer produces spoken prompts to elicit spoken responses from the user. VoiceXML prompts may be recorded or generated using Text-to-Speech (TTS) synthesis. Spoken user responses are processed using speech recognition and grammars defined in the VoiceXML program. Users may also respond through a keypad (DTMF[1]), as defined in the program.

Meet the Technical Parents

On hearing the term "VoiceXML," people new to the technology often notice the Extensible Markup Language (XML) connection but fail to catch the "computer speech recognition and synthesis" implication. In fact, VoiceXML draws heavily from the lineage of both, and its greatest technical innovation is to make computerized voice technology available and accessible to the masses.

Speech Recognition and Synthesis

The history of the research and development of computer speech recognition and synthesis is long and somewhat frustrating. The possibility of communicating with a computer the way people communicate with each other has seemed tantalizingly close since the dawn of computing, but it still has not been realized. In one of those unexpected paradoxes of high technology, it turns out to be easier for a computer to beat a person at chess than it is for it to achieve a child's ability to talk.

---

[1] DTMF stands for Dual Tone Multi-Frequency, which is techno-speak for the sounds a Touch-Tone phone makes when you press the keys.

Considerable amounts of intellectual capital have been spent developing techniques to automate the recognition and comprehension of language. Efforts have spanned many venerable fields of study, including linguistics, computer science, mathematics, statistics, and psychology. In the pursuit of results, techniques have run from the heights of elegant, abstract mathematical theory to the depths of grubby, empirical pragmatism. The bottom line: Automated speech recognition has improved, and continues to do so, but it is still far from perfect.

Speech synthesis has had a similar record of continued improvement. At the end of the day, computers still talk funny, but people can understand computers better than computers can understand people.

Sound, Speech, and Meaning

Something you hear is *sound.* A sequence of sounds people make with their voices with the intent to communicate is *speech. Meaning* is the message conveyed when speech is successfully understood.

During a conversation, several distinct processes occur. *Speaking* can be defined as the generation of understandable sounds using the voice. *Hearing* is the perception of those sounds as speech and the chunking of sounds into units of speech. *Cognition* is the assembling of speech units into an understandable, meaningful message. This speech processing model is illustrated in Figure 2-1.

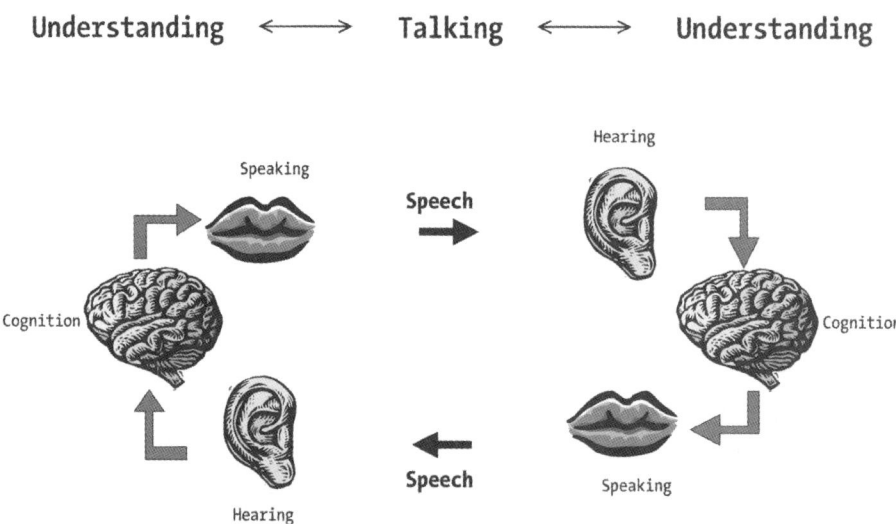

Figure 2-1. Speech processing model

When people of a certain age hear about "talking to a computer," they often conjure up images of HAL from the film *2001: A Space Odyssey*. HAL was an amazing computer that could talk and see. He sounded a little nerdy, but he could carry on a conversation with no problem whatsoever, and his eyesight was excellent. In the year 2001, HAL is still amazing. Today's computers approach HAL in their ability to speak understandably and to recognize the words that a person speaks. However, in the area of cognition, HAL is still far beyond our current technological capabilities. Consider the fact that HAL could not only understand natural human language, but he could also lip-read it (despite his personal lack of lips!).

HAL engenders the false expectation that you can talk to a computer and have a conversation, just as you can strike up a conversation with someone standing in line at the post office. That happens to be exactly what computers can't yet do. That is why VoiceXML encompasses speaking and hearing but has no cognition model other than standard computer programming.

Speaker-Dependent versus Speaker-Independent Speech Recognition

Speech recognition technologists make a critical distinction between *speaker-dependent* and *speaker-independent* speech recognition. A person must *enroll* with a speaker-dependent voice system before using it. Enrolling means going through a process of training the computer to recognize an individual's voice—that is, by having the person read text that the computer provides in the person's habitual environment. Once the computer has "imprinted" on an individual, it can recognize a significant portion of that person's vocabulary in any context, but it makes more errors recognizing other people's speech than it did before enrollment. Notice that when speaker-dependent systems train, they are training not only on the individual's voice, but on the environment as well (for instance, your voice as it sounds through a headset microphone in your office). Therefore, a controlled environment is a necessary ingredient for speaker-dependent speech recognition. Some dictation systems even go so far as to suggest re-enrolling if you change your microphone.

On the other hand, speaker-independent speech recognition strives to recognize what a person is saying without knowing anything about the person or his or her environment. This means that the recognizer must be able to accommodate all the variables that people unconsciously adjust for: accents; differences between men's, women's, and children's voices; level of excitement; and so on. These natural voice variations are compounded by a variety of environmental obstacles: background noise; poor phone connections; fidelity variations between phones, speakerphones, and headsets; and so on.

Using speaker-dependent speech recognition, current systems make errors at tolerable rates. Dictation systems such as Dragon NaturallySpeaking and IBM ViaVoice make errors at a rate that some people find annoying, but still useful. Speaker-independent speech recognition works with reasonable success when the recognizer is working with a constrained grammar. In other words, success is greatest when the recognizer is not trying to understand what someone says out of the blue; it works when it has the simpler job of matching what the user said against a predefined set of options (for instance, a list of names or a menu of commands). Speaker-independent speech recognition does not work in unconstrained situations. You still can't just walk up to a computer and strike up a conversation.

VoiceXML uses speaker-independent speech recognition. VoiceXML interactions are programmed, structured dialogs where the computer is always aware that the user is using a finite vocabulary of possible utterances.

Markup Languages

Markup languages had their heyday before graphical interfaces and the Web. Markup languages were a way to embed text-formatting instructions into text documents. The text and markup language were entered into a text file using a text editor (which in those pre-GUI days were line-at-a-time monsters). To produce a formatted document, a special formatting program (a word processor) read the text file, interpreted and stripped out the markup instructions, and produced a text file that would print nicely on a selected printer. Because pre-GUI days were also pre–laser printer days, the printer might have been a line printer, a dot matrix printer, or (for the utmost in quality) a daisy wheel printer. All these technologies—markup language–based text processors, command-line text editors, and impact printers—were authoritatively eclipsed by GUIs, WYSIWYG (What You See Is What You Get) editors, and laser printers.

However, the markup language approach solved some difficult publishing problems that WYSIWYG word processors could not. Standard Generalized Markup Language (SGML), a standard developed by IBM, continued to serve a small but loyal market, and as a result it was still vital when someone began envisioning a "World Wide Web."

SGML, HTML, and XML

HTML is a blessing and a curse to its aged parent SGML. It's a blessing because it breathed life into a stagnant technology. It's a curse because it did so with a brash, youthful disregard for the elegance and refinement of its progenitor.

SGML aimed to solve a tough information management problem in technical publishing. Designers and manufacturers of complex systems, such as airplanes, weapons, and electronics systems, are forced to also be publishers of the large volume of technical documentation that must accompany their systems: user manuals, maintenance guides, specifications, and so on. The complexity of the publication and maintenance processes for technical documents rivals (and sometimes exceeds) the complexity of the design and manufacturing processes described therein. (Consider the case where upgrading a single part in a deployed system may require modifications to multiple copies of multiple documents delivered to the customer.)

SGML enables technical publishers to represent complex, interrelated information electronically such that

- The format is neutral with regards to publication technology.

- The information is accessible at subdocument granularity.

- The granules of information can be reused across multiple documents.

SGML is a *metalanguage*, a language used to define other languages. The other languages actually get used to solve problems. HTML and XML are examples of languages defined in the SGML family. In its intended use, SGML is used by a publisher to define a language specific to the problem at hand. For example, Norton Aircraft might define a Norton Aircraft Markup Language (NAML) specific to its airplane part numbering system. Norton Aircraft then captures the technical information for an airplane in NAML.

SGML and its derivatives are *markup languages*. That means the information content is stored interspersed with *tags* that describe the meaning of the information. The analogy is to a publisher's markups, where an editor marks proofs with coded instructions that refer to adjacent text or graphics. *Presentation markup* annotates content with instructions about how to present the content in a given medium (for example, on a video screen). *Content markup* provides information about the meaning and logical structure of the content, which is the same no matter how the content is presented. An SGML language may include a combination of presentation and content markup tags, but in practice, languages tend to fall in one category or the other.

HTML draws power from SGML, but it is an expedient rather than an elegant application of SGML in two senses. First, the syntax of HTML is almost, but not quite, SGML compliant (HTML tags such as <br> aren't proper SGML). Second, HTML muddies the distinction between content and presentation. HTML is a presentation markup language because it describes how things should appear in a Web browser. For example, the HTML <bold> tag describes how text should appear visually, but it provides no hint as to why it should appear that way. Other tags such as <H1> (header level 1) sound like they are describing the logical structure of the document, but in use, they really refer to particular rendering styles.

In contrast, content markup tags content by its meaning (for example, <informalAside>...</informalAside>) and leaves rendering decisions to the renderer. For example, a voice interface might render an informal aside in a whisper, while a Web interface might simply italicize the text. Decisions about rendering into a particular medium can be made while generating presentation markup from content or they can be preprogrammed into the media browser itself.

Development of XML was spurred by a desire to generalize and extend the success of HTML. Technically, the approach was to popularize SGML by creating a simplified subset that would be useful to the broad audience of businesses trying to exchange data over the Web. In its full generality, SGML has some finicky and complex nooks and crannies that are only used to solve the hardest problems. XML removes some of the most obtrusive complexity (and hence some of the power) of SGML by defining a restricted family of SGML-compliant languages. This family shares a strict, but tractable, syntax that mere mortals can learn and use. Notice that in the grand scheme of things, SGML and XML are both metalanguages, while HTML is a single SGML application (that is, an instance).

WML and VXML

HTML has two younger siblings: Wireless Markup Language (WML) and VoiceXML (VXML). In the "family" analogy, one might say that HTML is a young teenager, WML is a toddler, and VXML is a newborn. Both WML and VXML are XML-compliant markup languages.

The term "Wireless Markup Language" seems to imply that there is something special or unique about wireless communication that requires separate handling from other types of communication. In fact, WML does not rely on or exploit the "wireless versus wired" distinction in any essential way. WML is better understood as a low-bandwidth, low-resolution markup language. In other words, WML is targeted at being rendered in environments (devices) with low communications bandwidth, limited display capabilities, and limited computing resources. It was simply a mark of the times that in the late 1990s wireless devices happened to be low-bandwidth, low-resolution devices. In the coming years, when wireless bandwidth improves and mobile gear has small, high-resolution displays, wireless devices will probably render HTML (or its successor). On the other hand, future toasters and other relatively low-tech household devices may render WML on small, cheap displays, even though they are connected by a wired household LAN.

The difference between WML and HTML (syntactic differences temporarily aside) is really one of capability rather than one of paradigm. At the 30,000-foot level, WML and HTML follow the same usage paradigm: computer displays information and choices visually, user enters data and makes choices with his or her hands (through a mouse, keyboard, or keypad). VoiceXML implements a different usage paradigm than its siblings: In VoiceXML, the computer and person take turns speaking and listening to each other. Thus, VoiceXML differs from WML and HTML in that it implements a fundamentally different model for human/computer interaction.

Why Merge Speech and the Web?

Some benefits of putting speech recognition, speech synthesis, XML, and the Web together are as follows:

- *Extend the reach of the Web.* People can access the Web from anywhere they can make a phone call. People get increased access to goods and services and businesses get increased access to their customers.

- *Make the Web easier to use.* VoiceXML relaxes the requirements on being able to use the Web from "literacy plus hand-eye coordination" to "being able to carry on a conversation." These relaxed requirements include people with sight disabilities (for example, blindness) as well as people who are illiterate or have cognitive disabilities (for example, dyslexia).

- *Increase the available options for computer/human interfaces.* Until VoiceXML, developing a voice-based interface (for instance, Interactive Voice Response) was an expensive, programming-intensive activity requiring specialized hardware and software. With VoiceXML, developing a voice-based interface is inexpensive and viable even for low-end applications.[2]

- *Reduce infrastructure costs.* Businesses currently maintain separate infrastructures for call centers and network computing. VoiceXML offers the possibility of saving money by merging these functions into one Web infrastructure.

---

[2] For an example of a low-end application, play the Tellme blackjack game by calling (800) 555-8355 and saying "entertainment" at the main menu followed by "blackjack." (Tellme is a VoiceXML vendor, and its voice site is completely written in VoiceXML.)

Making Voice User Interfaces Easy to Build and Use

Speech technology has traditionally been an expensive, high-end technology available only to businesses with enough money, solid technical capabilities, and a strong business need for it. Combining voice technology with the simplicity of markup languages makes it dramatically simpler and cheaper to "program" a Voice User Interface (VUI). Furthermore, voice technology's spread has been impeded by the fact that it is error-prone and still cannot handle natural language. The Web provides a relatively simple framework for interaction with computers. Within this framework, current voice technology is acceptable and useful. Speech recognition can adequately handle the basic Web requirements of navigating menus, traversing links, and entering data into forms. Combining recordings with TTS synthesis is sufficient to develop intelligible voice interfaces that can handle the Web's open-ended store of content.

Summary

This chapter reviewed some of the technologies converging in the emergent voice-enabled Web. These technologies include speech recognition, speech synthesis, and markup languages. Each is a powerful technology in its own right, and each has its own history and drivers. This background sets the stage for the next chapter, which explores how the architecture of Web applications draws on these underpinnings.

The Evolution
of Web Application
Architectures

THIS CHAPTER BRIEFLY TRACES the architectural evolution of the Web from a simple
mechanism for sharing published information electronically to its current role as
a public infrastructure for communication, interaction, and commerce. In the big
picture, enabling the Web with voice is just one piece of the larger mosaic that
comprises the Web. At a more detailed level, voice-enabling technologies such as
VoiceXML are just beginning on a growth path that has already been taken by
vision-enabling technologies such as HTML.

The Good Old Days: Browsers, Servers, and Content

Before the Web, you could share information over the Internet through tools such
as Gopher, but the textual presentation of the information was crude. The Web
superimposed a publishing paradigm on shared information: On the Web, information is structured as a related set of documents that are published and
rendered electronically. From this publishing paradigm derived some of the basic
technologies of the Web. For example, HTML derived from SGML, a languishing
technology for representing structured electronic documents. The stateless
nature of the core HTTP protocol is consistent with the publishing paradigm:
Rendered documents are viewed by readers. Does anyone "interact" with a book?

Architecturally, the requirements to publish documents to the Web were simple. To publish on the Web, you scrounged up a server, installed some free
software, ran a phone line to somebody that was already wired, and listened for
HTTP requests on port 80. A document was published as one or more files placed
in a directory tree on the file system.

A key architectural innovation popularized by the Web is the distinction
between content and presentation. *Content* is information that is stored and
shipped around between machines on the Internet. To be useful to humans, content must be *presented* (rendered) in a format that people can comprehend and
manipulate. The Web introduced the concept of a browser as the mediator between

a person and content fetched from the Web. In visual terms, the browser acts as a window in which various types of content can be rendered. The browser:

- Provides functions needed to locate and download content from servers.

- Does everything required by the host environment to act as a well-behaved graphical application.

- Renders HTML.

- Calls on specialized rendering software to render nontextual content.

Early on, the relationship between content and its rendition was simple: Content arrived in files, content was typed (by MIME types and/or file extensions), and content types had renderers. Things rapidly became more sophisticated with plug-ins, applets, ActiveX controls, and so on, and the distinction between content and computer programs was blurred.

> **NOTE** *The Internet Engineering Task Force (IETF) maintains a list of Multipurpose Internet Mail Extension (MIME) types. A MIME type is a standard identifier for a particular type of content. The identifier usually consists of a content type and a subtype—for example, "text/plain" or "image/gif." MIME types are heavily used in the "Content-type" header on HTTP messages, and they play a vital, but largely unsung, role in enabling the whole multimedia Web experience. For more information, visit the IETF's MIME Request for Comments document at* `http://www.ietf.org/rfc/rfc1521.txt?number=1521.`

HTML is the glue that ties together related content and drives the browser. The browser renders its way through an HTML stream, and along the way it must call on other renderers to render images, sounds, spreadsheets, and so on. In a sense, HTML is a rendering language that is "interpreted" by the browser.

Before the browser paradigm, developing a GUI was a programming-intensive activity. Software developers wrote software programs that embedded calls to an underlying windowing system API, such as Windows, Motif, Apple, X, and so on. The programs were expensive to write, debug, and deploy, and they were specific to the underlying windowing system. With the advent of the Web browser, anyone with a text editor and basic knowledge of HTML could program a GUI that could run anywhere.

Sessions and Dynamic Content

As the Web became popular, the simple model of Web users "viewing" static documents became inadequate. For example, there's a lot of useful data that people want to view in databases, and databases are not documents in the Web sense. Correlated with the demand for a more inclusive notion of "document" was the desire to be able to tailor the information presented to the task and person at hand. Given that the document wasn't really rendered until it hit the browser's screen, why not "create" documents on demand? Why did documents have to live in files anyway? The needed ingredients were a way to identify the person doing the browsing so that information could be tailored for him or her and a way for the Web server to initiate some general-purpose computing that returned an HTML stream that could be served to the client.

Sessions

As originally conceived, the HTTP protocol was stateless and anonymous. A browser requested a document from a server, the server returned it, and the transaction was done. Any browser that made the same request got exactly the same document returned.

Some gross but effective techniques for maintaining information about a user's interaction with a Web site were rapidly hacked into place. Cookies and URL rewriting are the most common. Both are techniques for piggybacking information about user identity onto HTTP requests: Cookies store information in HTTP headers, while URL rewriting stores information in URL search strings.

Generating Content Dynamically

On the server side, techniques for creating HTML documents on the fly were quickly developed. An early and popular technology was Common Gateway Interface (CGI). In CGI, a certain part of the namespace of a Web server (`http://.../cgi-bin`) is treated specially by the Web server. Rather than serve the files in this part of the namespace as content, the Web server treats the files as executable (script). The Web server synthesizes a command line, passes any HTTP request parameters as command-line arguments, and throws it over to the operating system to execute. From the operating system, the Web server receives a handle to retrieve and pass through the HTML generated by the executed program. As far as the browser knows, it visited a URL and got an HTML stream back.

CGI has the advantages of being simple, flexible, and popular with all kinds of people, because the programs that generate content can be written in anything from Perl to shell script to C++. However, CGI suffers from architectural problems: poor scalability and dubious security. Relying on an OS to start, schedule, and tear down a process for every hit is slow and computationally expensive. Security is an issue because CGI scripts often access other, security-conscious subsystems (for example, databases), and the issue of maintaining end-to-end security from a user through a browser through a Web server through a CGI script to a database management system (DBMS) is not addressed architecturally.

Application Servers

The early techniques for managing user state and generating content on demand, while minimally secure and far from perfect, enabled the evolution of Web servers from document vending machines into sophisticated environments for running complex distributed applications.

Early attempts to improve on CGI focused on directly extending the capabilities of the Web server. A server-side include (SSI) is a mechanism for embedding executable instructions into the content being served. As the server parses through content, it recognizes and acts on server commands, which produce the actual content served to the browser. Server extension APIs such as ISAPI and NSAPI enabled programs running on the server to interact with the Web server directly. Unfortunately, these direct extensions were implemented directly in the Web server software, making Web servers proprietary. The extensions also complicated Web server implementations by compounding technical issues concerning threading and resource management that are much simpler in a pure Web server.

The development of component-based server extensions sidestepped the propriety issue. This approach leaves Web servers as they are but defines a complementary component-hosting server that interacts with the Web server through existing protocols. The component hosting server, or application server, provides a robust, general-purpose environment for components. The application server handles the OS-like functions of resource management, thread management, I/O, and so on, while the components implement transformations on content streams. This makes server-side components relatively easy to program and deploy and enables Web servers to do what they do best: serve content. Of course, the application server is tied to the component architecture it implements, so the issue of propriety was moved but not solved.

GUIs, WUIs, and VUIs

As summarized in Table 3-1, GUI, WUI, and VUI represent the major markup language–based browsing interfaces to the Internet. GUI is the most fully developed of the three and is exemplified by products such as Netscape Communicator and Microsoft Internet Explorer. WUI, the next most developed interface, is implemented by "microbrowsers" embedded in wireless phones and personal digital assistants (PDAs). VUIs are just beginning to appear as browsing interfaces to the Internet, and they are driven by the standardization of VoiceXML 1.0.

Table 3-1. Markup Languages and Browsers

USER INTERFACE	BROWSING TECHNOLOGY	ORGANIZING PARADIGM	USAGE MODE
GUI (graphical)	HTML, XHTML	Page	Monitor, keyboard, and mouse
WUI (wireless)	WML	Card	Portable handheld
VUI (voice)	VXML	Dialog	Phone

The markup languages for these three types of interfaces are all based on XML. XML is a markup metalanguage derived from SGML. XML simplifies some of the complex and little-used features of SGML, but it still provides a flexible and extensible base for defining specialized markup languages. For more on XML, see Chapter 11.

HTML

HTML was originally conceived as the "stitching" needed to weave together the "World Wide Web" of multimedia documents. In this role, HTML is appropriate because it is simple and platform independent, and it provides a lingua franca for linking together documents. Basic HTML had a simple model of interaction with the user. The browser rendered documents and forms onto screen real estate owned by the browser. The user could "interact" with the browser by clicking a link, entering text into a form field, or pressing a form button to submit data to a server.

Surprisingly, this simple model was rich enough to support the rapid morphing of HTML into a platform for building GUIs. As the Web took off, it became possible for anyone with a text editor to put together a rudimentary GUI in a matter of minutes, changing forever the economics of developing graphical interfaces. More sophisticated HTML-based GUIs were enabled by the following innovations:

- Extension of the concept of "content rendering" to include software components (plug-ins, applets, ActiveX, and so on) invoked by the browser to control small pieces of the screen

- Architectural enhancements to bind the GUI to server-side programs in a user session

- Enhancements to HTML itself

The net result is that today it is possible to build very sophisticated GUIs using HTML and the Web. However, you can't do it using your trusty old text editor. In fact, HTML may be on the path to becoming a purely generated language created by programs such as WYSIWYG GUI editors and application servers solely to drive browsers and looked at by humans only in the direst need. (If you have doubts about this trend, go to your favorite Web page and have your browser display the HTML source.)

> **NOTE**   *HTML is not, strictly speaking, a true XML application. Some syntactically sloppy shortcuts in HTML violate the strict syntax rules of XML. Extensible HTML (XHTML) is a slightly reformulated version of HTML that does conform to XML. XHTML is an up-and-coming standard now and is expected to supplant HTML soon. Although there are no major conceptual or functional differences between HTML and XHTML (as far as Web browsing goes), there are subtle but important technical differences. As a well-behaved member of the XML family, XHTML enables a suite of powerful XML-based technologies that HTML does not. These technologies are explored in Chapter 11. For more information on XHTML, visit XHTML.org (`http://www.xhtml.org/`).*

WML

WML is a modernized, "lite" derivative of HTML that is optimized for running on devices that have low communication bandwidth, limited computing resources, and small, low-resolution displays. (It sounds like a dirty job, doesn't it?) To meet these performance constraints, WML is compiled into a compact binary representation before being sent to the handheld. The markup was designed to be renderable by a WML browser (microbrowser) that is simple and has a small memory footprint. To reduce the number of network exchanges, WUIs are organized into "decks" of "cards." An entire deck is downloaded at once, but the browser displays only one card at a time.

WML is not a subset of HTML for the following reasons:

- There are tags in WML that are not in HTML.

- WML is an XML application, while HTML is not.

- WML, although a simpler language than HTML, has a more sophisticated model of browsing. WML has the concept of "decks" of "cards," where one card at a time is displayed. HTML has a simpler "one file, one page" model.

Linguistic hairsplitting aside, WML WUIs really work like lightweight HTML GUIs. There's a screen, text and graphics, and links to click and buttons to push. The overall structure of how the user interacts with the interface is the same for WML and HTML.

> **NOTE**   *Visit* `http://www.wirelessinanutshell.com/` *to learn more about WML.*

VoiceXML

Unlike HTML, which has roots in publishing, VoiceXML comes from a programming language background. It has the earmarks of a programming language: control constructs, variables, event handlers, nested scoping, and so on. VoiceXML was designed from the beginning to be a lightweight, easy-to-learn, interpreted programming language for developing VUIs.

VoiceXML structures interactions with the user into dialogs. A dialog consists of a sequence of prompts spoken by the computer and responses spoken by a person. The person can speak responses or key them in using a keypad. VUI dialogs are by nature sequential and linear, in contrast to GUI windows, which are multitasked and two-dimensional.

Architecturally, VoiceXML interfaces are event-driven interfaces just like GUIs. In a dialog, the computer speaks a prompt and then waits for the user to respond to it. The computer then waits until a speech recognition event occurs. A speech recognition event is initiated by the speech recognition engine, which is continuously analyzing the user's speech and attempting to match it to expected responses in the dialog. There are a number of possible speech recognition events, including "recognized response blah blah blah," "got a response but didn't recognize it," "no response," and so on. Therefore, unlike GUIs and WUIs, where the events that drive the interface are low-level, unambiguous occurrences (button pressed, mouse clicked, and so on), events in VoiceXML interfaces are the result of complex, computation-intensive, potentially erroneous processing.

Summary

At its inception, the Web was envisioned as a medium to publish, share, and interlink electronic documents. As the Web became more popular, the focus shifted from electronic publishing of static documents to an interactive infrastructure for generating, processing, and displaying information. The content comes from a variety of sources, including files, databases, and computer programs. A browser interprets markup language embedded in the content, renders it to a particular medium, and interacts with the user. HTML renders to a computer display (and a sound card) and interacts with the user through a keyboard and mouse. WML works with low-capability handheld devices. The newcomer to the scene, VoiceXML, renders content as speech and interacts with the user using speech recognition and speech synthesis technologies.

Part Two
The VoiceXML Language

HAVING ESTABLISHED A technical context for voice in general, it's time to focus on the specifics of the VoiceXML language. As languages go, VoiceXML is not particularly tough. However, developing interfaces for voice is quite different than developing graphical or text-based interfaces. Voice and graphical interfaces differ in structure, in how errors are created and perceived, and in how information is processed. Some of the material in this part is the usual "syntax and semantics" common to all introductions to programming languages. Much of the material, however, is intended to help you think about and design high-quality voice interfaces.

Chapter 4 introduces the Simplified Personal Information Manager, a voice-enabled Web application that animates the tutorial in this part and the prototype in the next part. Chapter 5 introduces the concepts that the VoiceXML language is built around. Chapter 6 dives into the nuts and bolts of setting yourself up (in terms of hardware and software) as a VoiceXML developer. With your environment in place, Chapter 7 provides a step-by-step tutorial that acquaints you with all the key features of VoiceXML 1.0. Building on your understanding of what VoiceXML can do, Chapter 8 offers guidance about how to design a good voice interface using VoiceXML. Chapter 9 provides a reference-style discussion of the machinery behind features explored in the tutorial. Finally, Chapter 10 explores some advanced topics and issues that become apparent when you develop real-world VoiceXML applications.

Simplified Personal Information Manager Example

THROUGHOUT THE REST of this book, you will work with a simplified personal information manager (SPIM) application. A SPIM is a slimmed down personal information manager (PIM) with the following features: address book, appointment calendar, and to-do list. A SPIM is accessible through voice, wireless, and Web interfaces. As you work through the examples in the book, you will develop fully functioning components of your SPIM, but your intent should not be to implement a complete, robust PIM.

This example was chosen for the following reasons:

- It is simple to understand and useful. Many people are familiar with some kind of PIM.

- It can be used in a variety of situations and environments. Some use cases naturally involve Web access, some involve wireless access, and some involve voice access.

- It can be developed in useful increments, so I can illustrate points on an ongoing basis.

In the following sections, I analyze the SPIM as a serious but petite application. The core use cases are elaborated and diagrammed in Universal Markup Language (UML).[1] The basic diagrams used here are pretty intuitive, so you should be able to grasp the intent of the diagrams without knowing UML.

---

[1] UML is a notation for object-oriented analysis and design. It was developed by Rational Software and is called "universal" because it incorporates the methodologies championed by Booch, Jacobson, and Rumbaugh, as well as others. For more information on UML, the Rational Rose object-oriented design and development tool (which was used to draw the diagrams here), and pretty much anything to do with developing object-oriented software, visit the Rational Software Web site (http://www.rational.com/).

Use Case Analysis

A full PIM can be used in so many ways that a full use case analysis would proba-bly involve dozens, if not hundreds, of use cases. In the sample application, you will leave room for future growth and build menus assuming there's a greater variety of functions than you'll actually implement here. For pedagogical pur-poses, you will focus on three representative use cases for the SPIM. They are "representative" in terms of both the underlying technology involved and how it is used.

The use cases are as follows:

- Editing information about a contact (for example, name, address, phone numbers, and so on)

- Handling a scheduled appointment that you're late for

- Reviewing your list of things to do today

The sections that follow elaborate on these cases.

Top-Level Use Case

The top-level use case diagram in Figure 4-1 shows the intentionally limited scope of the SPIM. In a "real" PIM, there would be many more use cases at this level—for example, "call a contact," "schedule an appointment," "add an address to an existing contact," and so on.

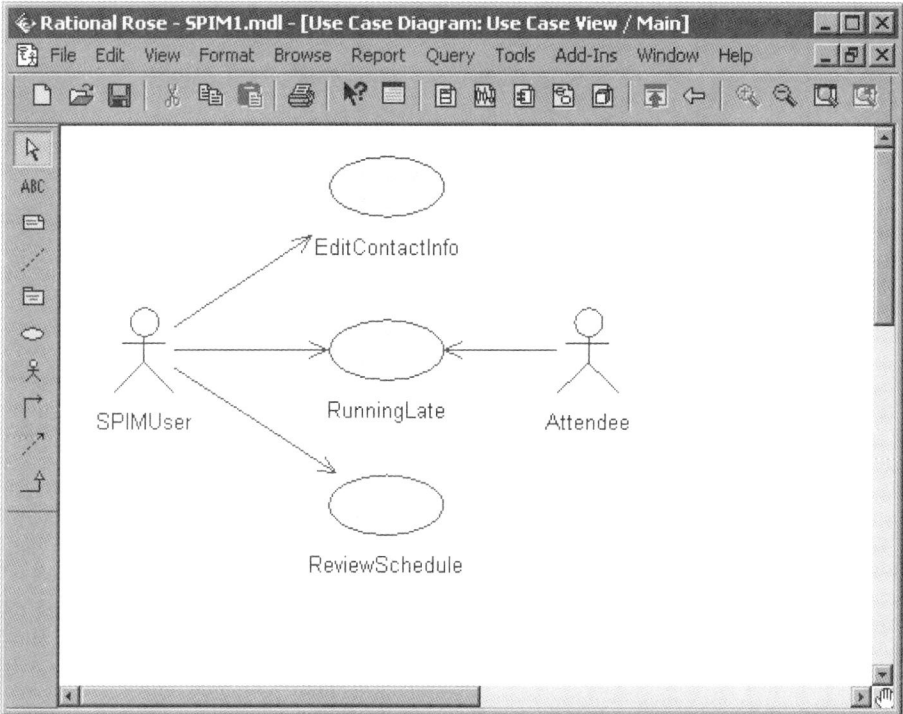

Figure 4-1. SPIM top-level use case

During use case analysis, SPIMUser's access mode (eye or ear) is not assumed or implied unless the access mode is intrinsic to the requirements of the use case. For example, the use case in the next section (titled "Edit Contact Information Use Case") should be the same regardless of access mode, because it is an essential function of the system. On the other hand, a hypothetical "Dial Roadside Assistance from My Broken-Down Car" use case could, arguably, presume that the user is accessing the system through a VUI or WUI, but not a GUI.

The sections that follow drill down another level into these scenarios. Notice that every case starts with the Authenticate use case. This shared case models the process of identifying the current user to the system. Conventionally, authentication is performed by a username/password-based login, but it may use other mechanisms for voice (as you will see in Chapter 12).

Edit Contact Information Use Case

You receive a change of address notice in the mail from a friend. You're not going to call the friend right now or schedule a meeting with him or her, but you want to record the address change. First, you look up the existing contact information for your friend, and then you selectively modify it. To look it up, you can either browse your address book (if it's small) or search your address book by name. Once you have the information at hand, you can either review it in summary form (the types of addresses you have on file) or in detailed form (a full listing of address contents). Then you update the fields that have changed. Figure 4-2 illustrates this use case.

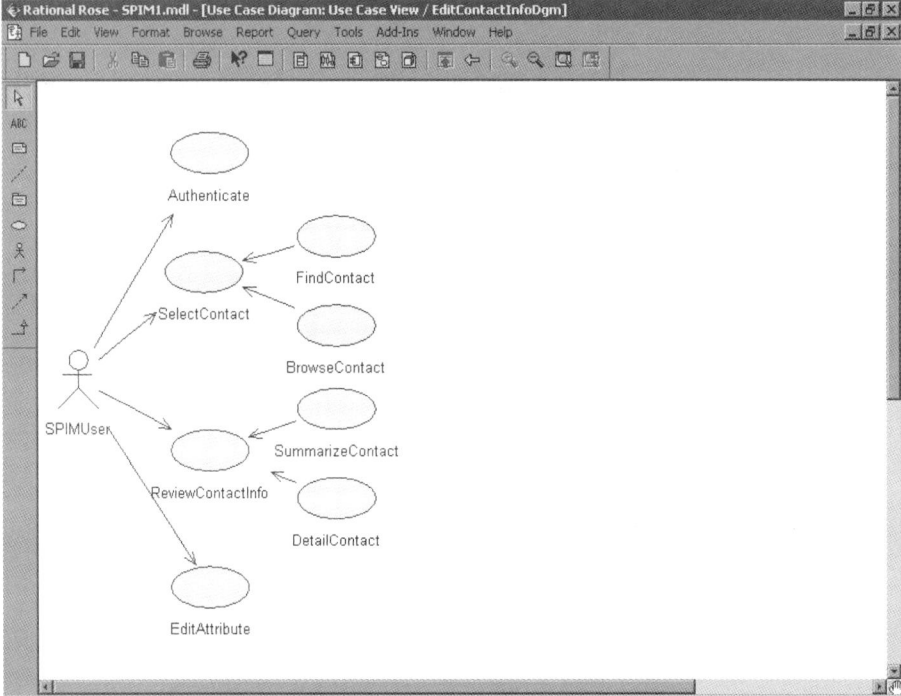

Figure 4-2. Edit Contact Information use case diagram

Running Late Use Case

Your schedule is jammed solid and you've just escaped from a meeting that ran over. You don't have time to fiddle around with rescheduling things, so you want to notify your next appointment that you'll arrive late. You access your SPIM, get the relevant contact information for your next appointment, and communicate the fact that you'll be late by the best means possible: e-mail, phone call, wireless text message, or voice mail. Figure 4-3 illustrates this use case.

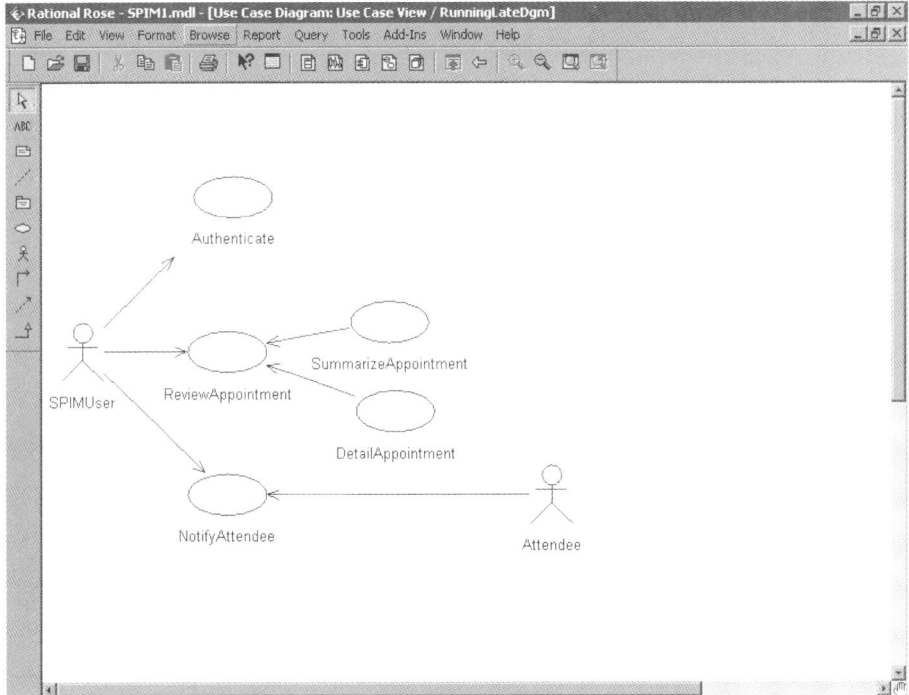

Figure 4-3. Running Late use case diagram

Review Schedule List Use Case

To refresh your memory on what you have scheduled for the upcoming week, you want to review your appointments on a day-by-day basis. In your SPIM, you identify the day you're interested in and then review that day's planned activities. As you progress through your list of appointments, you want to scan quickly, ignore things you already recall, and selectively focus on particular items of interest. Figure 4-4 illustrates this use case.

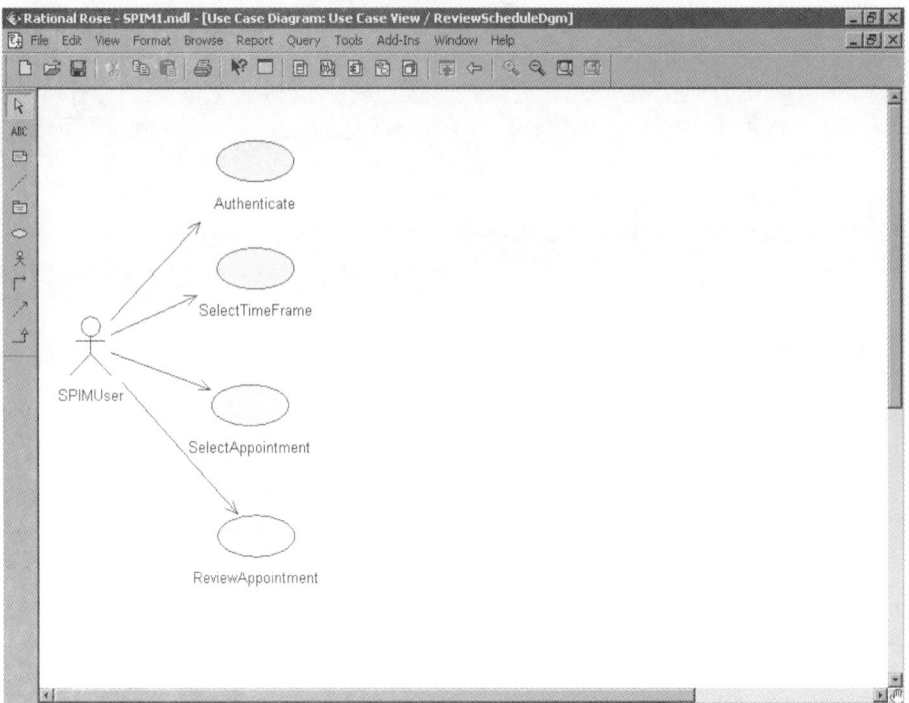

Figure 4-4. Review Schedule use case diagram

Object Model

The core objects in a SPIM are as follows:

- A *contact* is an entity that you communicate with. To initiate communication with a contact, you can use an *address* that is appropriate for your chosen communication method (a phone number for a phone call or fax, an e-mail address for e-mail, and so on).

- An *appointment* is a scheduled event that involves you and one or more contacts with whom you will interact. The *venue* specifies how the interaction will occur (physical meeting, teleconference, and so on).

- A *schedule* is a list of appointments that fall in a given *time span* (this afternoon, today, tomorrow, and so on).

Figure 4-5 captures the relationships between these objects.

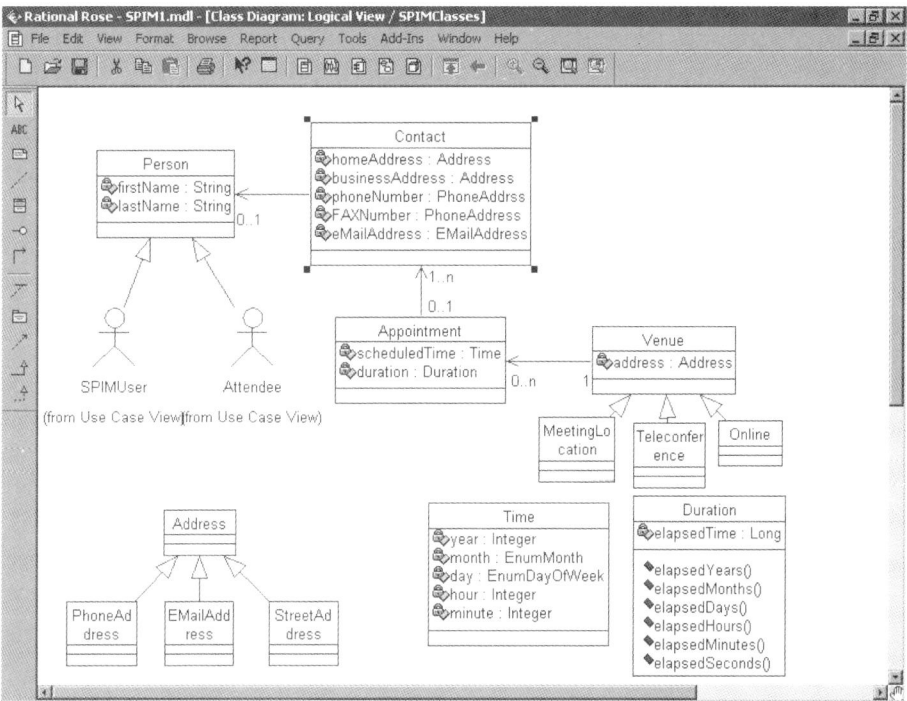

Figure 4-5. SPIM class diagram

Summary

In this chapter, I've laid out the skeleton of a simple, but realistic, application example. The core use cases were elaborated and diagrammed in UML. From the use cases, a basic object model was derived and diagrammed. Applying this level of formality to the example is intended to drive home two points.

- The examples presented throughout the book are not "concocted" examples that show off technology features but never occur in practice. Rather, the examples are practical because they derive from a real application.

- Voice-enabled applications are not a new, different kind of application. The best practices of application design, development, and software engineering apply to voice-enabled applications.

In the chapters that follow, you'll use the SPIM application to lead you into VoiceXML programming.

CHAPTER 5

VoiceXML Concepts

THIS CHAPTER INTRODUCES VoiceXML. It begins with a brief history of how VoiceXML was developed and provides an overview of VoiceXML technical concepts. This sets the stage for subsequent chapters, which drill down into specific topics using the SPIM application to illustrate how speech user interfaces are expressed in VoiceXML.

VoiceXML History

The major driver for development of VoiceXML has been the desire of the telephony industry to make existing telephone networks a vital part of the Information Age. Obviously, telephone companies and our society as a whole have a strong investment in the telephone and Public Switched Telephone Network (PSTN). Access to the Internet over dial-up connections was and is a major component of the Internet's success. Technically, however, the encoding and transmission of digital data over telephone networks originally intended for analog voice communication is somewhat inefficient. On the other hand, using voice to access the Internet would capitalize directly on the existing, proven, and highly tuned capabilities of Plain Old Telephone Service (POTS).

AT&T, Lucent Technologies, and Motorola began discussing the possibility of developing a common language for voice-enabled applications in 1998. The VoiceXML Forum was formed in 1999, and IBM became the fourth founding member. The initial specification, VoiceXML 0.9, was released in August 1999. A process of public review and response to comments culminated in the release of the VoiceXML 1.0 specification in March 2000. Following development of the language definition, the VoiceXML Forum turned custody of the specification over to the World Wide Web Consortium (W3C). The Forum reorganized itself and broadened its charter to include more of a general role as a technology and industry advocate for the VoiceXML community. See Figure 5-1 for a detailed timeline of the previously described events.

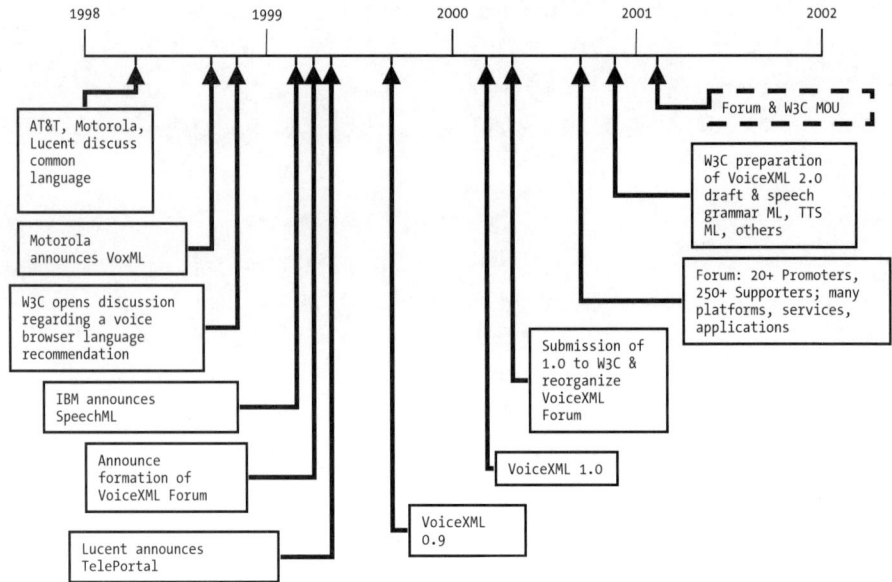

Figure 5-1. Timeline of speech and telephony activities (courtesy of the VoiceXML Forum)

The VoiceXML Web site (`http://www.voicexml.org/goals.html`) describes the Forum's goal as follows:

"The VoiceXML Forum is an industry organization founded by AT&T, IBM, Lucent and Motorola, and chartered with establishing and promoting the Voice Extensible Markup Language (VoiceXML), a new specification essential to making Internet content and information accessible via voice and phone."

Now the W3C is overseeing the ongoing specification of the VoiceXML language and other speech-related technologies, including

- Speech grammars

- Voice dialogs

- Voice synthesis

- Pronunciation lexicon

- Call control

- Natural language representation

- Multimodal systems

- Reusable dialog components

Visit the VoiceXML Forum's Web site (`http://www.voicexml.org/`) for information about VoiceXML Forum activities and members. Visit the W3C's Voice Browser Activity area (`http://www.w3c.org/Voice`) for information about the W3C's work on various voice-related technologies.

Voice Web Browsing

Accessing a Web site through the telephone is different than ordinary Web browsing in both user experience and technical implementation. A typical Web-browsing session goes something like this:

1. You sit down at a computer, open a Web browser, and type in a Web address (URL).

2. The Web browser sends a request to the Web server.

3. The Web server sends a response to the Web browser, which includes an HTML document.

4. The Web browser "renders" the HTML document onto your screen.

5. You view the display and navigate the site by clicking and typing.

Getting the same information from the same Web site using VoiceXML goes something like this:

1. You pick up a phone and dial the Web site's phone number.

2. A VoiceXML gateway answers your call and sends a request to the Web server.

3. The Web server sends a response to the VoiceXML interpreter, which includes a VoiceXML document.

4. The VoiceXML interpreter "renders" the VoiceXML document by speaking to you.

5. You listen and then respond by speaking or pressing keys on the telephone's keypad.

> **NOTE** *Even though you can use your wireless phone to access the Web using voice (VXML) or Web browsing (WML), you can't do both together. When using voice, the link is over the telephone network; when using wireless, it's over a WAP link. Currently, handheld devices can only communicate over a single type of link at a time. Even if your handheld device is capable of servicing both types of links simultaneously, there's no protocol to correlate what's happening on the phone with what's happening on the WAP link.*

From the user's perspective, the difference is in the medium by which input and output are conveyed. With a conventional Web browser, you receive the output from the computer through your eyes and send input to the computer with your hands. With VoiceXML, you receive output from the computer through your ears and send input to the computer with your voice (see Figure 5-2).

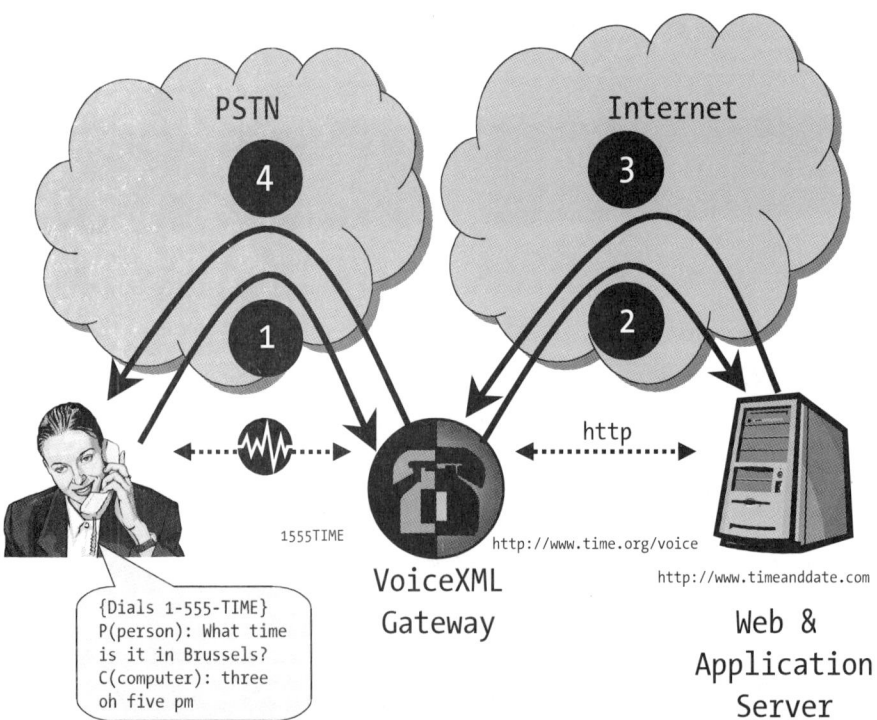

Figure 5-2. Voice Web browsing

From a technical perspective, HTML Web browsing involves two computers (browser and server) connected by one IP network (Internet or intranet). The Web browser uses the display, keyboard, and mouse of its host computer for input and output.

Browsing with VoiceXML involves a telephone, two computers (gateway and server), and two networks. An IP network connects the Web server to the VoiceXML gateway, and the PSTN connects your telephone to the VoiceXML gateway through an ordinary phone call. The VoiceXML gateway interacts with the Web server using the standard HTTP protocol, just like a Web browser. However, it "renders" the VoiceXML document by sending its output to, and receiving its input from, your telephone over the PSTN.

A VoiceXML gateway has the following subsystems (shown in Figure 5-3):

- *Network Interface:* Enables HTTP communication with Web servers

- *VoiceXML Interpreter:* The software that carries on a conversation with the user, as specified in a VoiceXML document

- *Text-to-Speech (TTS):* Translates text to the spoken word

- *Audio:* Plays and records audio files

- *Speech Recognition (ASR):* Translates user utterances into text

- *DTMF:* Translates keypad input into characters

- *Telephony Interface:* Enables communications with the telephone network (PSTN)

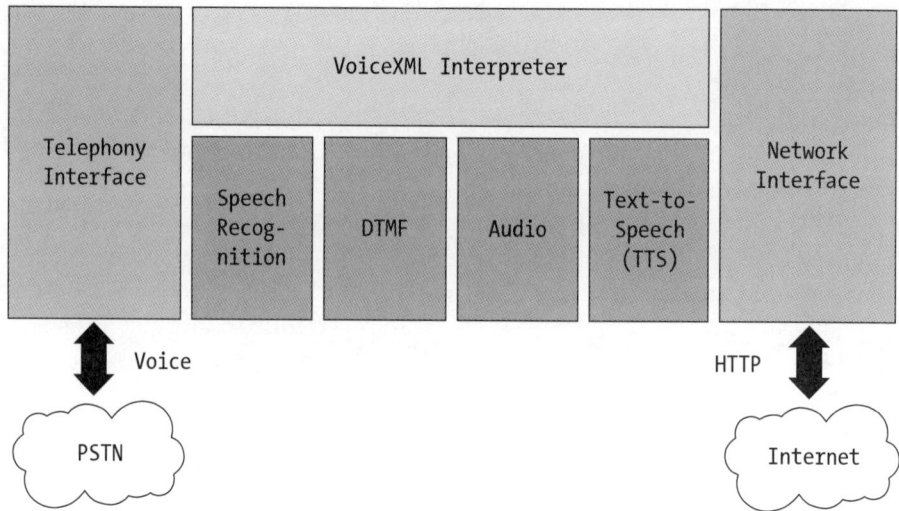

Figure 5-3. VoiceXML gateway subsystems

Elements of VoiceXML

In HTML, the basic element of retrieval is a page, which is a document with a certain address. When a Web browser receives an HTML document from a Web server, it renders the entire page to the screen at once. A VoiceXML document specifies an entire conversation, which consists of interchanges between the caller and VoiceXML interpreter. In each of these interchanges, the VoiceXML interpreter reads or plays a prompt and the caller responds with information or a command. The VoiceXML interpreter thus "renders" the VoiceXML document one exchange at a time. (In this respect, VoiceXML is more similar to WML, where the WAP phone displays one card at a time.)

Dialogs

In VoiceXML, *dialogs* are the building blocks for conversations. The VoiceXML interpreter "renders" a VoiceXML document by carrying on a conversation with the person at the other end of the telephone call. The person and the VoiceXML interpreter take turns speaking and listening. At any point in time, the conversation between the caller and gateway is "in" one dialog. During a call, the conversation moves among dialogs in the application. The VoiceXML document contains elements that specify what the VoiceXML interpreter can say or play to the user and what the user can say or key to the VoiceXML interpreter.

Navigation

Web sites are usually organized into a shallow hierarchy of topics. Visually, this hierarchy is shown as a row of links at the top of each page (or column of links at the left of each page). Visitors click these links to navigate through the hierarchy. VoiceXML *menus* provide the audio equivalent of visual pick lists. The computer speaks the list of available choices, and the user responds by saying the desired option. VoiceXML *links* enable people to jump directly to a destination at any time simply by saying the name of the link.

Forms and Items

VoiceXML *forms* serve the same purpose as HTML forms: They are used to collect information from the user and send it to a Web server. Both VoiceXML and HTML collect information in *fields.* HTML field values are entered as text in the browser, while VoiceXML field values are spoken by the caller and translated into text by the VoiceXML interpreter. In both cases, when all the fields have been filled in, the completed form is sent to the Web server through an HTTP GET or POST request.

To fill in a field, VoiceXML executes a *form item.* A form item may be a simple field elicitation that speaks a prompt (for example, "What city?") and captures the response. A form item may involve more complex processing, such as invoking another dialog, telephoning a third party, or executing a client-side script (ECMAScript, also known as JavaScript).

When executing a form, the VoiceXML interpreter will repeatedly process form items until it determines that all fields have been filled. Notice that executing a form item by no means guarantees that the corresponding field is filled. For example, the user may fail to respond to a prompt, or the computer may not be able to recognize what the user said.

Grammars

At any point in a VoiceXML dialog, there is a predefined set of valid responses that a person can speak. A *grammar* specifies a set of responses that can be recognized by the computer. A simple grammar may specify some fixed phrases to be used as commands (for example). A more complex grammar may specify a set of basic words (the vocabulary) and multiple alternative rules determining the order in which the words may appear to form expressions or sentences. A grammar is the primary input to the voice recognition technology that underlies the VoiceXML interpreter.

A grammar is specified inline, within a VoiceXML program, or in an external text file. VoiceXML 1.0 doesn't specify or require a particular grammar format, although two are widely used: JGSF (Java Grammar Specification Format) from Sun and GSL (Grammar Specification Language) from Nuance. The next release of VoiceXML is expected to require that VoiceXML interpreters support the XML form of the W3C speech grammar language, but it permits the interpreter to accept other formats as well (see Chapter 14 for a fuller discussion of this point).

Events

Programming languages such as C++ and Java use *exceptions* to handle errors. VoiceXML *events* are based on the exception concept. Events are *thrown* when certain conditions are detected either by the VoiceXML interpreter or by the VoiceXML program itself. *Event handlers* are fragments of executable code that are invoked to *catch* an event.

Due to the nature of speech, conversational dialogs are intrinsically real-time processes. Unlike graphical interfaces, where you can take a lunch break and pick up right where you left off, speech interfaces require responses within certain time periods and must explicitly accommodate real-time interruptions and distractions. In VoiceXML, events are not restricted to representing error conditions—they are used to represent all kinds of real-time interactions.

Summary

Beginning with a brief history of VoiceXML, this chapter introduced the key concepts that underlie VoiceXML. Browsing the Web by voice is a new activity enabled by VoiceXML that differs from using a conventional Web browser. To access a VoiceXML application, a person dials into a VoiceXML gateway, which contains all the hardware and software required to recognize speech, synthesize speech, and run the VoiceXML interpreter. The VoiceXML application is composed of dialogs that structure the interaction between person and computer. VoiceXML provides links, which are the verbal equivalent of hypertext links. VoiceXML forms are composed of items, each of which elicits a particular piece of information from a person. Grammars specify what responses are valid at every point in a dialog. Events are used to handle errors and manage a conversation in real time.

CHAPTER 6

Outfitting Your VoiceXML Expedition

VOICEXML IS A NEW and burgeoning technology, so the landscape of available VoiceXML tools and products is changing at "Web speed." This chapter provides a quick orientation to the basic development approaches and tools. I'm not going to try to cover the various characteristics and features of each tool, because that information will undoubtedly be obsolete by the time you get it. However, I will provide pointers to places where you can find up-to-date information.

Standalone versus Hosted Development

In a deployed VoiceXML application, the VoiceXML browser runs on a VoiceXML gateway. The VoiceXML gateway may be a privately owned server (for example, one owned by your company) equipped with expensive telephony and voice software, or it may be a service you buy from a VoiceXML hosting vendor. In either case, the application developer provides the VoiceXML software and the host provides the gateway environment in which the software runs. You contact the hosted gateway by calling a telephone number that connects to the VoiceXML application.

While the VoiceXML application is under development, the developer can run it in either a *standalone* or a *hosted* configuration. In a standalone configuration, the "gateway" runs on the developer's own workstation. The developer uses a headset and microphone to listen and speak, and all speech synthesis and recognition is done on the developer's workstation (see Figure 6-1). In a hosted configuration, a VoiceXML hosting vendor provides the developer with access to a VoiceXML gateway. The vendor gives the registered developer a phone number, a personal identification number (PIN), and a way to upload VoiceXML source code to the gateway. To run the application, the developer uploads the software, calls the phone number (which may the same number for all developers), and enters the PIN. The gateway locates the uploaded software for that PIN and executes it (see Figure 6-2).

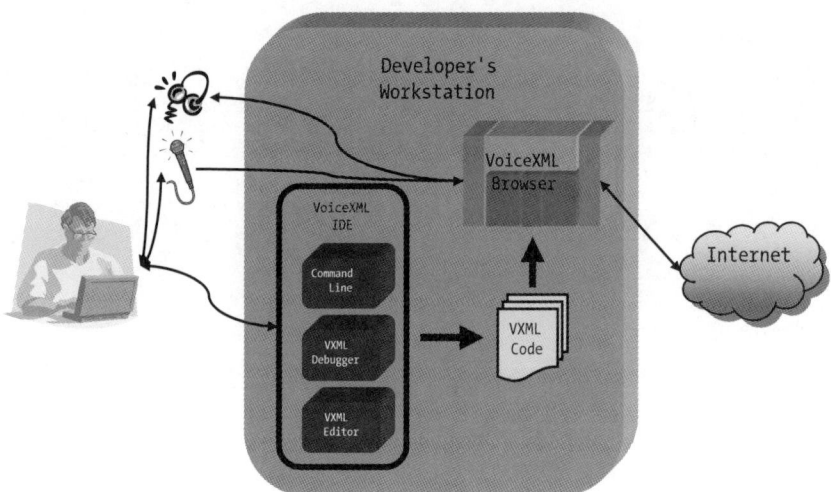

Figure 6-1. Standalone development configuration

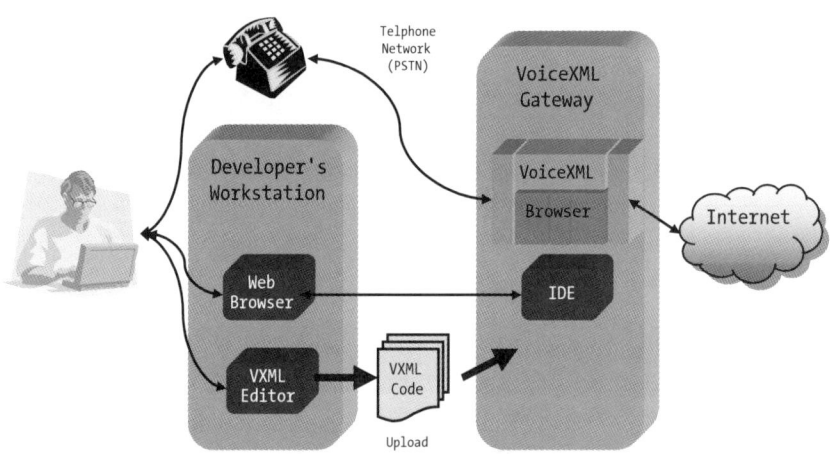

Figure 6-2. Hosted development configuration

In practice, the application will probably morph from a standalone configuration to a hosted configuration during the development cycle. In initial development, the standalone configuration is preferable because the code is changing rapidly and the tasks of uploading and phoning to try out every change are onerous. As the application stabilizes toward a software release, the developer needs to test the application in a hosted configuration (using the phone instead of the microphone), because that is how it will be deployed. When the application goes into production, it will be in a hosted configuration.

Development Environment

The basic requirements for developing a VoiceXML application are the same as those for developing an HTML application: an editor, a browser, and a Web server (for anything but the simplest apps). For developers still hoping that GUIs are a passing fad, a text editor and a command line can fit the bill. For the programming challenged, there are fully hosted Interactive Development Environments (IDEs) that provide sophisticated GUIs. VoiceXML browsers are not as commonplace as HTML browsers (yet), but a number are available at little or no cost to developers.

XML, and hence VoiceXML, is a text-based language. As a result, you can use any text editor to edit VoiceXML source. XML-specific editors provide niceties such as syntax coloring, text and tree views, and automatic validation. VoiceXML IDEs may provide drag-and-drop GUI-style editing. Take your pick or mix and match. A standard text format is a standard text format, so you don't have to restrict yourself to one tool.

When selecting a VoiceXML browser for development, the major choice is between a hosted and a standalone configuration. At one end of the spectrum, there are hosted development environments that don't require you to install any software on your local workstation—the whole IDE runs in a Web browser against a remote host. On the other end of the spectrum, there are standalone configurations, which require you to install all software locally and launch the VoiceXML browser from the command line or from within an IDE. The one you select is primarily a stylistic choice based on the development approach that's comfortable for you. Remember that, once written, a VoiceXML program can run (in theory) on any VoiceXML browser.

> **CAUTION** *VoiceXML gateway hosting vendors seem to be multiplying rapidly. Many of the sites appear to incorporate the "developer network" model. You, as a developer, sign up and get access to development tools, documentation, forums, FAQs, samples, and so on. These nontechnical features can help you get up to speed quickly and draw on the experience of others, but beware the siren song of "free" proprietary stuff that locks you in with the hosting vendor.*

When you select your development environment, think about where you're going to use it. If you're a frequent-flying, laptop-coding developer, you'll probably want to go with a standalone configuration that can be loaded entirely onto your laptop. If you're a curious amateur with not much disk space left on the old home computer, a hosted configuration that minimizes local resource requirements is probably a good idea.

One feature to be aware of is the VoiceXML interpreter's acceptance of both voice and text input. When accepting text input, speech recognition is short-circuited, so the text input is treated as output from the speech recognition engine. Text may be entered in interactive mode, where you hear the spoken prompts and respond by typing in text or picking from a menu that shows expected responses. Text may also be entered in batch mode, where the VoiceXML interpreter reads text from a script file. The ability to enter text is very useful in a number of situations, including when you are

- Doing development on an airplane, in a shared office, or in a (semi-) public place where saying responses out loud might be embarrassing and/or distracting to others

- Developing a VUI for a language you are not fluent in

- Performing automated testing (for example, regression testing)

- Developing while you have a cold or other impediment that makes your voice hard to recognize

- Going through rapid code/test sequences and you want to avoid repeating the same sequence of responses over and over

- Developing on an underperforming machine whose resources shouldn't be squandered on speech recognition

VoiceXML 1.0 versus VoiceXML 2.0[1]

The VoiceXML 1.0 specification was released in May 2000. Public release of the VoiceXML 2.0 specification is expected in late 2001 (according to W3C). At the time of this writing, there are quite a number (dozens) of VoiceXML 1.0–compliant browsers and IDEs available. There are a handful of tools claiming

---

[1] "VoiceXML 2.0" is the unofficial name, used throughout the VoiceXML community, of the next release of the VoiceXML language specification. The W3C doesn't use this name, and its web page simply states the next working draft from the Voice Browser Working Group is due in late 2001. Therefore, the version number assigned by the W3C may or may not be 2.0. In fact, the scope of changes that are anticipated to appear in the next specification may be more consistent with a "point-rev" (e.g. VoiceXML 1.1) than a "full-rev" (e.g. VoiceXML 2.0). In any case, the phrase "VoiceXML 2.0" should be understood to be an informal reference to the next release of the specification, whatever its official name turns out to be.

VoiceXML 2.0 compatibility (which is surprising, because there is no published standard to comply with). To avoid the pain associated with running at the bleeding edge of technology, the code samples, examples, and tutorials in this book are based on VoiceXML 1.0. Where appropriate, I have called out changes that are expected to be included in VoiceXML 2.0. Given that the differences between VoiceXML 1.0 and VoiceXML 2.0 are expected to be evolutionary, not revolutionary, sticking with the more established and mature VoiceXML 1.0 toolset seems prudent.

Some Available Software Options

For a comprehensive list of companies involved with VoiceXML (many of whom are vendors), visit the VoiceXML Forum's Member page (`http://www.voicexml.org/member_companies.html`). To find a variety of XML editors, visit XML.com's XML Editors page (`http://www.xml.com/pub/rg/XML_Editors`) and Scripting News' XML Editors page (`http://scriptingnews.userland.com/directory/1026/xmlEditors`). Tables 6-1 and 6-2 list some VoiceXML-related tools that are currently available.

This book's companion CD contains the following software to get you started:

- *IBM WebSphere Voice Server SDK (trial edition):* A standalone voice browser.

- *IBM WebSphere Studio (entry edition):* A VoiceXML IDE that provides integrated VoiceXML editing and integration with the ViaVoice SDK for testing and debugging.

- *XML Spy:* An XML IDE for editing XML Schemas, DTDs, XML files, and XSL transformations. It integrates with external XSL transformation engines for testing XSL transformations.

Table 6-1. Selected VoiceXML Editing/Authoring Tools

PRODUCT	COMMENTS	URL
TIBCO Extensibility	Full suite of XML tools for editing schemas, instances, validation, and so on	`http://www.extensibility.com/`
XML Spy	Integrated GUI for XML/XSL development	`http://www.xmlspy.com/`
IBM WebSphere Studio	Web development IDE integrates VoiceXML support	`http://www-4.ibm.com/software/ webservers/studio/`

Table 6-2. Selected VoiceXML Browsers Available for Experimentation

PRODUCT	CONFIGURATION	URL
BeVocal Café	Hosted	`http://cafe.bevocal.com/`
Cambridge Voice Studio	Standalone	`http://www.cambridgevoicetech.com/ devsite/Developers.asp`
HeyAnita FreeSpeech	Hosted	`http://freespeech.heyanita.com/default.asp`
IBM WebSphere Voice Server SDK	Standalone	`http://www-4.ibm.com/ software/speech/enterprise/ep_11.html`
Informio Developer Network	Hosted	`http://idn.informio.com/`
Motorola Mobile ADK	Standalone	`http://mix.motorola.com/audiences/ developers/madk_intro_dev.asp`
Nuance V-Builder	Standalone	`http://www.nuance.com/products/toolkits.html`
Tellme Studio	Hosted	`http://studio.tellme.com/`
VoiceGenie Developer Workshop	Hosted	`http://developer.voicegenie.com/`
Voxeo Designer	Standalone	`http://community.voxeo.com/index. cfm?pageid=B1F070D5-4E49-467D-91979A961F1516C9`

Speech Developer Accessories

To look good and be effective, every VUI developer needs one or more headsets (microphone plus earphones). At a minimum, you'll need a telephone headset and a phone. You'll use this gear while testing your VoiceXML application in its deployed state, and you'll use it while developing in a hosted configuration. Using a headset is more comfortable than using a fixed microphone and it enables you to type while you talk. Because you'll want to test your deployed application in a realistic fashion, getting a top-quality telephone headset is probably *not* a good idea: You want to use consumer-quality equipment, just like all the people who will call into your site.

If you're doing development in a standalone configuration, and/or you're interested in learning about voice technologies other than VoiceXML, you'll want to invest in a comfortable, high-quality headset that connects to your computer. Don't skimp on quality here. If you want to try using other speech technologies, such as dictation systems (for example, IBM ViaVoice, Dragon NaturallySpeaking, L&H Voice Xpress, or Philips FreeSpeech), the software will require you to use a high-quality microphone (and will refuse to enroll you unless you use one).

> **TIP** *Strictly speaking, you could use your computer's speakers and get by with simply adding a microphone. However, if you do any of your development within earshot of other human beings, they will probably appreciate your thoughtfulness in using a headset so they don't have to hear the endless playing and replaying of prompts as you build your application.*

Summary

Getting set up to develop VoiceXML applications requires you to perform a few simple steps:

- Decide whether you want to work in hosted or standalone mode.

- Register with a gateway hosting service (hosted) or acquire and install VoiceXML browser software (standalone).

- Install an XML-capable editor or IDE for entering and editing VoiceXML source (based on your preferences).

- Get yourself a good-looking and comfortable headset.

To make things easy, all the software you need to get started is included on the book's companion CD.

CHAPTER 7

VoiceXML Language Tutorial

IN THIS CHAPTER, YOU'LL develop VoiceXML code to implement some core functions of the SPIM application. Along the way, you'll explore most (but not all) features of VoiceXML (some advanced features are discussed separately in Chapter 10). The example files are all contained on the companion CD. Under the Tutorial directory on the CD, there are subdirectories labeled Step1, Step2, and so on, through Step10. The tutorial refers to these steps as it progresses.

From this tutorial, you'll learn the salient points of VoiceXML without executing the sample code. However, if you're a hands-on type, I suggest you get outfitted (as described in the previous chapter) and try out the examples as you go.

To make the tutorial examples executable in today's voice browsers, the examples conform to VoiceXML 1.0. Where appropriate, comments related to features anticipated in VoiceXML 2.0 are inserted parenthetically [VXML 2: this is a parenthetical comment] or called out as follows:

> **VXML 2:** *This is an example of a comment related to VoiceXML 2.0.*

"Hello, World!"

Before diving into the SPIM, let's take a look at a very basic VoiceXML program. The following VoiceXML application simply speaks the phrase "Hello, World!" (using speech synthesis) and then exits. See Listing 7-1 (from SmallExamples\Example1.vxml).

Listing 7-1. Hello, World!

```
<?xml version="1.0"?>
<!DOCTYPE vxml SYSTEM "http://www.voicexml.org/voicexml1-0.dtd">
<!-- This is a simple "Hello, World!" voice application. -->
<vxml version="1.0">
  <form id="hello">
    <block>Hello, World!</block>
  </form>
</vxml>
```

As with any other well-formed XML file, the first line identifies the version of XML. The DOCTYPE directive is an XML directive that tells the XML parser to parse according to the specified "schema." Following the DOCTYPE directive is a sample of the ghastly format of SGML (hence XML, hence VoiceXML) comments: The delimiters are <!-- and -->. The <vxml> tag identifies its content as VoiceXML 1.0 code. This application is composed of a single form, which contains a single line of executable content. When the VoiceXML interpreter encounters text, it reads it aloud. As an alternative, you can replace the text with a recorded greeting, as in SmallExamples\Example2.vxml.

```
<block> <audio src="SmallExamples/HelloWorld.wav"/></block>
```

SPIM Menu Navigation

The SPIM menu structure is shown in Figure 7-1. To start a SPIM session, the user dials the phone number of the VoiceXML gateway that is hosting the SPIM. The user then identifies him- or herself to the gateway and requests the SPIM application (if the phone number is not dedicated to the SPIM). For the purposes of the SPIM, assume that the user has been identified—somehow—at the point that the main menu becomes active.

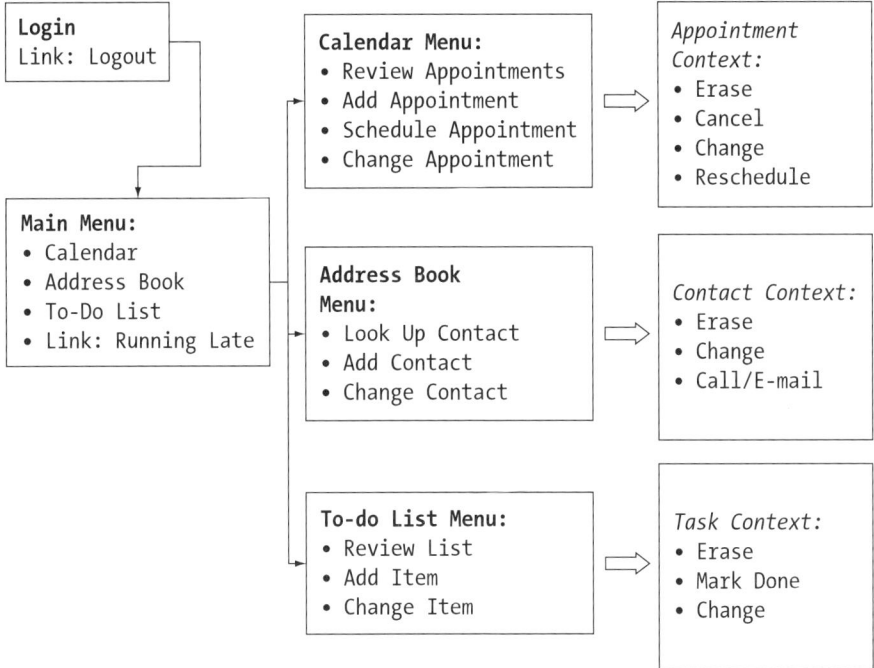

Figure 7-1. The SPIM menu hierarchy

SPIM Main Menu

The SPIM main menu has three choices (Calendar, Address Book, To-Do List) and one link (for the Running Late function described in Chapter 4). The following code implements the basic structure of this main menu in a single document (see Listing 7-2 from Step1\SPIMMainMenu.vxml). When the VoiceXML interpreter executes the document, it starts executing the first form or menu in the document.

A <menu> consists of a spoken prompt and a set of choices. When the <menu> is executed, the prompt is read and then the system listens for the user to say one of the choices. The choices are specified in the body of the <choice> tag. When a choice is recognized, the system starts executing the form or menu identified by the value of the next attribute, which is interpreted as a URI.

Listing 7-2. Main Menu

```
<menu id="topLevelChoices">
    <prompt>Your choices are: <enumerate /></prompt>
    <choice next="#calendar">Calendar</choice>
```

```
    <choice next="#toDo">To-Do List</choice>
    <choice next="#addressBook">Address Book</choice>
  </menu>
```

The prompt for a menu either can be coded explicitly or can use the <enumerate/> tag. The <enumerate/> tag simply returns the list of all available choices. In the example, the line

```
<prompt>Your choices are: <enumerate /> </prompt>
```

is equivalent to

```
<prompt>Your choices are: Calendar, To-Do List, Address Book </prompt>
```

In the example, the targets of the next attribute start with the pound sign (#). In URI-ese, # indicates an intradocument link. In the absence of an explicit document address, the current document is assumed, so #calendar refers to the form whose ID is "calendar" in the current document. For this example, the forms are "stubbed out," so that they will simply say a message and exit.

A menu or form field specifies a prompt/response exchange between the caller and the computer. A link is a transition that the caller can activate at any time the computer is listening for a response. Whereas a menu choice generally corresponds to only one spoken phrase, a link specifies a grammar. The grammar may be as simple as a single word or phrase, or it may be more complex. The example link in Listing 7-3 will be activated when either of two phrases is recognized: "late" or "I'm late." Like a menu choice, the voice interpreter goes to the target of the next attribute when the link is activated. The most obvious differences between menu choices and links are that links do not specify prompts and there is no <enumerate/> tag for links.

Application with Multiple Dialogs

In this step, you'll add another level to the SPIM dialog hierarchy. The first task is to convert the stubbed-out forms into menus (which in turn point to stubbed-out forms). The result is in Step2. However, the document is starting to get lengthy and confusing to read, so you're going to break it out into multiple documents.

The relationship between VoiceXML dialogs and documents is analogous to the relationship between functions (subroutines) and files in a programming language such as C or C++. The language does not specify any fixed relationship, but there are subtle considerations involving information hiding, readability, maintainability, and so on. In any nontrivial VoiceXML application, developers will need to establish coding standards that cover this issue (and other issues).

The result of breaking the dialogs out is in Step3. In Listing 7-3, notice that the URIs associated with menu choices in the main menu have been adjusted to point to the new documents.

Listing 7-3. Dialogs Broken Out into Multiple Documents

```
<?xml version="1.0" encoding="UTF-8"?>
<vxml version="1.0" application="SPIMApplication.vxml">
  <menu id="topLevelChoices">
    <prompt>Your choices are: <enumerate />
    </prompt>
    <choice next="/Step3/Calendar.vxml#calendarActions">Calendar</choice>
    <choice next="/Step3/ToDo.vxml#toDoActions">To-Do List</choice>
    <choice next="/Step3/AddressBook.vxml#addressBookActions">Address
Book</choice>
  </menu>
  <link next="#Late">
    <grammar type="application/x-jgsf">late | I'm late</grammar>
  </link>

  <form id="Late">
    <block>
      <prompt>You are late.</prompt>
    </block>
  </form>

 </vxml>
```

In the spirit of reorganizing everything at once, the dialogs have also been grouped into a single VoiceXML application. Documents associate with applications by specifying the application attribute on the <vxml> tag. Its value is a URI that points to the root document of the application. Whenever a document is loaded by the VoiceXML interpreter, the interpreter ensures that the application root document is loaded. Therefore, any grammars, dialogs, links, variables, and so on active in the root document are active whenever any other document in the application is loaded. The application root document in Listing 7-4 establishes a scope that is shared by all documents in the application.

Listing 7-4. Basic Application Root Document

```
<?xml version="1.0"?>
<vxml version="1.0" application="/SmallExamples/SPIMApplicationBasic.vxml">
  <!--Application root document for the SPIM application
```

```
     contains common links that are always active-->
  <meta name="Content-Type" content="text/x-vxml" />
   <var name="userName" expr="'Ken'"/>
  <form>
    <block>
      <prompt>Hi, <value expr="userName" />!</prompt>
      <goto next="/Step3/SPIMMainMenu.vxml#mainActions" />
    </block>
  </form>
</vxml>
```

The application root document shown in Listing 7-4 (from SmallExamples\SPIMApplicationBasic.vxml) contains a variable called username. This variable can be referenced by any document in the application as application.username. For this basic example, the variable is simply initialized to the string "Ken." The application root contains a single form that greets the user ("Hi, Ken!") and dispatches immediately to the main menu. It's actually not necessary for the root document to contain any executable forms; it can also function as a passive repository for shared variables and links used in other documents.

Visiting Documents

The Web is based on HTTP, and HTTP is based on the paradigm of hypertext linking. As a result, it is not surprising that VoiceXML provides several tags for transitioning between dialogs.

<goto> and <submit>

The application root document oversees authentication of the user and then invokes the main menu using a <goto> tag:

```
<goto next="SPIMMainMenu.vxml#mainActions" />
```

The next attribute specifies the URI of a dialog to execute. URIs are resolved relative to the current document. (See Table 7-1 for examples.)

Table 7-1. Sample <goto> Tags

TAG	MEANING
`<goto next="#localForm" />`	Execute the dialog called "localForm" in the current document.
`<goto next="SomeDocument.vxml" />`	Execute the first dialog in the document "SomeDocument.vxml" in the same directory as the current document.
`<goto next="SomeDocument.vxml#dialog1" />`	Execute dialog "dialog1" in the document "SomeDocument.vxml" in the same directory as the current document.
`<goto next="../AnotherDocument.vxml />`	Execute the first dialog in the document "AnotherDocument.vxml" in the parent directory of the current document.
`<goto next="http://www.apress.com/vxml/test/TestDocument.vxml#sampleDialog" />`	Execute "sampleDialog" at the given Web address.

A close relative of <goto> is <submit>. The <submit> next attribute specifies a Web address to visit. The namelist attribute specifies a list of names of variables whose values are to be passed by an HTTP GET or POST request. The following <submit> tag is used to send the user name and current time to the server:

```
<submit namelist="application.user when" next="LateAppointment.jsp" />
```

The .jsp suffix on the URI indicates that the target of the <submit> is a (Java) server page. The server page processes the submitted arguments and dynamically generates a VoiceXML document that is returned to the VoiceXML interpreter. During development of a VoiceXML application, it is best to start with static VoiceXML and deal with the complexities of dynamic generation once the basic framework of the application is firm. So, for the first run through, hand code all dialogs, even ones that will be generated in the working application. Evidence of this technique can be seen in the following pair of lines:

```
<!--<submit namelist="application.user when" next="LateAppointment.jsp"/>-->
    <goto next="LateAppointment001.vxml" />
```

During early development, the <goto> tag transfers control to the hand-coded version of the target page. After everything works together, the <goto> statement will be commented out and the <submit> tag will be used instead.

Subdialogs

In your sample SPIM application, authentication will be performed by a utility program that is part of the security infrastructure rather than part of the SPIM application proper. To model this for the future, you'll invoke an authentication routine from the application root and plan on substituting the real implementation later.

The VoiceXML <subdialog> functions like the "call" statement in some programming languages. When another dialog is invoked using <subdialog>, the dialog executes and then returns control to the caller. Optionally, the caller can specify input and/or output parameters to the subdialog. However, unlike programming languages, which typically have special syntax to distinguish parameters from local variables in a subroutine or method, VoiceXML does not provide any special syntax for parameters.

> **NOTE**   *There is a subtle distinction between dialogs that are invoked through* <subdialog> *and those invoked through* <goto>. *If invoked as a subdialog, a form returns control to the caller by executing a* <return> *tag. However, it is a semantic error to execute a* <return> *tag when executing as the result of a* <goto>. *So it's not clear how to code forms that can be invoked either way.*

In Listing 7-5 (from Step4\SPIMApplication.vxml), a <subdialog> tag is used to invoke the login form in the Authenticator document. The name attribute on the <subdialog> tag implicitly declares a local variable that will hold the output parameters, if any, of the subdialog. Input parameters are passed through <param> tag(s), which immediately follow the <subdialog> tag. The names specified in the <param> tags should match the names of local variables declared in the form being called, but this is not enforced by the VoiceXML interpreter. The <filled> tag is executed when the subdialog has placed output parameters in the output variable.

Listing 7-5. A Subdialog

```
<subdialog name="login" src="/Step4/Authenticator.vxml#login">
    <!-- Input parameters are passed to subdialog local variables-->
    <param name="application" expr="'SPIM'" />
    <param name="enableAnonymous" expr="false" type="boolean" />

    <filled>
        <!-- When the subdialog has set values for the "login" object
             assign the id to the application variable "userName" -->
        <assign name="userName" expr="login.userId" />
    </filled>
</subdialog>
```

In Listing 7-6 (from Step4\Authenticator.vxml), there are three variables declared local to the form: Two correspond to input parameters and one corresponds to the output parameter. When the login form is invoked as a subdialog, the local variables are initialized with values specified in the caller's <param> tags. When the <return> tag is executed, values are copied from local variables listed in the namelist attribute into the output variable in the caller.

Listing 7-6. Login Form

```
<form id="login">
    <var name="application" />      <!-- Input param -->
    <var name="enableAnonymous"/>      <!-- Input param -->

    <var name="userId" />         <!-- Output param -->
    <block>
    <!-- For the time being, always set user ID to "Ken" -->
    <assign name="userId" expr="'Ken'" />
    <return  namelist="userId" />
    </block>
</form>
```

Form Handling

Forms are the workhorses of VoiceXML for gathering information from the user. In Step5, you take a first crack at the form used to add a new appointment to the address book. This an ambitious task, because there are several data items to gather:

- Whom the appointment is with (should be a known contact)

- When the appointment is scheduled

- The duration of the appointment

- The medium of the appointment (a telephone call, a face-to-face meeting, and so on)

- The location of the appointment (home, work, and so on)

Directed Form

The simplest approach is to go through the list of data items you need and ask the user for them one by one. This corresponds to the simplest kind of input form: a directed form. In a *directed form,* the computer prompts the user explicitly for each item and does not proceed to the next item until the current item has been successfully elicited. A directed form for gathering information for a new appointment is shown in Listing 7-7 (from Step5\AddAppointment.vxml).

Listing 7-7. Directed Form

```
<?xml version="1.0" encoding="UTF-8"?>
<!DOCTYPE vxml SYSTEM "http://www.voicexml.org/voicexml1-0.dtd">
<vxml version="1.0" application="/SPIMApplication.vxml">
  <meta name="Content-Type" content="text/x-vxml"/>
  <meta name="Source" content="Step5/AddAppointment.vxml"/>
  <!-- SPIM Example: Dialog to add an appointment
    to the calendar                      -->

  <form id="addAppointment">
    <block>
      <prompt>You are adding a new appointment.</prompt>
    </block>

    <field name="appointee">
      <prompt>Who is the appointment with?</prompt>
    <option value="ken abbott"> Ken </option>
    <option value="dennis mccarthy"> Dennis </option>
    <option value="susan abbott"> Susan </option>
    </field>
```

```
<field name="year">
  <prompt>What year?</prompt>
  <grammar type="application/x-jgsf">
      2001 | 2002 | 2003 | 2004 | 2005 | 2006 | 2007
  </grammar>
</field>

<field name="month">
  <prompt>What month?</prompt>
  <grammar type="application/x-jgsf">
January | February | March | April | May | June |
July | August | September | October | November | December</grammar>
</field>

<field name="date" type="date">
  <prompt>What date?</prompt>
</field>

<field name="time" type="time">
  <prompt>What time?</prompt>
</field>

<field name="where">
  <grammar type="application/x-jgsf">home | work | office | other</grammar>
  <prompt>Will it be at home, office, work, or other?</prompt>
</field>

<field name="medium">
  <grammar type="application/x-jgsf">
  call | meet | teleconference | other
  </grammar>
  <prompt>Call, meet, teleconference, or other?</prompt>
</field>

<block>
  <prompt>You have a <value expr="medium" />
    with <value expr="appointee" />
    on <value expr="month" />
        <value expr="date" />
        <value expr="year" />
    at <value expr="hour" />
    at <value expr="where" />.
</prompt>
```

```
        <!-- At this point, the data for the appointment
          should be submitted to the server -->
      <clear />
      </block>
    </form>
</vxml>
```

The form consists of a set of fields, one field for each data item. The <field> tag implicitly declares a variable that will contain the value of the field. Each field has its own prompt and its own grammar describing valid responses to the prompt. When the form is executed, the VoiceXML interpreter starts at the top of the form and works its way through the fields one at a time. The interpreter speaks the prompt and waits for a spoken response. If the user doesn't respond within a default time-out period, or the response could not be matched to the grammar, the interpreter informs the user of the error and prompts again for the same information.[1] When the interpreter recognizes a valid response, it assigns the recognized speech to the field variable and moves on to the next field.

The "appointee" field uses <option> tags to identify a set of alternative responses to the prompt. The body of the tag contains a grammar specifying one or more equivalent responses. When any one of the responses is recognized, the value from the value attribute is assigned to the field variable. If the dtmf attribute is specified, and then the keypad value is also an alternative. For example:

```
<field name="personName">
<option value="'ken abbott'" dtmf="1"> [Ken | Kenneth] [Abbott] </option>
```

The previous code will cause the value 'ken abbott' to be assigned to the variable personName if any of the following are recognized: "Ken," "Kenneth," "Ken Abbott," "Kenneth Abbott," "Abbott," or keypress "1." The <enumerate> tag will work in conjunction with <option> tags, but the results may not be what you expect if the body of the option contains a grammar rather than a single phrase. Grammars are discussed in detail in Chapter 9.

The "year" and "month" fields specify alternates using more concise field-level grammars. When one of the alternatives is recognized, the recognized value (as text) is assigned to the field variable.

The "date" and "time" fields make use of built-in grammars. There are seven: boolean, date, time, digits, currency, number, and phone (see Table A-6). The idea

---

[1] It's up to the interpreter to set the default policy for how many times it will reprompt. The application is also free to specify event handling and not rely on the default policy.

is that these basic building blocks are implemented by the VoiceXML interpreter in a locale-sensitive fashion.[2]

While directed forms are simple and effective, long ones don't stand up well to repeated use. A person often doesn't mind going through a list once or twice when it's new. Once the person understands what's expected, he or she may find it very frustrating to waste time going item by item. In addition, people find the strict "turn-taking" (computer speaks, the person responds; computer speaks, the person responds; and so on) conversationally awkward. In general, directed forms are best used for brief, structured interactions such as taking a credit card number or eliciting a person's address.

A partial solution to the frustration factor is to enable *bargein*. This means that the computer listens for a response at the same time it speaks the prompt. If the person knows what to say, they can "barge in" by speaking over the prompt and interrupting the strict turn-taking. Bargein is enabled by setting the `bargein` attribute of the <prompt> tag to `true`. As a rule, bargein should be enabled whenever possible. However, it is not foolproof. The computer may have trouble recognizing the start of a response, or it may have trouble hearing the response. The latter situation often occurs when talking over a telephone. The echo suppressors in the phone network do not work perfectly and they can make a phone act like a nonduplex device, where only one person can talk and be heard at the same time.

Mixed-Initiative Forms

To achieve a more conversational style of interaction than computer-directed forms, VoiceXML supports mixed-initiative forms. They are called "mixed-initiative" because both the computer and the person can direct what fields are filled and in what order. Another significant feature is that multiple fields can be filled by a single utterance.

In Listing 7-8, the directed dialog has been converted to a mixed-initiative dialog. This involves the following VoiceXML constructs, which I'll cover in turn:

---

[2] The interpreter should provide input grammars that recognize these basic elements and format the responses into a canonical format, and it should provide speech synthesis that reads the canonical format in the appropriate local idiom. In theory, you could write standard VoiceXML that manipulates dates and currencies without regard for locale. In practice, VoiceXML 1.0 is murky and underspecified in describing how these types behave, so use of these constructs is at least VoiceXML interpreter dependent, if not locale dependent as well.

- Form-level grammar

- <initial> tag

- <help> tag

Listing 7-8. Mixed-Initiative Dialog

```
<?xml version="1.0" encoding="UTF-8"?>
<!DOCTYPE vxml SYSTEM "http://www.voicexml.org/voicexml1-0.dtd">
<vxml version="1.0" application="/SPIMApplication.vxml">
  <meta name="Source" content="Step6/AddAppointment.vxml"/>
  <!-- SPIM Example: Dialog to add an appointment
    to the calendar                 -->

  <form id="addAppointment">
    <grammar type="application/x-jgsf">
      <![CDATA[
    [call | meet | teleconference | videoconference]{this.medium=$}
    [Dennis | Susan | Ken] {this.appointee=$}
    [on
              (Sunday | Monday | Tuesday | Wednesday |
               Thursday | Friday | Saturday)
               {this.day=$}]
    [at
              ((one | two | three | four | five | six |
                seven | eight | nine | ten | eleven | twelve)
                [am | pm]) {this.hour=$} ]
    ]]>
    </grammar>

    <initial name="appointment">
      <prompt>Add appointment. You may say help at any time.</prompt>
      <help>
        <prompt>Say something like call Dennis on Thursday at three
pm.</prompt>
      </help>
    </initial>

    <field name="appointee">
      <prompt>With whom?</prompt>
      <grammar type="application/x-jgsf">Dennis | Susan | Ken</grammar>
```

```
  <help>
    <prompt>
        Say the name of the person you are making an appointment with.
    </prompt>
  </help>
</field>

<field name="day">
  <prompt>What day of the week?</prompt>
  <grammar type="application/x-jgsf">
        Sunday | Monday | Tuesday | Wednesday | Thursday | Friday | Saturday
  </grammar>
  <help>
    <prompt>Days are Sunday through Saturday.</prompt>
  </help>
</field>

<field name="hour">
  <grammar type="application/x-jgsf">
     (one | two | three | four | five | six |
      seven | eight | nine | ten | eleven | twelve)
     [am | pm]
 </grammar>
  <help>
    <prompt>Say something like three pm.</prompt>
  </help>
</field>

<field name="where">
  <grammar type="application/x-jgsf">home | office | other</grammar>
  <prompt>Where?</prompt>
  <help>Say work, home, office, or other.</help>
</field>

<field name="medium">
  <grammar type="application/x-jgsf">
     call | meet | teleconference | other
  </grammar>
  <prompt>Call, meet, teleconference, or other?</prompt>
  <help>
      <prompt>
      Say one of call, meet, teleconference, or videoconference.
    </prompt>
```

```
      </help>
    </field>

  <block>
    <prompt>You have a <value expr="medium" />
      with <value expr="appointee" />
      on <value expr="month" />
          <value expr="date" />
          <value expr="year" />
      at <value expr="hour" />
      at <value expr="where" />.
    </prompt>
    <!-- At this point, the data for the appointment
      should be submitted to the server -->
    <clear />
  </block>
  </form>
</vxml>
```

Form-Level Grammar

The form-level grammar is the key to mixed-initiative dialogs. It describes a set of valid responses and specifies how elements of the response are assigned to field variables. In the example, the form-level grammar is enclosed in a <![CDATA[ ]]> tag. This impressive-looking tag is a generic XML tag that turns off XML parsing for its contents. It is useful for specifying inline grammars, because grammar syntax includes special characters. If the special characters were parsed, they would have to be written using XML escape sequences (for example, "<" must be written as "<"; "&" becomes "&"; and so on). Using the CDATA tag avoids confusion and keeps the grammar readable.

Consider the following grammar:

```
[call | meet | teleconference | videoconference]{this.medium=$}
 (Dennis | Susan | Ken) {this.appointee=$}
 [on (Sunday | Monday | Tuesday | Wednesday
          | Thursday | Friday | Saturday) {this.day=$}]
 [at ((one | two | three | four | five | six |
      seven | eight | nine | ten | eleven | twelve) [am | pm])
  {this.hour=$} ]
```

The previous grammar will match any of the following utterances (as well as others):

"Call Dennis."
"Meet Susan at 1."
"Teleconference Ken on Thursday."
"Meet Dennis on Sunday at 9 p.m."

The curly-braced entities are tags used by VoiceXML. Tags appear immediately after phrases in the grammar. When the phrase is recognized, the body of the tag is substituted for the recognized text and returned to the VoiceXML interpreter, which treats it as executable script. For example:

1. The person says "Call Dennis."

2. The recognizer recognizes the phrase "call."

3. In the first tag body, $ is replaced by the recognized text ("call").

4. The recognizer recognizes the phrase "Dennis."

5. In the second tag body, $ is replaced by the recognized text ("Dennis").

6. The recognizer returns the tags to the VoiceXML interpreter.

7. The VoiceXML interpreter interprets the two tags: {this.medium="call"} and {this.appointee="Dennis"}, resulting in form fields "medium" and "appointee" both being filled in from the utterance.

The <initial> Tag

The <initial> tag acts like the first field in a mixed-initiative dialog. Like a <field>, it has a prompt, but its grammar is the form-level grammar. After the initial prompt is spoken, the computer attempts to match the response against the form-level grammar. If one or more field variables are set as a result of recognizing the response, the <initial> tag is considered to have been "filled," and processing continues on to the next field. However, if the response is erroneous or not recognized, the user will be prompted again.

The <initial> prompt is a general solicitation for the user to provide as much information as he or she is able. If the user knows what to say and speaks clearly, the <initial> prompt may be the only prompt he or she responds to in the form. If the user provides some, but not all, of the information, the computer reverts to a directed form to fill in the missing pieces.

As a result, Dialog 7-1 and Dialog 7-2 are both acceptable.

Dialog 7-1. Mixed-Initiative Dialog (Single Utterance)

C (computer): Add appointment. You may say help at any time.
P (person): Call Susan on Friday at 10 a.m. at work.
C: You have a call with Susan on Friday at 10 a.m. at work.

Dialog 7-2. Mixed-Initiative Dialog (with Prompting)

C (computer): Add appointment. You may say help at any time.
P (person): Call Susan at 10 a.m.
C: What day?
P: Friday.
C: Where?
P: Work.
C: You have a call with Susan on Friday at 10 a.m. at work.

Handling Events

So far, you've focused on the "talking" aspects of VoiceXML. Just as a conversation between people involves more interaction than just the transcript of the words spoken, so does scripting a VoiceXML interaction involve more than just defining prompts and responses. A good VUI must anticipate and handle all the vagaries of working in the real world: interruptions, noise, misunderstandings, lack of attention, soft voices, foreign accents, poor phone lines, unexpected disconnects, nonstandard vocabularies, and so on. The more you study speech, the greater appreciation you develop for natural human languages as frameworks for communicating reliably using an inherently error-prone medium. However, as pointed out before, VoiceXML has no cognitive model and is not capable of natural language.

What VoiceXML does have is a rich event model, which provides the basic hooks for dealing with many of the real-time issues in scripting a speech interaction. Looking back at Step6\AddAppointment.vxml, you see that the explicit scripting took into account two kinds of events: recognition events and help events.

Recognition events are events triggered by the VoiceXML interpreter when a phrase in an active grammar is recognized with acceptable certainty. For the most part, recognition events are handled invisibly by VoiceXML. For example, the language-defined semantics for the <initial>, <field>, and <choice> constructs rely implicitly on recognition events happening in the interpreter. Recognition events can also be handled explicitly by using the <filled> tag. For example, the fragment in Listing 7-9 simply plays back what the computer heard when it recognized the response to the <prompt>.

Listing 7-9. "Filled" Event Handler

```
<initial name="appointment">
    <prompt>Add appointment. You may say help at any time.</prompt>
    <filled>
      <prompt> You said:
                    <value expr="appointment$.utterance">
            </prompt>
    </filled>
  </initial>
```

The help events coded into Step6\AddAppointment.vxml are triggered by the VoiceXML interpreter. Presumably, the interpreter triggers help events when it recognizes piteous phrases such as "help me" (the triggering phrases are not specified by VoiceXML 1.0). Help events are one element of a larger set of built-in events defined by VoiceXML (see Chapter 9 for more information).

Let's look at sample transcripts that are supported by Step6\AddAppointment.vxml. The first example is the best-case scenario, where the person knows what to say and responds correctly to the prompt (see Dialog 7-3).

Dialog 7-3. Dialog with Knowledgable Person

C (computer): Add appointment. You may say help at any time.
P (person): Call Pete on Friday at 10 a.m.
C: You have a call with Pete on Friday at 10 a.m.

In Table 7-2, the person asks for help, the <help> prompt is read, and the user responds correctly.

Table 7-2. Mixed-Initiative Dialog with Help

SPEECH	VOICEXML

C (computer): Add appointment. *You may say help at any time.*	`<initial name="appointment">`
	  `<prompt>`
	  `Add appointment. You may say help at any time.`
	  `</prompt>`

P (person): Help.
 	
 C: Say something like call *Dennis on Thursday at three pm.*
	`<help>`
	    `<prompt>`
	    `Say something like call Dennis on Thursday at three pm.`
	    `</prompt>`
	 `</help>`

P: Call Dennis.	`<grammar type="application/x-jgsf">` `<![CDATA[` `[call	meet	teleconference	`      `videoconference]{this.medium=$}`      `[Dennis	Susan	Ken] {this.appointee=$}`      `. . .`      `]]>`   `</grammar>`
C: What day of the week? *P: Wednesday.*	`<field name="day">` `<prompt>What day of the week?</prompt>` `<grammar type="application/x-jgsf">` `Sunday	Monday	Tuesday	Wednesday |`      `Thursday	Friday	Saturday`      `</grammar>`
C: What time will you meet? *P: 8 p.m.*	`<field name="hour">` `<prompt>What time will you meet? </prompt>` `<grammar type="application/x-jgsf">` `(one | two | three | four | five | six |` `seven | eight | nine | ten | eleven |` `twelve) [am	pm]`      `</grammar>`

Table 7-2. Mixed-Initiative Dialog with Help (continued)

SPEECH	VOICEXML
C: *Where will you meet?*	`<field name="where">`
	`  <grammar type="application/x-jgsf">`
	` home	office	other`
	`  </grammar>`
P: *Work.*	`<prompt>Where will you meet?</prompt>`
C: *You have a call with Dennis on Wednesday at eight pm at work.*	`<block>`
	`  <prompt>`
	`  You have a <value expr="medium" />`
	`  with <value expr="appointee" />`
	`  <value expr="day" />`
	`  at <value expr="hour" />`
	`  at <value expr="where" />.`
	`  </prompt>`
	`  <goto next="#newAppointment" />`
	`</block>`

If the person doesn't speak, the prompt will generate a `timeout` event after a default amount of time. There is no explicit handler for a time-out, so the default handler for the `timeout` event simply repeats the prompt and waits some more (see Table 7-3).

Table 7-3: Dialog with `noinput` *Events*

SPEECH	VOICEXML
C (computer): *Add appointment. You may say help at any time.*	`<initial name="appointment">`
	`  <prompt>Add appointment. You may say help at any time.</prompt>`
P (person): *{silence}*	`{times out}`
C: *Add appointment. You may say help at any time.*	`{VXML default noinput handler}`
P: *{silence}*	`{times out}`
C: *Add appointment. You may say help at any time.*	`{VXML default noinput handler}`

In Table 7-4, the person responds inappropriately, so a nomatch event is generated. There is no explicit handler, so the default handler says "I didn't get that," repeats the prompt, and waits some more.

Table 7-4. Dialog with nomatch *Events*

SPEECH	VOICEXML
C (computer): Add appointment. You may say help at any time.	`<initial name="appointment">` `<prompt>Add appointment. You may say help at any time.</prompt>`
P (person): {mumble} *C: I didn't get that. Add appointment. You may say help at any time.*	{VXML nomatch event} {VXML default nomatch handler}
P: {dtmf "1"} *C: I didn't get that. Add appointment. You may say help at any time.*	{VXML nomatch event} {VXML default nomatch handler}

Tapered Prompting

The default handlers get the job done, but they do not structure a well-designed interaction. Mechanically repeating the same prompt in response to a recurring situation leads to stalemate and an angry user. Applying the technique of *tapered prompting* can provide a better experience. In tapered prompting, the prompts are varied based on prior experience. For example, help prompts may "taper up," starting very concise and getting more verbose as the user requests more help, as in Dialog 7-4.

Dialog 7-4. Tapered Help

C (computer): Add appointment. You may say help at any time.
P (person): Help.
C: Say something like call Dennis on Thursday at three pm.
P: Help.
C: You are adding an appointment to your calendar. Say something like call Dennis on Thursday at three pm.
P: Help.
C: You are adding an appointment to your calendar. An appointment involves another person, a scheduled time, and a location. You will be asked for these individually.
C: Who are you meeting with?

On the other hand, interrogational prompts may get terser as the person uses them and learns what's expected, as in Dialog 7-5.

Dialog 7-5. Tapered Interrogation

C (computer): Add appointment. You may say help at any time.
P (person): Call Dennis.
C: What day will you meet?
P: Wednesday.
C: What time will you meet?
P: 8 p.m.
C: Where will you meet?
P: Work.
C: You have a call with Dennis on Wednesday at eight pm at work.
C: Add appointment.
P: Call Dennis on Saturday.
C: Time?
P: 3 p.m.
C: Where?
P: Home.
C: You have a call with Dennis on Saturday at three pm at home.

In Step7\AddAppointment.vxml, improved error handling has been wrapped around the form fields to handle more errors and provide some tapering. nomatch, noinput, and help handlers have been added. The handlers use the count="n" attribute to modify which handler is activated after at least n invocations. The basic strategy is to provide two layers of help prompting, a terse level and a verbose level, and to permit the help handler to switch the form into directed mode. The nomatch and noinput handlers invoke the help handler if the events recur. The directed form fields provide a terse and verbose interrogational prompt for each field.

See Table 7-5 for an elaboration of how the tapered help prompting is implemented using event counters. Notice how the dialog switches from mixed-initiative mode to directed mode by setting the value of "directedDisabled" in the <help count=3> handler. Because the entry condition (cond attribute) on the <initial> tag fails, the interpreter does not visit the <initial> tag again. The interpreter looks for the next form item whose variable has not been set and continues prompting in directed mode.

Table 7-5. Tapered Help Prompting

SPEECH	VOICEXML
C (computer): Add appointment. *You may say help at any time.*	```<grammar`` `src="/NewAppointment.gram#appointment"` `type="application/x-jgsf" />` `<initial name="appointment"` `cond="document.disableDirected">` `<prompt>` `Add appointment. You may say help at any time.` `</prompt> ...` `</initial>```
P (person): Help. *C: Say something like call Dennis* *on Thursday at three pm.*	```<help count="1">`` `<prompt>` `Say something like call Dennis on Thursday at three pm.` `</prompt>` `</help>```
P: Help. *C: You are adding an appointment* *to your calendar. Say something like* *call Dennis on Thursday at three pm.*	```<help count="2">`` `<prompt>` `You are adding an appointment to your calendar.` `Say something like call Dennis on Thursday at three pm.` `</prompt>` `</help```
P: Help. *C: You are adding an appointment* *to your calendar. An appointment* *involves another person, a scheduled* *time, and a location. You will be* *asked for these individually.*	```<help count="3">`` `<prompt>` `You are adding an appointment to your calendar.` `An appointment involves another person,` `a scheduled time, and a location.` `Please answer some questions about the appointment.` `</prompt>` `<!-- Switch over to directed mode. Stay in directed` `       mode until this form is reentered. -->` `<assign name="document.disableDirected"` `  expr="false" />` `<reprompt />` `</help>` `<field name="appointee" >```
C: Who are you meeting with?	```<prompt count="1">`` `Who are you meeting with?` `</prompt>` `...` `</field>```

Table 7-5. Tapered Help Prompting (continued)

SPEECH	VOICEXML
P: Dennis.	
	```<subdialog```
	``` src="/Step7/GetDayAndHour.vxml#getDayAndHour"```
	``` name="when">```
	``` <param name="i_day" expr="dialog.day"/>```
	``` <param name="i_day_prompt" expr="'What day?'" />```
	``` <param name="i_hour" expr="dialog.hour" />```
C: What day?	``` <param name="i_hour_prompt" expr="'What time?'" />```
P: Tomorrow at 3 p.m.	``` <filled>```
	``` <assign name="day" expr="when.day" />```
	``` <assign name="hour" expr="when.hour" />```
	``` </filled>```
	```</subdialog>```
. . .	```{field by field processing continues}```

Prompt Counting

The prompt-counting mechanism may not work exactly as you expect. In the previous example, the person can specify as many appointments as he or she wants. It would be nice if the first time through, the computer read the long prompt and then used the terse prompt for subsequent appointments. However, this is not how the prompt counter works. Every time a field is cleared, its prompt counter is reset to zero. All fields are implicitly cleared when the form is reentered (by a <goto>), or when a <clear/> is executed (as in the example).

Therefore, the only time the terse prompt <prompt count=2> is heard is when a </reprompt> is issued from within the body of the <field>. The desired behavior—only saying the verbose prompt once—can be achieved by keeping your own count with an application-scoped variable, as shown in Listing 7-10 (from Step7\ManualCounter.vxml). The count can be used as a guard condition on <prompt> by explicitly testing it in the cond attribute.

Listing 7-10. Manual Prompt Counter

```
<!-- This variable should be in document or application scope-->
  <var name="myFieldCounter" expr="1" />
  <form>
    <var name="mlname" expr="'VXML'" />
    <field name="theField">
      <grammar type="application/x-jgsf">something</grammar>
      <prompt cond="document.myFieldCounter == 1">
          This is a verbose prompt!
      </prompt>
      <prompt cond="document.myFieldCounter != 1">terse!</prompt>
      <filled>
        <script>document.myFieldCounter +=1;</script>
      </filled>
    </field>
```

Queries and Sets

One of the biggest challenges in designing a VUI is browsing through collections of data. The nature of speech forces a linear style of browsing, which can be very time-consuming and tedious. In the SPIM application, this problem occurs when reviewing appointments for a given time period. The number of appointments that a person has can vary widely from day to day, so some days a person may have more than a dozen and other days that person may only have two or three.

To implement the Review Appointments function, you need to establish the time period of interest. The sample form Step8\ReviewAppointments.vxml shows some dialogs that perform this function. Notice that in this case, the imprecision of language can actually be very useful—for example, people find it comfortable to say something like "tomorrow afternoon," but they may find it tedious to have to completely spell out "March 23, 2001, 12:00 a.m. to 6:00 p.m." Furthermore, people can have different opinions about what "afternoon" includes. You'll want to take advantage of these compact linguistic patterns that people use to communicate effectively.

The strategy in the VoiceXML form is simply to capture a valid specification of a time period from the user. The recognized text will be shipped to a server program to interpret precisely what was intended. (This is consistent with the principle that VoiceXML is a presentation language, not a processing language.) The server program will interpret what the user said, restate the time period in precise terms (that is, in a query language), retrieve all the appointments in that time period, and return the collection (as generated VoiceXML) to the user (see Figure 7-2).

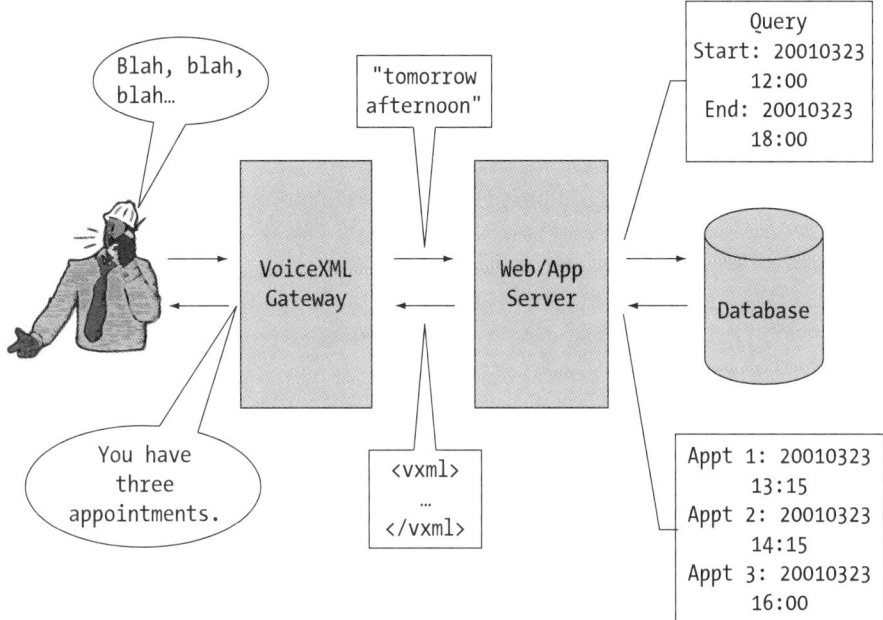

Figure 7-2. Reviewing appointments

Recognizing a Time Period

To specify the period of interest for reviewing appointments, a person should be able to specify various permutations of the following time periods (and others):

Today
Tomorrow afternoon
Next Thursday
March twenty third two thousand one after two fifteen pm
Saturday from three through six
July eighteenth two thousand one from seven fifteen am through July nineteenth eight thirty pm

To recognize a person's specification of a time period of interest, the JGSF grammar defined in SearchAppointment.gram (Listing 7-11) is used. In Listing 7-11, notice that the more basic productions (for example, days of the week) appear first and are followed by more complex rules that use the basic ones. The most comprehensive production is <timeframe>. In the course of recognizing an utterance as a <timeframe>, the parser also has to recognize component <day>s, <hour>s, <timespan>s, and so on.

Listing 7-11. Grammar for Specifying Time Periods

```
public <dayofweek> = ( today | tomorrow |
   [ a week from | next ] (Sunday | Monday | Tuesday | Wednesday | Thursday |
                        Friday | Saturday ));
public <hour> = (((one | two | three | four | five | six | seven | eight | nine
               | ten | eleven | twelve)
         [o'clock | fifteen  | thirty | forty-five] [am | pm] ) |
         ( noon | midnight )) {this.hour=$};

public <month> = (January | February | March | April | May | June | July |
               August | September | October | November | December );
public <dayofmonth> = (thirtieth | thirty-first | twentieth | tenth ) |
               [twenty] ( first | second | third | fourth | fifth | sixth |
               seventh | eighth | ninth ) |
               (eleventh | twelfth | thirteenth | fourteenth | fifteenth |
               sixteenth | seventeenth | eighteenth | nineteenth);
public <year> = [two thousand] (one | two | three | four | five | six | seven );

public <date> = <month> <dayofmonth> [<year>] |
               <dayofmonth> [of] <month> [year];
public <day> =  <dayofweek>  | <date> ;

public <timespan> = ( afternoon | morning | evening | all day );
public <relativetime> = after | before | around | about;
public <timeframe> = <day> {this.startday=$} [(
            [[from] <hour> {this.starthour=$}]
            [through [<day> {this.endday=$}] [<hour> {this.endhour=$}]] |
            <relativetime> {this.relativetime=$} <hour> {this.starthour=$} |
            <timespan> {this.timespan=$} )] ;
```

Notice that as various component phrases of a <timeframe> are recognized, the phrases are assigned to form field variables (by the expressions in curly braces, as discussed in the "Form-Level Grammar" section). Table 7-6 shows some examples of accepted utterances and the values assigned to field variables after the utterance is recognized.

Table 7-6. Parsing Time Frame Utterances

TIME FRAME SPECIFICATION	VOICEXML FIELD VARIABLES
Tomorrow	this.startday="tomorrow" this.starthour=undefined this.relativetime=undefined this.endday=undefined this.endhour=undefined this.timespan=undefined
March twenty third two thousand one after two fifteen pm	this.startday="March twenty third two thousand one" this.starthour="two fifteen pm" this.relativetime="after" this.endday=undefined this.endhour=undefined this.timespan=undefined
Thursday evening	this.startday="Thursday" this.starthour=undefined this.relativetime=undefined this.endday=undefined this.endhour=undefined this.timespan="evening"
July eighteenth two thousand one from seven fifteen am through July nineteenth eight thirty pm	this.startday="July eighteenth two thousand one" this.starthour="seven fifteen am" this.relativetime=undefined this.endday="July nineteenth" this.endhour="eight thirty pm" this.timespan=undefined

CAUTION *VoiceXML 1.0 does not specify grammar formats or the mechanism for communicating values from the recognizer back to the VoiceXML interpreter. Therefore, any VoiceXML 1.0 program has platform dependencies based on the grammar format and the passing of data. The previous example is fairly standard in that it uses JSGF and the tagging mechanism is supported by at least some voice platforms, including the IBM platform included with this book.*

> **VXML 2:** *VoiceXML 2.0 will specify the grammar format and will specify the mechanism for passing data from the recognizer to a VoiceXML program. However, at the time of this writing, the specification of the data-passing mechanism was still under development. The basic mechanism is expected to be similar to that used previously: The grammar will be tagged in such a way that recognized phrases are assigned to form field variables.*

Formatting a Query String

The grammar discussed in the preceding section is used by the form Step8\ReviewAppointments.vxml#getTimePeriod. The form works somewhat like the mixed-initiative dialog you used to define a new appointment (see the "Directed Form" section). The person can respond to the <initial> prompt with a full or partial specification of a time period. If the response is sufficient to specify a time period, the response is sent to the server for processing. If the response does not fully specify a time period, form getHourAndDay is invoked to get the precise hour and day. Notice that you are not forcing the person to be completely precise. If the person says "tomorrow afternoon" and nothing more, this is taken to be a full, valid specification, even though (formally) one could argue that "tomorrow afternoon" could also specify a start time that requires an end time (for example, "through Friday morning").

The following code declares field variables, but does not prompt for them:

```
<field name="startday" cond="false"></field>
<field name="relativetime" cond="false"></field>
<field name="timespan" cond="false"></field>
<field name="starthour" cond="false"></field>
<field name="endday" cond="false"></field>
<field name="endhour" cond="false"></field>
```

The fields are either filled in by the response to the <initial> prompt or the <subdialog> references. The <subdialog> tag contains the gross-looking attribute

```
cond="(startday == null) ||
   (endday==null &amp;&amp;relativetime == null &amp;&amp;timespan == null)"
```

The expression in parentheses uses XML escape codes, but the conditional expression is equivalent to the somewhat more easily read

```
startday==null || ( endday==null && relativetime == null && timespan == null)
```

The form item (in this case, subdialog invocation) is executed if its cond attribute evaluates to true. So, the meaning of this expression is "If the start day of the time period was not specified, or the start day was specified but not followed by an ending day, a relative time (for example, 'after 3'), or a time span (for example, 'evening'), then execute the subdialog to elicit a specific start day and time."

The "checkpoint" form item reads back the information gathered thus far and asks the user if he or she wants to review the appointments or start over. If the user wants to review the appointments in the time period, the query string is formatted using ECMAScript, as shown in Listing 7-12. The formatting puts information in a canonical order and makes sure that undefined values are not inserted.

Listing 7-12. ECMAScript Formatting

```
<var name="queryString" />
<script>
  <![CDATA[queryString =  startday +
    ( timespan == null ? "" : timespan ) +
    ( starthour==null ? "" :
    ( relativetime==null ? "" : relativetime) + starthour  ) +
    ( endday == null ? "" : " through " + endday + (endhour==null?"":endhour) ) +
    '.';]]>
</script>
```

This script makes use of ECMAScript and the <![CDATA]]> tag for compactness. It makes heavy use of the C-style <boolean>:<true-case>? <false-case> operator to avoid inserting the string "undefined" into the resulting query string. ("undefined" is the string representation of a null or undefined ECMAScript variable.) See Table 7-6 for examples of utterances and resulting variable values. Once the query string is formatted, it is passed to the server by a <submit> tag.

Browsing the Results

Based on results of the query, server components will generate VoiceXML code to browse the qualifying appointments (see Figure 7-3). Step8\BrowseAppointments001.vxml is an example of generated code. (Part III of this book gets into the details of how it is generated—for now just assume that it happened somehow.) Notice that specific information—variables, prompts, grammars, and so on—is coded directly into the generated VoiceXML.

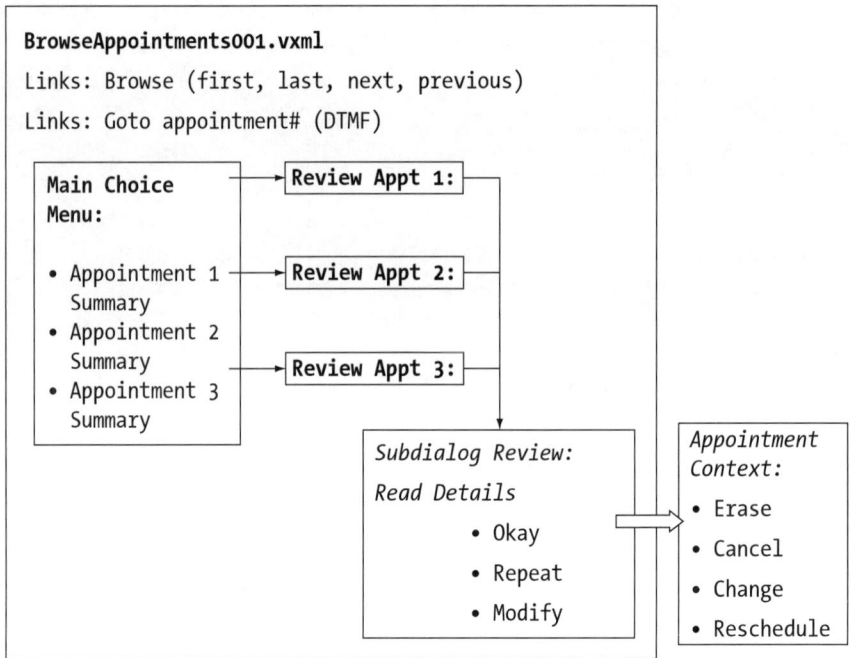

Figure 7-3. Structure of generated browsing code

The generated code contains two kinds of prompts for each appointment. There is a short prompt (for example, "Dennis at thirteen hundred.") that is used in the browse menu and a long prompt that gives the details (for example, "Weekly status meeting with Dennis and Fred at work on Thursday, May third from thirteen hundred hours to fourteen hundred hours.").

To implement browsing, links are specified at document scope. There are voice links ("first," "last," "next," and "previous") for moving relative the current appointment, and DTMF links, which go directly to the nth appointment. The links are at document scope so that they can be used in any of the dialogs in the generated voice browser. The generated code enables bargein at most prompts, so that a person can cut off the computer at any time. In Dialog 7-6, the person barges in three times. The first time, the person uses the keypad to go directly to the last appointment and escape from the reading of summaries. The second and third time, the person uses voice commands to cut off reading of unwanted details.

Dialog 7-6. Dialog with Bargein

C (computer): You have three appointments. One: Dennis at thirteen hundred.
    Two: Dentist at . . .
P (person): (barging in) DTMF "3."

C: *Appointment three. Dinner with Susan at Robertos Frito Misto on Thursday, May 3 from nineteen hundred hours to twenty one hundred hours. Your choices are okay, repeat, or modify appointment.*

P: *Repeat.*

C: *Dinner with Susan at Robertos . . .*

P: *(barging in) Previous.*

C: *Appointment two. Semiannual cleaning . . .*

P: *(barging in) First.*

C: *Appointment one. Weekly meeting with Dennis . . .*

Event Links

The navigational commands are implemented as links that throw events. This allows some processing to be performed when the link is activated, as shown in Listing 7-13.

Listing 7-13. An Event Link

```
<link event="browse.previous">
     <grammar type="application/x-jgsf"> previous </grammar>
   </link>
   <catch event="browse.previous">
     <script> current = Math.max( current-1, 1);</script>
     <goto expr="'#review'+current"/>
   </catch>
```

When a person says "previous," the link is activated and the application-defined event "browse.previous" is thrown in the dialog that was active when the user spoke. If there are no other "browse.previous" event handlers in nested forms or subdialogs, the document-scope "browse.previous" event handler will be invoked in the active dialog.[3] The event handler uses ECMAScript to do some simple math on a cursor variable that always identifies the current appointment, and then it goes to the generated review form for the new current appointment.

The behavior of event links is somewhat counterintuitive. At first glance, you would assume that a document-scoped link would throw a document-scoped event. However, that isn't really the case, because the whole point of links is to make a common set of actions available in all nested dialogs. Throwing the event at document scope would always terminate any nested dialogs, rather than give them a shot at handling the event. To see how this works, consider the example in Listing 7-14.

---

[3] See Chapter 9 for a detailed discussion of how this works.

Listing 7-14. Scope of Events Thrown by Links

```
<vxml>
    <link event="special.help">
        <grammar type="application/x-jgsf">double help</grammar>
    </link>
    <catch event="special.help">
        <prompt>Call 911!</prompt>
        <exit/>
    </catch>
    <form id=withSpecialHelp>
        <initial>
        <prompt>I am at your service.</prompt>
    </initial>
    <catch event="special.help" count="1">
        Please tell me whatever is on your mind.
        <reprompt/>
    </catch>
    <catch event="special.help" count="2">
        <throw event="special.help"/>
    </catch>
    </form>
    <form id=withoutSpecialHelp>
        <initial>
        <prompt>What do you want?</prompt>
    </initial>
</form>
</form>
</vxml>
```

In form "withSpecialHelp," the event is handled within the nested dialog the first time and then explicitly propagated out to document scope the second time (see Dialog 7-7).

Dialog 7-7. Nested Event Handler

C (computer): *I am at your service.*
P (person): *Double help.*
C: *Please tell me whatever is on your mind. I am at your service.*
P: *Double help.*
C: *Call 911! (exits)*

...

In form "withoutSpecialHelp," there is no nested event handler, so the event is handled by the document-level event handler (see Dialog 7-8).

Dialog 7-8. Document-Level Event Handler
C (computer): What do you want?
P (person): Double help.
C: Call 911! (exits)

"Punching Up" Prompts

Synthesized speech can be hard to understand because it comes out as an unemphasized stream, without the normal patterns of emphasis and pause that people use to highlight their speech. Consider the contrast between a person reading the two following sentences:

> "there are two reasons why small businesses fail one insufficient investment and two lack of forecasting."

> "There are two reasons why small businesses fail: 1.) insufficient investment, and 2.) lack of forecasting."

In the second case, a person will add pauses around and emphasis on the numbers to signal that he or she is labeling the following phrase.

To achieve a similar effect in the prompts, where numbers label options, the generated prompt in form "mainChoice" contains embedded <break> tags. The size attribute of <break> can be none, small, medium, or large, or the msecs attribute can specify the pause length in milliseconds. The generated prompts look like this:

```
You have three appointments:
      <break size="large"/>
             <sayas class="number">1</sayas>
             <break size="small"/>Dennis at thirteen hundred, . . .
```

The breaks serve to delineate the numbers as labels, so that people intuitively understand that they are menu options. The <sayas> tag is used to inform the VoiceXML interpreter that its content should be read as a number, which is one of the say-as types (see Appendix A for a list of say-as types).

NOTE   *It is easy to confuse built-in grammars, built-in types, and say-as types, but they are different. Built-in grammars and built-in types are used by the speech recognizer to recognize common speech patterns such as phone numbers, strings of digits, sequence of keypresses, and so on. Say-as types are markup instructions to the voice synthesizer, identifying how the text is to be rendered into speech (as an acronym, for example). Although there are both built-in types and say-as types for currency, phone numbers, and so on, they are unrelated.*

VXML 2:   *VoiceXML 2.0 is expected to use speech markup tags defined in the W3C's Speech Synthesis Markup Language Specification for the Speech Interface Framework* (http://www.w3.org/TR/speech-synthesis). *The tags in this specification have slightly different names and syntax than their VoiceXML 1.0 equivalents. For example,* <sayas> *from version 1.0 becomes* <say-as> *in Speech Synthesis Markup Language (SSML),* <pros> *becomes* <prosody> in SSML, <emp> *becomes* <emphasis> in SSML, *and so on. Version 1.0's* <break msecs="30"/> *becomes* <break time="30ms" /> in SSML.

Telephony Features

In the SPIM application, when the person says "I'm late," a link is activated and Step9\RunningLate.vxml is executed. The dialog there fetches the current time, reads it to the person, and submits a query to the server. A server page uses the submitted current time (because client and server may be in different time zones) and the user ID to look up the current appointment. Based on the available contact information (for instance, is there a listed fax number?), the server page generates a document like Step9\LateAppointment001.vxml. The generated dialog provides a menu of options for contacting the person being met: phone, fax, or e-mail (in the example).

The telephone call to the person is initiated through a <transfer> tag, as shown in Listing 7-15.

Listing 7-15. Transfer Tag

```
<transfer name="callOutcome" dest="phone://5085551234" bridge="true"
          connecttimeout="20s">
```

```
<filled>
  <if cond="callOutcome == 'busy' || callOutcome == 'network_busy'">
    <prompt>Sorry, the line was busy.</prompt>
    <elseif cond="noanswer" />
    <prompt>Sorry, there was no answer.</prompt>
    <else />
    <prompt>Your call lasted
        <value expr="callOutcome$.duration" /> seconds.
    </prompt>
  </if>
</filled>
</transfer>
```

The dest attribute specifies a URI that is interpreted by the VoiceXML inter-preter. If the bridge attribute is true (bridging transfer), the VoiceXML interpreter suspends while the call is underway and resumes execution when the call completes. If the bridge attribute is false (blind transfer), the interpreter exits as soon as the call connects. For bridging transfers, the end of the call causes the "call-Outcome" variable to be set and the <filled> handler to execute. Possible outcomes are busy, noanswer, network_busy, near_end_disconnect, far_end_disconnect, and network_disconnect.

The variable "callOutcome$.duration" is an example of a VoiceXML shadow variable. Shadow variables are implicitly declared and set by the VoiceXML inter-preter after executing a form item. Syntactically, they are accessed as ECMAScript objects named *name*$, where *name* is the form item variable. Not all tags set shadow variables—see the VoiceXML specification for more information.

Summary

In this tutorial, you've taken a rapid tour of most of the essential features of VoiceXML. Starting with a "Hello, World!" example, you've explored the following features of VoiceXML:

- Menus

- Dialogs, documents, and applications

- Dialog navigation

- Directed forms and mixed-initiative forms

- Event handling

- Generation of VoiceXML to browse sets

- Telephony

With this knowledge in hand, you should be able to design and implement standalone VoiceXML programs. In the next two chapters, you'll look at some more advanced features of VoiceXML. After that, you'll explore some of the broader architectural issues involved in integrating VoiceXML with distributed Web applications.

CHAPTER 8

VUI Design Principles and Techniques

THE FOLLOWING SECTIONS provide introductory guidance about best design practices for VUIs. Comprehensive coverage of the entire VUI design process is beyond the scope of this book. The intent here is to make you aware of some of the key issues that must be addressed in VUI design and provide an overview of some of the techniques that are available to address those issues.

Core Principles

Among speech interface designers, there's a credo: A good GUI and a good VUI are both a pleasure to use, a bad GUI is hard to use, but a bad VUI isn't used at all. This will be a major issue as VoiceXML puts voice technology in the hands of developers everywhere. You may remember in the early days of the Web, when HTML tools were just becoming available, that the number of truly awful Web site designs took off. Well, that's where VoiceXML will be very soon, and you can expect many unusable VUIs to be written.

Keep It Simple, Do It Well

Be realistic about what can be accomplished through a VUI. Focus on handling the easiest 80 percent of requests simply and cost-effectively.

A famous French proverb states, "Nothing succeeds like success." It seems obvious: A good interface is one that gets the job done. However, who has not experienced the frustration of calling a customer service phone number and immediately being thrust into a Kafka-esque maze of voice prompts and menu choices, none of which meet your need?

There is tension between the needs of people calling in ("users") and businesses that provide the service ("providers"). Users want to have their needs quickly and courteously met. From the user's perspective, nothing beats having a well-trained and empowered person on the vendor's end of the line. From the provider's perspective, well-trained and empowered customer service representatives are expensive. Vendors want the call center to please customers in a cost-effective manner.[1] As Table 8-1 shows, users and providers do not use the same criteria when measuring VUI usefulness and effectiveness.

Table 8-1. Satisfaction Criteria for VUI

USER CRITERIA	PROVIDER CRITERIA
Can I get the information or perform the transaction I want?	Does it reduce the load on customer service reps?
Is the result worth my effort to get it?	Are users satisfied with the experience?
Do I feel like I'm receiving a valuable service?	Does it increase the number of users I connect with?

By these criteria, a VUI that gracefully and elegantly ends up routing most calls to a human operator is not meeting provider needs. On the other hand, a VUI that never routes a call to a human operator is not meeting the needs of some users. Achieving a balance between the sometimes conflicting requirements of users and providers is part of the design process. Skewing the balance too heavily to the provider's side results in a VUI that is overly comprehensive, loaded with options, and frustrating to use. Skewing the balance too heavily to the user's side results in a VUI that is expensive to build and operate.

When designing a VUI, be realistic about its capabilities. Don't assume that the VUI should be able to do everything a GUI can. Use the 80/20 rule: Aim to simply and effectively handle the easiest 80 percent of the load, and leave the other 20 percent to other means (usually human operators).

Accommodate Errors

Errors are not exceptions in speech and cannot be eliminated. A good VUI should be deceptively simple—simple in its basic dialog structure, but complex in its capability to perform in the presence of a multitude of errors.

Communication by speech is inherently a complicated and error-prone process. Computer programmers are biased to treat errors as defects—failings to be eradicated. However, when you develop VUIs, you have to overcome this bias: Errors are essential and inherent. The goal is not to eliminate errors, but rather to contain them and tolerate them. Natural languages are marvelously error

---

[1] All lofty rhetoric aside, a reason businesses are interested in VUIs is to reduce (or eliminate) the cost of maintaining call centers. VoiceXML will accelerate this interest because it opens the possibility of collapsing two infrastructures (call center and Web) into one.

tolerant. People can communicate effectively despite mispronunciations, jack-hammers in the background, misunderstandings, verbal stumbles, interjections, false starts, incomplete sentences, poor grammar, uncouth accents, and so on. Developing a good VUI has a lot in common with programming a real-time process control system like that which runs a power plant. There's a lot going on in real time: There are basics laws of physics at work, relative timing of events is crucial, and errors that occur need to be managed so that they damp down rather than amplify over time.

As mentioned previously, VoiceXML has no cognitive model, and so it is not an appropriate instrument for implementing natural language. More precisely, VoiceXML cannot match the expressiveness of natural language, though it can borrow profitably from the error tolerance of natural language. The goal of a good VoiceXML VUI is to be deceptively simple—simple in that the basic structure of dialogs should be simple and easy, and deceptive in that the "simple" dialogs should be possible in the face of a multitude of errors. In terms of the effort invested in developing a VUI, the minority of effort should be spent on the basic dialogs. The majority of effort should be spent on detecting errors, recovering from them, and getting the conversation back on track.

Design for Everyone, Everywhere

People don't all speak alike. Bear in mind that users will possess a wide variety of voices, speech skills, and vocabularies. The Web is a public place: A voice-enabled Web site can expect to hear from people with all kinds of backgrounds, speech skills, vocabularies, and voices. In designing a VUI, keep the response vocabulary simple and generic. Avoid disenfranchising nonexpert users by using specialists' jargon. Make sure that the VUI can adapt to situations where speech recognition isn't working well.

Speech recognition technology currently achieves the highest recognition rates for adult native speakers of English, and it achieves lower rates for children and non-native speakers. In addition to natural variations in people's speech, speech recognition professionals also refer to "sheep" and "goats"[2]: "Sheep" are people for whom speech recognition works exceptionally well, and "goats" are people for whom it works exceptionally poorly. Only the voice recognizer knows what separates them. People can't predict whose voice will be recognized easily and whose won't. The best policy is to design the interface so it can handle all kinds of voices in all kinds of environments.

---

[2] From *How to Build a Speech Recognition Application*, by Bruce Balentine and David P. Morgan, Glossary.

Speech Design

The goal of designing an effective VUI in VoiceXML is to create a small speech dialect that is constrained in vocabulary and phrase structure, effective for the task at hand, and tolerates errors. In other words, you're not trying to make the computer talk at the level of a person. You're trying to get a person to speak at the level of the computer.

While this may sound like interface blasphemy (making the person accommodate the computer!), it is not unprecedented. People comfortably and effectively use a variety of dialects daily, without feeling put upon or constrained. For example, people talk differently to a child than they do to an adult, because a child's speech and comprehension skills are less than those of an adult. Similarly, people talk to their pets all the time, and successfully communicate attitudes and emotions, even though the speech is (in human terms) nonsense. When talking to a non-native speaker, people unconsciously adjust their speech patterns to communicate more effectively. A computer is less linguistically competent than a person is, whether that person is a child or adult, so it makes sense that people adopt a restricted form of speech to facilitate communication.

In terms of speech design, it's important that the designer make the computer speak like one. People's speech expectations are based on their perceptions of whom they're talking to. If a person doesn't realize he or she is speaking to a child, for example, that person will perceive that he or she is talking to a very strange adult. Similarly, if a computer attempts to sound like a person, people will have expectations of a person rather than a computer. So the designer should present the computer as what it is: an automated speaker of a simplified dialect. Unfortunately, people's expectations of computer speech tend to spontaneously fly to the HAL model, but this can be addressed by good design.

Modeling

In talking with one another, and with computers, people tend to model their speech on the other party's. If the second party speaks tersely and rapidly, the first party will tend to speak tersely and rapidly as well. This unconscious mimicry applies to many aspects of speech: vocabulary choice, phrase structure, volume, pitch, rate, and so on. Modeling is one of the most powerful tools available to a speech designer for tacitly cluing in users to acceptable forms of speech. The following are dos and don'ts for using modeling in a VUI:

- *Do* use computer prompts that are brief and to the point. The style of the computer's speech should instill the impression that the conversation is a professional one—not friendly or unfriendly, but directed to a purpose.

- *Do* start out with examples of acceptable speech when you provide help rather than try to explain what's going on. People are more often confused about the form of what they can say to the computer than they are about the meaning.

- *Don't* use long, wordy prompts in the vernacular because people will respond in kind.

Disfluency

One of the biggest inhibitors of continuous speech recognition is that people do not speak continuously. People's speech is peppered with "um"s, "ah"s, "er"s, pauses, and other fillers. People correct their own speech on the fly: "Give me two—no, three sodas," "I want—need—a cup of coffee." People may abandon forms of speech in midstream: "I was just wondering . . . oh, never mind." People subconsciously filter out these disruptions in the normal flow of speech, both as listeners and speakers, and consequently do not realize how frequent these *disfluencies* are. One way to gauge how much you expect disfluency in speech is to think about how unnatural synthesized speech sounds. It sounds unnatural for at least two reasons: its prosodic limitations (for example, lack of modulated pitch and emphasis) and its total (inhuman) fluency.

Disfluency causes problems in speech interfaces because they are resolved at multiple levels. Pauses and fillers can be fairly effectively filtered by a voice recognizer, but they also can lead to errors (for instance, inserting an extra word) that will baffle a semantic analyzer. Self-corrections occur at the semantic level and are hard to model in grammars.

The occurrence of disfluencies increases rapidly as a function of the length of an utterance. The longer a person speaks without a break, the greater the number of disfluencies. Therefore, the main tool for dealing with disfluency in speech design is limiting the length of utterance. There are tradeoffs in this approach, however. When a person starts using a VUI, there is a lot of disfluency due to the person's uncertainty about what to say. As the person becomes more familiar with the VUI and becomes more adept at speaking in a way the computer can understand, he or she wants to make longer utterances for efficiency's sake. Heed the following tips about how to design a VUI to minimize the effects of disfluency:

- *Do* structure dialogs using mixed-initiative combined with directed forms. This enables users to convey as much information as they are able in a single utterance, but it elicits information in smaller snippets if there are problems communicating.

- *Don't* try to address disfluency through grammar design. It can greatly increase the grammar complexity and slow down recognition, but the chances of ultimate success are slim.

Synthesized Speech

Listening to synthesized speech requires more concentration and effort than listening to human speech. People vary their intonation, pitch, volume; introduce pauses; and provide any number of behavioral "clues" that cue the listener as to the structure and meaning of the spoken content. Without these cues from the computer, people are working with less information and have to try harder to decipher what's being communicated. This also means that lapses in attention are harder to recover from, and long messages are harder to comprehend. Although techniques for maximizing the comprehensibility and effectiveness of synthesized speech depend on the particular speech synthesizer being used, here are some general tips on using speech synthesis:

- *Do* use recorded prompts wherever possible. Any fixed prompts (for example, menu choices) should be recorded. Speech synthesis should be reserved for reading information that varies (for example, a person's appointments today).

- *Do* pay attention to prosodic features when using synthesized speech. For example, when reading lists, introduce pauses to demarcate individual items.

- *Don't* use synthesized speech to read long lists to a person and expect the person to comprehend or remember the lists. The interface should be designed so that lists contain no more than four or five items. This may require introducing dialogs to refine the person's focus of interest (for example, rather than reviewing all 15 of today's appointments, start with five of this morning's appointments).

> **NOTE** *See Table 9-1 in Chapter 9 for a list of the VoiceXML tags that affect how synthesized speech sounds.*

Getting the Most Out of Speech Recognition

Recognizing speech is not an exact, analytical science. It is a probabilistic art and incorporates elements of sophisticated guessing. There are some design principles that can help you make the most of this inexact but powerful tool. The basic principle is to make expected responses as distinct as possible. Unfortunately, a person's intuition about phrases that sound "close together" or "different" isn't a very good predictor of how a voice recognizer will perform. As anyone who has used a computer dictation system knows, voice recognizers make the oddest mistakes. This means that grammars need to be field tested for recognition problems.

Some gross properties of responses, however, do have a strong effect on recognition. The main property is response length. The best responses are brief phrases that give the recognizer some meat to chew on, but are not so long that disfluencies crop up. So, for example, "Speak louder" is preferable to "Louder." This is particularly true for background grammars. In VoiceXML, several grammars may be active at once:

1. Field grammar (awaiting a response to a prompt for information)

2. Form-scoped links

3. Document-scoped links

4. Application-scoped links

5. Voice interpreter default grammars (help, cancel, and so on)

Lower numbered grammars are "in front of" higher numbered grammars in the sense that in case of a toss-up, the recognizer prefers to match to lower numbered grammars. The shortest prompts should be reserved for the closest grammars (field and form), and links with broader scope should be longer phrases that can be recognized in a variety of contexts.

Numbers and letters are problematic because they are so short. For example, "six" (the shortest spoken digit in English) is commonly both falsely inserted (recognized but not spoken) and falsely deleted (spoken but not recognized) by recognizers. This does not mean that numbers and letters aren't recognizable and shouldn't be responses, but it does mean the designer should be aware of potential problems. Some possible solutions are to allow DTMF input where numbers are expected and to use the International Communications alphabet for letters (alpha, bravo, charlie, delta, and so on instead of a, b, c, d, and so on). The following are some techniques for effective use of speech recognition:

- *Do* use short phrases or multisyllabic words for links (for example, "Start over," "Speak louder").

- *Do* reserve the shortest, commonest responses for field-level responses.

- *Do* allow use of DTMF where precise input of numbers is important.

- *Don't* share recognition errors with the person. While the person may find it reasonable to ask for clarification with a question such as "Did you say Austin or Boston?", the computer will spontaneously come up with something goofy such as "Did you say Austin or hippopotamus?" Instead, ask for clarification directly (for example, "I didn't get that. What city?").

- *Don't* make field and form grammars needlessly broad (for instance, with lots of synonyms), because they will interfere with recognition of background links.

Interface Design

When using a good VUI, a person will feel oriented, in control, and able to anticipate what will happen next. A person is oriented if he or she can relate the current dialog to the task he or she wants to perform. A person feels in control if the person feels he or she knows what to do to affect the way the interaction with the computer proceeds. To be able to anticipate what will happen next, a person needs a mental model of "what the computer is up to." (Notice that the computer has no cognitive model, and therefore is not really "up to" anything. However, a good interface will superimpose a model purely for the person's benefit.)

Ironically, some of the biggest challenges in designing a good VUI bear a strong resemblance to challenges faced by developers in the days of command-line interfaces and small-screen displays. Probably the biggest challenge is keeping the person cued about what he or she can do next. In VUIs, this means knowing what you can say in response to a voice prompt; in command-line systems, it means knowing what commands (and options) you can type at the command prompt. The other big challenge is presenting information in small enough chunks that people can absorb and use it. In VUIs, reading long lists of options is time-consuming, frustrating, and ineffective. On small screen displays, printing out more than a screen full of data caused some of the data to scroll off the screen. In both cases, you have to rely on human memory to retain what's important.

The eventual resolution of command-line issues turned out to be windowed GUIs. Commands became menu options, options became property sheets, and windows became scrollable. This resolution is unfortunate for VUI designers, because the graphical solution cannot be transferred to voice. For a variety of reasons, VUIs must succeed as an alternative to GUIs, and they must work where GUIs don't. Hopefully, during the upcoming decade we will see the evolution of interface techniques and technologies for handling the shortcomings of voice as a medium, just as in the past decade we've seen the development of GUI technology to supplant command lines.

Turn-Taking and Error Amplification

A big challenge in VUI design is handling issues related to turn-taking. Because there are no behavioral or visual cues accompanying the conversation, it is very common for the two parties to lose track of whose turn it is. Once a conversation goes off track, it can rapidly degenerate into chaos (see Dialog 8-1).

Dialog 8-1. Inexperienced User[3]

P (person): Umm, I'd like to know, ahhh . . .
C (computer): I'm sorr–
P: I'd like to know . . . the number of sh–
C: I'm . . .
P: I want to sell half my shares of Motorola.
C: I didn't understand.
P: I'd like to SELL . . . half my shares . . .
C: I didn–
P: . . . of Motorola
C: I didn't under–
P: I'd like to SELL . . . Motorola.
C: I didn't understand.

In this example, an inexperienced user pauses because of uncertainty about how to proceed. The computer interprets the pauses as the end of unrecognized responses and responds with an error prompt. The user pauses when the computer speaks, trying to yield his or her turn, but the computer is busy digesting the remnant of the user's previous attempt to spit out a whole sentence, which it can't recognize, and so on. The dialog spirals out of control, as the user attempts to get through to the brain-damaged computer by increasing volume and overstressing "sell," which guarantees that the computer will not recognize the speech. At this point, the only solution is to separate the combatants for a cooling-off period.

---

[3] From *How to Build a Speech Recognition Application,* by Bruce Balentine and David P. Morgan, pg. 99.

This is an example of *error amplification*, in which an initial small error rapidly escalates into a wholesale breakdown in communication. It can be initiated by virtually any kind of error that confuses turn-taking. This kind of error escalation is familiar to designers of real-time process control systems, and it is also known as *cascading errors*. A major goal of interface design is to structure the interface so that when anything goes astray, the interface will get the person to a state where he or she is once again oriented, in control, and knows what's coming.

To help stabilize dialogs and prevent error amplification, build *safe points* into the interface. A safe point is a known state of the application, usually a high-level menu, at which the person and computer can resynchronize turn-taking and generally get a fresh start. The tricky part about safe points is figuring out when to transition to them. If things are going badly, the person and computer may not be listening well to each other, and so normal prompting may be ignored. A last-ditch technique to stabilize a dialog is to prompt the user with a modal prompt that requires a "yes" or "no" response:

Computer: Do you want to continue adding appointments to your calendar? Say yes or no after the beep. {beep}

A "no" answer would initiate transfer to a safe point. Such a prompt can occur after a certain number of errors occur in a row.

See the end of the following section for some tips that affect both turn-taking and orientation issues.

Lost in Space

Because speech is not persistent, people must rely on their memory to know "where they are" in a conversation. Such short-term memory is fragile and can easily be disturbed by any kind of distraction: avoiding a road hazard while driving, another person entering the room, a child interrupting his or her mother, a fire truck screaming by, and so on. When these distractions occur during a conversation, a person may recover by saying something like "Where was I?" The other person reorients the distracted one, and the conversation resumes.

Feeling "lost in space" and out of control should be dealt with in a good VUI. Distraction is a common source of disorientation. Disorientation also results when the computer goes down a path the person was not anticipating. The person is still thinking about the task at hand, but the computer's prompts have become irrelevant.

A good technique for maintaining orientation is to provide auditory cues along the way, so that the person receives some feedback about where he or she is. For example, different parts of an application might use different voices. In the SPIM example, you might use different voices for Calendar, Contact, and Appointment. *Earcons*, or auditory icons, can accentuate meaning of different types of prompts. For example, different tones can be used for confirmations, errors, and menu choices. This does not require that the conversation rely on tones for turn-taking (as in "Wait for the tone before speaking"). Bargein can be enabled so that experienced users do not have to wait, while inexperienced users will get greater contextual feedback. Music or other nonspeech audio can be used to signal that the computer is working (and hence is holding on to its turn).

A related technique is to include orientation tips in prompts generated when the person is silent or can't be understood.[4] For example, the user might receive the following prompt if they do not respond:

Computer: You are in your address book. Adding entry for Veronica Voice. What is the home phone number?

This technique should be used judiciously, in tandem with tapered prompting, because the additional orientation information increases the prompt length and may frustrate users who are making small errors but are not disoriented.

The following tips apply to good design with regard to turn-taking and orientation:

- *Do* be aware in designing all dialogs that distraction can strike at any time and that errors may be the result of a loss of orientation rather than a lack of knowledge.

- *Do* include some auditory feedback to maintain orientation and signal when it's the computer's turn.

- *Do* provide application safe points where the user can reorient him- or herself and resynchronize turn-taking.

- *Do* incorporate last-ditch error handling to avoid runaway error amplification.

- *Don't* use too many tunes, tones, or other nonspeech audio—it becomes tiring to listen to repeatedly.

---

[4] This is the audible equivalent of the technique used on U.S. interstate highway marker signs, which seem to have a formula for orientation. The signs show where you are (I95S), the next major destination (New York City 100mi), and the next destination (West Nowhere 2mi).

- *Don't* have the computer take drastic unilateral action (for example, transferring the user to an operator) without confirmation from the user.

- *Don't* force a lot of contextual information on the user unless he or she requests it.

Accommodating Different Experience Levels and Environments

People using your VUI will have varying levels of experience with voice interfaces in particular and with computers in general. One of the motivators for enabling Web applications with voice is to reach the user base that does not use PCs, digital networks, keyboards, and mice. So, at one end of the spectrum, novice users require an interface that is very simple, easy to use, and undemanding of the user. At the other end of the spectrum, advanced users require an interface that performs efficiently in a car, from a public phone, and in other mouse-less and keyboard-less environments.

Experience manifests itself in the following ways:

- Experienced users don't need constant cuing about what's expected of them. Too many cues can make experienced users impatient with unneeded prompts and more aggressive about barging in.

- Experienced users are more likely to retain their cool when errors crop up and to let the computer "catch up" when turn-taking errors occur.

- Experienced users require occasional help on options available in unfamiliar parts of the application, but they do not tolerate long help prompts.

- Experienced users can become disoriented as a result of distractions.

- Experienced users learn to speak to the computer so they will be understood, using constant volume, stress, and rate; enunciating fully; and so on. They are therefore capable of longer productive utterances than novices are.

It's tempting to think that the error rate decreases as user experience increases, but this may not be the case. The reason for this is that errors are a product not only of speech, but of environment as well. In fact, it's quite possible that experienced users will only use voice when other options are not available. So, when an experienced user is in the quiet of his or her home with a good microphone and no interruptions, he or she will use a mouse and keyboard. When the same user is at an airport with flight announcements randomly drowning out speech, he or she will use voice.

Environmental characteristics that affect how well the VUI performs include the following:

- *Background noise:* Recognizers are surprisingly good at screening out constant background noise, but both people and computers have trouble dealing with "bursts" of noise (for example, airport speakers, thunder, and so on).

- *Other people talking:* If you're sitting on your couch with your parrot chattering on your shoulder and Peter Jennings blaring on the TV, the computer is going to try to recognize everybody's speech—not just yours.

- *Voice fidelity:* The computer tries to recognize speech as received at the voice gateway. Anything between the larynx and gateway that degrades voice quality degrades performance. Low-quality microphones and poor telephone connections are the usual suspects.

Good interface design attempts to make the VUI adjust to speaker and environmental variations by trading off efficiency for robustness. With an experienced speaker and a good environment, dialogs should permit (but not require) longer utterances. With a naive user and a noisy environment, dialogs should collapse to brief, structured interchanges that are tedious but reliable. Essentially, this strategy adapts the dialogs to keep the error rate down. If there are many problems communicating, slow down and take it a step at a time.

Using VoiceXML mixed-initiative dialogs is a good way to permit a user to use longer utterances. The user can respond to the initial prompt with as much or as little information as he or she wants. The dialog then switches into directed mode and elicits information a piece at a time. This can require sophisticated grammar design, so that both short and long utterances are successfully recognized (see Table 8-2).

Table 8-2. Novice and Expert Mixed-Initiative Dialog

NOVICE USER	EXPERT USER
C (computer): Add appointment. You may say help at any time.	*C (computer): Add appointment. You may say help at any time.*
P (person): Help.	*P (person): Call Pete on Friday at 10 a.m. at work.*
C: Say something like call Joe.	*C: You have a call with Pete on Friday at ten am at work.*
P: Call Pete.	
C: What day?	
P: Friday.	
C: What time?	
P: 10 a.m.	
C: Where?	
P: Work.	
C: You have a call with Pete on Friday at ten am at work.	

As mentioned previously, falling back to a yes/no interrogation gives about as much reliability as is possible: The recognizer only has to match against two possible responses. People don't tolerate a "20 questions" style of interface in general, but it may be acceptable in extreme circumstances, as shown in Dialog 8-2.

Dialog 8-2. Fallback to 20 Questions

C (computer): Do you want the shirt in red, green, or blue?
P (person): {static}
C: Do you want the shirt in red, green, or blue?
P: {static}
C: Do you want red? Say yes or no.
P: No.
C: Do you want green? Say yes or no.
P: Yes.
C: Do you want small, medium, large, or extra large?

Because of this adaptability, the interface may become more complex, and there may be many valid responses to any given prompt. So, doesn't that make it more complicated to cue the user as to what's expected? Not necessarily. The support structure of the interface—help prompts, event handlers, and so on—should be primarily geared toward the simplest way of doing things. Even if there are ten ways to do something, the basic prompting should describe one way: the simplest way. The other nine options are still available, but they are not explicitly announced or described. The process of turning novices into experts should be treated as a training issue, not a prompting issue. Possible techniques for enlightening advanced users include offline tutorials and toggling a mode switch that switches the interface between "novice" mode and "expert" mode. Also, consider the following tips for accommodating different experience levels and environments:

- *Do* provide opportunities for expert users to use shortcuts.

- *Do* use mixed-initiative dialogs backed up with directed prompting for filling out forms.

- *Do* incorporate yes/no exchanges as the fallback when more complicated dialogs are not working.

- *Don't* clutter up basic prompts with a lot of tutorial material aimed at expert users.

- *Don't* assume that if a user encounters a lot of errors it means he or she is "slow"—it may mean that an expert user is in a tough environment.

Taking Time Out

When talking on the phone, people often engage in sidebar "mini conversations" with people around them, without explicitly interrupting the phone conversation. There are all kinds of amusing behaviors associated with these sidebars, including the following:

- Exaggerating facial expressions, mouthing words, pointing at a watch, and so on

- Pantomiming, as in the game charades

- Writing notes on paper or whiteboards

- Commenting in a sotto voce to someone nearby

- Putting a hand over the phone's mouthpiece or enabling the phone's mute feature to engage in a full-fledged conversation with someone else

While people seem to be able to converse through various types of conversational lapses, to a computer they sound like unrecognizable speech. The speech may be unrecognizable because it's disfluent, because the person's normal speech cadence is altered, because the computer hears things a person would filter out, or because a person misses timing on a response and speaks too soon or too late. Regardless of the reason, the person can suddenly find the computer reacting to "errors" and conversational turn-taking disrupted.

The VUI should provide ways for a user to pause or suspend a dialog at any point. When the user is using a microphone, issuing a command to turn the microphone off and on works well. On a phone, the computer cannot control the microphone, so a voice command that causes the computer to ignore input for a while is required. The command should be available at any prompt, as shown in Dialog 8-3.

Dialog 8-3. Taking Time Out for Distractions
C (computer): Please say the name of the person . . .
P (person): {barging in} Go to sleep.

. . .

P: Wake up.
C: Please say the name of the person to call.
OR
C: Please say the name of the person to call.
P: Give me thirty seconds.
{after 30 seconds}
C: Are you ready to continue?
P: Give me thirty seconds.
{after 30 seconds}
C: Are you ready to continue?
P: Yes.
C: Please say the name of the person to call.

> **CAUTION**   *VoiceXML does not provide an easy way to temporarily suspend the VoiceXML interpreter as described here. (In my opinion, this is a short-coming of VoiceXML.) Implementing the design described here requires the use of proprietary features of a particular voice platform.*

Summary

Careful VUI design is not an option—it is a requirement. A poorly designed VUI can be not only frustrating to the user, but also outright insulting and provocative. This chapter elaborated three core principles of VUI design: deceptive simplicity, error accommodation, and designing for everyone. Some basic behavior and psychological characteristics of speech were also introduced, along with tips and techniques for dealing with some of the common pitfalls and challenges of VUIs.

For pragmatic, hands-on tips about implementing speech recognition applications, I recommend reading *How to Build a Speech Recognition Application,* by Bruce Balentine and David P. Morgan. For a broader view of speech interfaces in general, I recommend *Designing Effective Speech Interfaces,* by Susan Weinschenk and Dean T. Barker (the companion Web site address is `http://www.wiley.com/compbooks/weinschenk/`). Also, the June 2001 issue of *VoiceXML Review* (`http://www.voicexmlreview.org/`) covers human considerations for VoiceXML applications.

CHAPTER 9

VoiceXML Programming Guide

THIS CHAPTER EXPLORES VoiceXML language elements individually and in detail. This chapter is intended to provide a conceptual elaboration of VoiceXML language elements for someone who is already familiar with the basics of programming voice applications. People who learn best "hands on" should go through the VoiceXML tutorial in Chapter 7 before tackling the material in this chapter. For a complete specification of VoiceXML syntax, see Appendix A or the VoiceXML specification.

Structure of a VoiceXML Program

Many of the structural concepts in VoiceXML (scope, events, and variables) may seem familiar to programmers who have used other languages. However, the way VoiceXML ties together the static structure of source code with the dynamic state of a running application has some subtleties that knowledgeable newcomers tend to gloss over. Some of these subtleties are a result of the real-time nature of speech processing, and some are the result of VoiceXML's essential nature as an interpreted markup language rather than a compiled programming language. The following sections establish some basic concepts that apply throughout the rest of the chapter.

Static Structure

The static elements of a VoiceXML program form a hierarchy. Conceptually, there is a single *application* that is composed of one or more *dialogs*. Each dialog structures an interaction with a person. Dialogs are structured sequences of alternating computer-generated prompts and human responses.

Physically, a VoiceXML program consists of a set of *documents*. Each document contains VoiceXML code defining one or more VoiceXML dialogs. One document is designated the *application root document*. All documents that specifically designate the application root document are considered part of the same application. Documents are usually just text files, and documents are the program units that are sent from a Web server to a VoiceXML browser.

A dialog is the basic executable unit of a VoiceXML program, akin to a sub-routine or function in conventional languages. Dialogs are implemented by one or more *forms* or *menus*. A form consists of a set of form items (variables and/or code blocks) and the "recipe" (control logic) for working with a person to assign values to items. A menu is a collection of alternatives, each with a unique prompt, from which a person may select one.

Scope

To share code and data between cooperating forms in an executing application, VoiceXML defines a *scope hierarchy*. The scope hierarchy mirrors the static struc-ture of the program and consists of five levels: session, application, document, dialog, and (anonymous).

A scope can contain variables, properties, event handlers, and grammars. Entities in session scope are defined by the VoiceXML interpreter and may not be changed by an application. These include default event handlers, default and platform-specific properties and variables, default event handlers, and built-in grammars. Entities are placed in application scope by declaring them in the application root document. Application-scoped entities are available whenever any part of the application is running. Document scope is shared by all dialogs within a document. Dialog scope is established by the currently active form or menu, and (anonymous) scope corresponds to the current item. (See Table A-2.)

Dynamic Execution Context

As a VoiceXML program executes, the flow of control moves from item to item within a form and from form to form. The VoiceXML interpreter maintains an execution context that corresponds to the current point of control. The execution context contains all entities that are currently *active* (in scope). Session- and application-scoped entities are active throughout a single invocation of an appli-cation. As the flow of control moves between forms, the interpreter may fetch and load documents containing the forms, causing the execution context to contain different document-scoped entities at different times. Similarly, the exe-cution context is adjusted to correspond to the currently executing form (dialog scope) and currently executing form item (anonymous scope).

When a variable is in scope (in the current execution context), it can be refer-enced by name in a VoiceXML <value> tag or embedded ECMAScript. When a property is set using the <property> tag, the interpreter places the value in the scope in which it was set.

When the speech recognition engine tries to match an utterance, it checks the utterance against all active grammars, starting with the grammars active in the closest scope and moving up the scope hierarchy. Typically, multiple grammars are active at once. For example, session-scoped grammars for the default <help>

and <cancel> responses are always active (although sometimes overridden). There is also an active grammar for every active link.

When an event handler is active, it is available for handling events that are thrown in the currently executing code. If there are event handlers defined in multiple scopes, there may be multiple handlers available when an event is thrown. The interpreter chooses the closest appropriate handler to process the event.

Input and Output

The following VoiceXML elements are used to specify input and output:

- <prompt>

- <audio>

- <grammar>

- <dtmf>

- <record>

The <prompt> and <audio> elements are used to prompt the user for input and to present output to the user. The <grammar> and <dtmf> elements are used to specify what a user can say or key, and how the user's speech or keystrokes are translated into text strings that can be sent to the Web server in HTTP messages.

Text that is to be read to the user is placed within a <prompt> element in a VoiceXML document. When the VoiceXML interpreter encounters a <prompt> element in the course of its conversation with the user, it feeds the text content of the element to its text-to-speech subsystem, which reads the text to the user.

Recorded audio is specified using the <audio> element. This element must be a child of a <prompt> element, where it can be used in place of, or in addition to, text. The <audio> element has an src attribute that specifies the URI of the audio file. To render an <audio> element, the VoiceXML interpreter fetches the file from a Web server and feeds it to its audio playback subsystem.

The <prompt> element has a Boolean attribute, bargein, that controls whether or not the user can interrupt a prompt. When it is set to false, the VoiceXML interpreter will read or play the entire prompt before responding to user input. When it is set to true (the default value), the user can respond before the VoiceXML interpreter has finished.

The <grammar> element is used to specify what the user can say and how the user's utterance is mapped to an action or field value. The <grammar> element can appear in a form or link. When the VoiceXML interpreter encounters a grammar, it feeds it to the speech recognition subsystem. The speech recognition subsystem listens to what the user says and attempts to match it with the grammar. When it does, it returns text to the VoiceXML interpreter. Speech grammars are expressed in a grammar language. The grammar can be the content of the <grammar> element or it can be in a separate file identified by the URI in the src attribute of the <grammar> element.

The <dtmf> element is used to specify what key sequences the user can enter as an alternative to speaking. The <dtmf> element is used in menus and forms. When the VoiceXML interpreter encounters a <dtmf> element, it feeds it to the DTMF recognition subsystem. The DTMF recognition subsystem listens for keystrokes and attempts to match them with the content of the <dtmf> element. When it does, it returns characters to the VoiceXML interpreter.

> **VXML 2:** *VoiceXML 2.0 is expected to require support for the Speech Recognition Grammar Specification for the W3C Speech Interface Framework (http://www.w3.org/TR/speech-grammar/). This specification treats "mode" (voice or dtmf) as an attribute of the grammar. The VoiceXML 1.0 <grammar> element specifies a Speech Recognition Grammar Specification (SRG) grammar whose mode is "voice". The VoiceXML 1.0 <dtmf> element specifies an SRG grammar whose mode is "dtmf".*

The <record> element is used to record what the user says without interpretation. It can appear in forms. When the VoiceXML interpreter encounters a <record> element, it uses the audio player/recorder subsystem to record what the user says. This audio stream can then be sent to a Web server for storage or further processing.

Navigation

VoiceXML has two elements for organizing and navigating a voice Web site:

- <menu>

- <link>

The <menu> element enables the user to select from a list of choices. A <menu> element generally contains a <prompt> element followed by <choice> elements. The interpreter reads or plays the prompt and then listens for the user's response. The user can make his or her selection using speech or the keypad. The content of the <choice> element specifies what the user must say to select it. The dtmf attribute of the <choice> element specifies what key the user can press to select it. Each <choice> element has a next attribute that specifies the URI of a dialog or document. When the user chooses one, the VoiceXML interpreter transitions the conversation to the next dialog.

The <link> element is the voice analog of the HTML hypertext link. A link has a trigger and an action. The trigger is a speech or DTMF grammar. When the user's input matches the link's grammar, the VoiceXML interpreter executes its action. The VoiceXML interpreter may transition to another document or dialog, or it may throw an event. The action is specified by the next or event attribute of the <link> element.

Forms and Fields

In VoiceXML, forms are the basic building blocks for structuring dialogs. Functionally, VoiceXML forms are similar to their ancestors, HTML forms: A form defines a set of fields that are filled in by the user. In HTML, fields are filled in by typing in text or using the mouse to make selections through radio buttons, check boxes, or pick lists. In VoiceXML, forms are filled in by speaking responses to prompts. VoiceXML forms have some features not found in HTML forms. In VoiceXML, multiple fields may be filled in by a single utterance. Also, VoiceXML subdialogs allow complex forms to be composed out of simple components in a nested manner.

The <form> element contains <field> elements for the form fields. The <field> element has a name attribute. Each field in a form has a form variable, whose name is the value of the field's name attribute. This variable holds the text value of the field.

A field typically contains a prompt, a recognition grammar, and a filled action. The <prompt> element within a <field> specifies the prompt to be read or played to the caller when the conversation enters the field. The <grammar> or <dtmf> element within a <field> element specifies the range of valid responses from the caller and how they are mapped into text values of the field variable. There are built-in grammars for common data types. These are specified by the type attribute of the field, rather than with an explicit <grammar> element.

A field may contain a <filled> element, which specifies an action to perform after the field has been filled. In simple forms, the last field contains a <filled> element, which in turn contains a <submit> element that sends an HTTP request to a Web server with the field values. A field can also contain event handlers such as <help>, <noinput>, and <nomatch>.

In a simple form, the conversation between the caller and the VoiceXML interpreter proceeds from field to field, in the order in which the fields appear in the VoiceXML document. The VoiceXML interpreter reads or plays the prompt in each field and compares the user response to the field's grammar. When the caller provides a valid response, the VoiceXML interpreter assigns a value to the field variable, performs the filled action, and goes on to the next field in the form. You can explicitly control the order in which the fields are visited by putting <goto> elements in the filled actions for the fields.

A <filled> element can also be a child of the <form> element and the same level as the <field> elements. The <filled> element at the form level has a namelist attribute that specifies a list of field names. When all of the fields in this list have been filled, the <filled> action is executed. The <submit> element for a form is usually placed within a form level <filled> element. In that way, the form will be submitted when the required fields have been filled, regardless of the order in which they were filled.

Dialog, Document, and Application

A VoiceXML document is a single file that is retrieved through HTTP from a Web server. The root element in a VoiceXML document is the <vxml> element. A VoiceXML document contains dialogs. There are two kinds of dialogs: forms and menus. Forms contain form items, each of which is a single interaction between a caller and the VoiceXML interpreter. When all of the fields have been filled, the form is typically submitted to the Web server, which returns another VoiceXML document. The conversation between the caller and VoiceXML interpreter transitions to that document. A menu is a single interaction between the caller and VoiceXML interpreter in which the caller is presented with a list of options and the VoiceXML interpreter transitions the conversation to another dialog based on the caller's choice.

The <vxml> element has an optional application attribute whose value is the URI of the application root document. By default, each VoiceXML document runs as an isolated application. When a document that specifies an application root document is loaded, the VoiceXML interpreter also ensures that the application root document is loaded. The application root document can define variables and links that are available for use by all documents in the application.

The conversation between a caller and the VoiceXML interpreter is always in one dialog. When the VoiceXML interpreter initially answers the call, it retrieves a VoiceXML document from a Web server, and the conversation is in the first dialog in that document. The conversation can move to another dialog in the same document or it can move to another document. Transitions are expressed in VoiceXML by links (<goto>), menus (<next>), and forms (<submit>).

Speech Recognition Grammars

Speech recognition grammars are used in links, menus, and forms to translate what a caller says into navigational commands or field values. VoiceXML has several means of specifying a speech recognition grammar:

- The `type` attribute of the <field> element

- The <choice> element in a menu

- The <option> element in a field

- The <grammar> element in a link, form, or field

VoiceXML interpreters have built-in speech recognition grammars for common data types: `boolean`, `date`, `digits`, `currency`, `number`, `phone`, and `time`. When a field specifies one of these as its `type` attribute, the VoiceXML interpreter uses the built-in grammar for the field.

Each choice in a menu has a speech recognition grammar fragment that is specified by the content of the <choice> element. A field can also specify a list of choices using the <option> element. The content of each <option> element specifies the speech recognition grammar fragment for that choice. In both cases, the VoiceXML interpreter assembles the speech recognition grammar for the menu or field from the <choice> or <option> elements.

The <grammar> Element

The <grammar> element is the most general construct for explicitly specifying a speech recognition grammar. The <grammar> element can appear in a link, form, or field. The grammar specifies what a caller can say to trigger an action or supply information.

The <grammar> element may specify either an *inline* grammar or an *external* grammar. An inline grammar is specified by the content of the <grammar> element. Alternatively, the grammar may be placed in an external file. In this case, the `src` attribute of the <grammar> element specifies the URI of the file, and the element is empty.

Grammars have scope, which determines when a grammar is active (that is, when it is being used by the speech recognition subsystem). If a grammar is inside a field, the scope of the grammar is the field. A field grammar is active only when the interpreter is visiting the field. If a grammar is inside a link, the scope of the grammar is the scope of the element that contains the link (dialog, document, or application). If a grammar is inside a dialog, by default its scope is that dialog. The scope of a dialog grammar can be extended to the entire document using the scope attribute of the <grammar> element.

Grammar Formats in VoiceXML 1.0

VoiceXML 1.0 does not specify a required grammar format. It is left up to the implementer of a particular platform to decide what grammar formats are recognized. Two widely used formats are Sun's Java Speech Grammar Format (JSGF) and Nuance's Grammar Specification Language (GSL). Some VoiceXML interpreter implementations support JSGF, while others support GSL. When you use an explicit inline grammar, you should specify the MIME type for the grammar format in the type attribute of the <grammar> element. The MIME type values for the two grammar formats are as follows:

- JSGF: "application/x-jgsf"

- GSL: "application/x-gsl"

Grammar Formats in VoiceXML 2.0

VoiceXML 2.0 is expected to require support for a draft standard grammar specification language called Speech Recognition Grammar . Visit http://www.w3.org/TR/speech-grammar/ for more of the specification's W3C working draft. The draft describes two syntaxes for the language: an Augmented Backus Naur Form (ABNF) syntax and an equivalent XML-compliant syntax. Only the XML-compliant syntax is expected to be required by VoiceXML 2.0. At the time of the writing of this book, this is a situation where one standard under development depends on another standard under development. See the section titled "Grammar and Speech Synthesis Specification" in Chapter 14 for a brief overview of the current state of the new grammar format.

The MIME type for the new grammar is "application/grammar" for the ABNF syntax and "application/grammar+vxml" for the XML-compliant syntax.

Speech Synthesis Markup

TTS synthesis is used to render text in <choice>, <prompt>, <enumerate>, and <audio> elements into speech. VoiceXML provides markup tags to direct how the generated speech should sound. Speech synthesis markup can affect pronunciation, pauses, emphasis, pitch, phrasing, and speaking rate.

VoiceXML 1.0 defined its own markup tags based on a draft Java Speech Markup Language specification (`http://java.sun.com/products/java-media/speech`). VoiceXML 2.0 is expected to make the 1.0 tags obsolete in favor of reference to a separate W3C draft specification, Speech Synthesis Markup Language Specification for the Speech Interface Framework (`http://www.w3.org/TR/speech-synthesis`). Table 9-1 summarizes the tags and their meanings.

Table 9-1. Speech Synthesis Markup Tags

VOICEXML 1.0 TAG	VOICEXML 1.0 ATTRIBUTES	SSML[1] TAGS	SSML ATTRIBUTES	USAGE
`<break>`	msecs size	`<break>`	time size	Insert a pause.
`<div>`	type="paragraph"	`<p>` or `<paragraph>`	xml:lang	Mark paragraph boundary.
`<div>`	type="sentence"	`<s>` or `<sentence>`	xml:lang	Mark sentence boundary.
`<emp>`	level	`<emphasis>`	level	Speak with emphasis.
`<pros>`	rate vol pitch range	`<prosody>`	pitch contour range rate duration volume	Specify prosodic attributes such as pitch, speaking rate, volume, and so on.
`<sayas>`	sub class	`<say-as>`	sub type	Identify the semantic type of a word or phrase (for example, currency or time). See Table A-9 in Appendix A.
`<sayas>`	phon	`<phoneme>`	ph alphabet	Specify phonetic pronunciation.
		`<voice>`	gender age category variant name	Set voice characteristics of the speaker.
		`<mark>`		Ignored.

[1] Based on Speech Synthesis Markup Language Specification for the Speech Interface Framework, W3C Working Draft 3 January 2001.

> **NOTE** *VoiceXML standardizes the syntax of speech markup, but it is still up to the voice platform to make decisions about how to interpret (render) the various markups. In fact, the platform may ignore speech markup. As a result, text marked up as a "teenage girl speaking emphasized phone number" may sound like your daughter on one voice platform and like the wrestler next door on another.*

The details of how speech is synthesized and how markup tags are interpreted are technical and platform dependent. See Table A-1 in Appendix A for more detailed information about the syntax of markup tags. For more information on the meaning of the speech markup language, see the VoiceXML specification or the Speech Synthesis Markup Language Specification for the Speech Interface Framework (http://www.w3.org/TR/speech-synthesis). For information about how markup tags are rendered into speech, see the documentation for your chosen voice platform.

Events and Handlers

Events are named objects that represent the occurrence of a particular situation or condition. Events can be generated in three ways: by the VoiceXML interpreter itself, by executing a <throw> element, or by specifying the event attribute on a <link> or <return>.

Event handlers are code fragments that are executed when an event occurs. As in other programming languages, event handlers nest hierarchically in scope, and the "closest" handler is invoked when an event is thrown.

The simplest form of event handling is provided by the shorthand <catch> elements.

- <error> is shorthand for <catch event="error">.

- <help> is shorthand for <catch event="help">.

- <noinput> is shorthand for <catch event="noinput">.

- <nomatch> is shorthand for <catch event="nomatch">.

VoiceXML specifies predefined events and errors, which are thrown by the VoiceXML interpreter. If you do not specify explicit handlers for these events, the VoiceXML interpreter invokes its default handlers. You can also make up your own events. You must explicitly throw your events using the <throw> element. Your event handler must specify a matching event name.

When an event is thrown, either by the VoiceXML interpreter or by your application, the interpreter selects the <catch> element "best qualified" to handle the event based on the following:

> *Scope:* The menu or form item being visited at the time the event is thrown must be in the scope of the event handler.

> *Event name:* The event name specified by the event attribute of the <catch> element matches the name of the event being thrown. The names match if they are identical, or if the <catch> name is a prefix of the thrown event name (see the VoiceXML specification for details).

> *Count:* The count of the <catch> element must be less than or equal to the event count.

VoiceXML defines more predefined events than it defines special elements, so some predefined events can only be caught by <catch> elements (see Table 9-2).

Table 9-2. VoiceXML 1.0 Events

EVENT NAME	TYPE	TRIGGERED BY	CAUGHT BY	MEANING
-	info	VXML	<filled>	A phrase in an active grammar was recognized.
cancel	info	VXML, <throw>	<catch>	The user has requested to cancel playing of the current prompt.
telephone. disconnect.hangup	info	VXML, <throw>	<catch>	The user has hung up.
telephone. disconnect.transfer	info	VXML, <throw>	<catch>	The user has been transferred unconditionally to another line and will not return.
exit	info	VXML, <throw>	<catch>	The user has asked to exit.

Table 9-2. VoiceXML 1.0 Events (continued)

EVENT NAME	TYPE	TRIGGERED BY	CAUGHT BY	MEANING
help	info	VXML, \<throw\>	\<catch\>, \<help\>	The user has asked for help.
noinput	info	VXML, \<throw\>	\<catch\>, \<noinput\>	The user has not responded within the timeout interval.
nomatch	info	VXML, \<throw\>	\<catch\>, \<nomatch\>	The user input something, but it was not recognized.
error.badfetch	error	VXML, \<throw\>	\<catch\>, \<error\>	A failed fetch. This may be the result, for example, of a missing document, a malformed URI, a communications error during the process of fetching the document, a timeout, a security violation, or a malformed document.
error.semantic	error	VXML, \<throw\>	\<catch\>, \<error\>	A run-time error was found in the VoiceXML document—for example, a divide by 0, a substring bounds error, or an undefined variable was referenced.
error.noauthorization	error	VXML, \<throw\>	\<catch\>, \<error\>	The user is not authorized to perform the operation requested (such as dialing an invalid telephone number or one the user is not allowed to call).

Table 9-2. VoiceXML 1.0 Events (continued)

EVENT NAME	TYPE	TRIGGERED BY	CAUGHT BY	MEANING
error.unsupported. format	error	VXML, <throw>	<catch>, <error>	The requested resource has a format that is not supported by the platform—for example, an unsupported grammar format, audio file format, object type, or MIME type.
error.unsupported. element	error	VXML, <throw>	<catch>, <error>	The platform does not support the given element. For instance, if a platform does not implement <record>, it must throw error.unsupported. record. This enables an author to use event handling to adapt to different platform capabilities.
- application defined -	app	<throw>	<catch>	Application-defined events should follow the Java naming convention: <org name>. <app name>.<event> (for example, com.company.spim. nocontactfound).

Form Items and the Form Interpretation Algorithm

A form contains fields and other form items. The VoiceXML interpreter presents the form items to the caller one at a time. (The specification calls this "visiting" a form item.) The form interpretation algorithm (FIA) specifies this process. The main loop of the FIA has three phases:

1. Select the next form item to visit.

2. Collect an input or event.

3. Process the input or event.

Each form item has a variable and a guard condition. The form item's variable and guard condition are used in the select phase to determine which form item will be visited next. The default behavior of a form is to visit each form item once in the order they occur in the form. The initial value of each form variable is undefined by default. The FIA selects the first form item whose value is undefined. After a form item receives a value, the FIA moves on to the next form item. You can change the order in which form items are visited by including an explicit <goto nextitem="..."> element in the <filled> action of a form item.

In the collect phase, the VoiceXML interpreter reads or plays the prompt for the form item and activates the field grammar. Then it waits for the user to say or key a response that matches any active grammar or for an event to be thrown. After either event occurs, the FIA moves on to the process phase.

In the process phase, if there was a grammar match on a link, the interpreter executes the link's transition. If there was a grammar match on the field being visited or its form, values are assigned to variables and <filled> actions are executed. If there was a grammar match on another form (document or application scope), the FIA transitions to that form. If an event was thrown, the interpreter identifies and executes the applicable <catch> element.

The form items are subdivided into two categories: field items and control items. The field items are used to collect user input and store it in variables. The field item elements are as follows:

<field>: Define a field in a form.

<record>: Capture raw user input without speech recognition.

<transfer>: See the section on telephony later in this chapter.

<object>: Invoke platform-specific features that return values.

<subdialog>: Analogous to a function call in a programming language. Invoke another dialog and return values collected by that dialog.

There are two control elements:

<block>: Contains procedural statements for prompting and computation, but does not gather input. The contents of a block are executed

during the collect phase, and its variable is then set to true. The process phase is skipped for <block> elements.

<initial>: Supports mixed-initiative forms. It usually contains a prompt for a form-level grammar.

Mixed-Initiative Dialogs

In a directed dialog (simple form), fields are filled one at a time, with a separate prompt and response for each field. It's called "directed" because the computer directs the whole conversation—the person simply supplies information. In a mixed-initiative dialog, the user can fill multiple fields with a single utterance, which resembles a normal bidirectional conversation with another person. At some points in a mixed-initiative dialog, the computer will be in the position of passively waiting for the user to speak and then taking action based on what was said. In the SPIM tutorial, the dialog used to add an appointment to the calendar is implemented as a mixed-initiative dialog: The computer prompts with an open-ended question ("Next Appointment?"), and the user can respond with a variety of utterances, from short ("Meet with Joe") to detailed ("Call Fred Tuesday, December third at fourteen hundred hours"). The computer extracts all the information it can from the utterance it recognized, and then it steps through a directed dialog to elicit information not extracted from the initial utterance.

A VoiceXML mixed-initiative dialog contains a form-level grammar and an <initial> item. The <initial> item is syntactically and functionally like the first field item in the form. When the form is activated, the <initial> prompt is read and the computer then waits for a response that satisfies the form-level grammar. During the recognition process, the recognizer encounters tags embedded in the grammar. The grammar tags associate grammatical constructs with data items that the VoiceXML interpreter places in VoiceXML program variables. (For example, a grammar tag may set a variable named "place" when the grammar matches a placeName phrase.) Because the interpreter may encounter multiple grammar tags in the course of recognizing a single utterance, it is possible to set multiple form item variables in one complex utterance.

An <initial> element has event handlers, event counters, and catch clauses like other form items, except that there is no <filled> handler. The form item variable for <initial> is either undefined or true. If the item variable is undefined, the FIA will consider the <initial> item "unfilled" and will revisit it until the variable becomes defined. The variable is set to true by the VoiceXML interpreter if any other form item variable is set as a result of processing grammar tags while recognizing a valid utterance. The item variable may also be explicitly set within the body of an event handler.

Once the <initial> form item has been "filled," other field items are processed as in plain directed dialogs. However, the FIA will not visit any field item whose variable has been set. Thus, form items whose variables were set by grammar tags are considered filled and will not be visited. In this way, a user may respond to the <initial> prompt with information that populates one or more form fields, and the computer will prompt for only those fields that were not populated.

Executable Content

Executable content is procedural code that can appear in <block> form items or event handlers. In regard to scripting capabilities, VoiceXML is layered closely on ECMAScript. (A VoiceXML interpreter is, of necessity, an ECMAScript interpreter as well.) The VoiceXML elements for data manipulation and control flow correspond closely to underlying ECMAScript data structures and control constructs and generally follow ECMAScript semantic rules.

The <var> element declares and optionally initializes a VoiceXML variable. Based on where the declaration appears, the variable is placed in one of the VoiceXML scopes: application, document, dialog, or (anonymous) (local to a block or event handler). Once declared, a variable may be used in VoiceXML or ECMAScript expressions interchangeably. Variables in containing scopes may be qualified with their scope: application.username or document.x. A declared but uninitialized variable has the value ECMAScript "undefined." The <assign> element is used to assign the result of an ECMAScript expression to a variable.

The FIA tests if a form item variable is set to "undefined" to determine if the field item is eligible for a visit. The <clear> element is used to reset one or more form item values to "undefined"[2] and reinitialize the form item prompt and event counters. By default, the <clear> element resets all form item variables, effectively resetting the form to its unfilled state.

ECMAScript expressions appear in the cond and expr attributes of many VoiceXML elements. Any ECMAScript code may appear in the body of a <script> element.

Conditional logic in VoiceXML is handled by the <if> element and its optional subelements, <else> and <elseif>. There is no element for looping. The <goto> and <submit> elements are used to unconditionally transfer control to another location (URI). When either of these elements is executed, the document identified by the URI is loaded. Execution begins at either the first form in the document or the form identified by the fragment in the URI (that is,

---

[2] ECMAScript provides no syntax to denote the value "undefined," so the ECMAScript equivalent of <clear namelist="variable"> is something inscrutable such as variable = void 0;.

if the URI ends with "#formName"). The main difference between the two is that <submit> allows a list of variables to be submitted through an HTTP POST or GET.

The <return> element is used to stop processing of a dialog called as a sub-dialog. Control returns to the point of invocation. The <return> element specifies either a result (an ECMAScript variable) to pass to the caller or an event to throw in the caller's scope. The <exit> element returns control the VoiceXML interpreter, terminating the VoiceXML application.

Telephony

The <transfer> element is a form item used to transfer a caller to another phone number. In a *bridging transfer,* the VoiceXML interpreter suspends while the call takes place and resumes when the call ends. In a *blind transfer,* the VoiceXML program terminates as soon as the call connects.

The <disconnect> element disconnects the caller and throws an event. The event may be caught to perform cleanup before exiting.

Platform and Performance Features

VoiceXML offers a number of ways to set and configure parameters in the under-lying voice platform. These features are discussed in Chapter 10.

Summary

This chapter provided reference-style coverage of all the major VoiceXML language elements. The VoiceXML specifications, available at http://www.voicexml.org/ and http://www.w3.org/Voice, are the ultimate source of information on the VoiceXML language. The specifications are quite readable, and unlike many specifications, they contain numerous examples that explain the intent of language features.

Advanced VoiceXML Topics

THIS CHAPTER EXAMINES some of the more advanced uses of VoiceXML. These advanced topics begin to explore how a VoiceXML program is constructed and how it interacts with its host environment. The discussion here covers some of the issues involved in developing and deploying a real-world VoiceXML application. It sets the stage for an architecture-oriented discussion of how VoiceXML interacts with other components in a distributed system.

Resource Fetching

In VoiceXML, a *resource* is a VoiceXML document, an audio file, an object, a grammar, or a script. Table 10-1 lists the VoiceXML tags that initiate fetching of resource content from a URI and what kind of content each tag fetches.

Table 10-1. Tags That Fetch Resources

TAG	CONTENT DESCRIPTION	MIME TYPES
<choice>	VoiceXML document	text/x-vxml
<goto>		
<link>		
<subdialog>		
<submit>		
<audio>	Audio recording	audio/basic, audio/x-law-basic, audio/wav
<dtmf> <grammar>	Grammar file	application/x-jgsf, application/x-gsl, others
<object>	External object	varies
<script>	ECMAScript source file	application/x-javascript

All tags that fetch resources share attributes that control how fetching works. Default values for these attributes are set by VoiceXML interpreter properties. The "Using Properties" section of this chapter provides information about how to set properties. See Table 10-2 for a summary of the attributes and values available.

Table 10-2. VoiceXML 1.0 Resource-Fetching Attributes

ATTRIBUTE	MEANING	PROPERTY CONTAINING DEFAULT VALUE
fetchtimeout	Specifies how long to wait before throwing an error. badfetch event. Example values: "100ms," "10s."	fetchtimeout
fetchhint	An optimization hint to the interpreter. prefetch suggests that the content may be downloaded before it is used. safe suggests that the content be downloaded on demand. stream suggests that the interpreter start processing the content when it is received, rather than waiting for the download to complete.	audiofetchhint documentfetchhint grammarfetchhint objectfetchhint scriptfetchhint
fetchaudio	The URI of an audio clip to play while the document is being fetched. This is a good way to keep the computer's conversational turn when a long delay may confuse the user. If attribute and property are not set, no clip is played.	fetchaudio
caching	Specifies the caching policy for the content. The VoiceXML interpreter, like most Web browsers, is capable of caching content to avoid unnecessary downloads. Caching policy safe is conservative and should be used when content is volatile. Caching policy fast provides the best performance with static content.	caching

Audit Trail

It's common when you reach an automated voice response system to hear a prompt something like this: "Please listen carefully to the following options, because our menu options have changed. For good service, press 1. For mediocre service, press . . . ." The change in options is good news, because it means that the Interactive Voice Response Unit (IVRU) operators are monitoring actual system usage and tuning the interface for best performance. The following are some tuning techniques that should be applied routinely:

- Move the most frequently used options to the front of the list.

- Restate prompts and/or restructure dialogs that prove prone to errors.

- Add/remove task-specific options as demand varies. (For example, add a special top-level option to request tax information during February, March, and April.)

These maintenance operations are only possible if the VUI is gathering historical data about its own operation. This type of self-monitoring is well known to Web site operators, who monitor clickstreams and server performance statistics for a variety of purposes, including managing and predicting load, inferring customer preferences, triggering generation of dynamic content, and so on.

The wrinkle introduced by VoiceXML is that maintaining a high-quality VUI requires detailed information about low-level conversational interactions. For example, a VUI designer can make good use of information such as "In form XYZ, the count=3 handler was invoked less than 10 percent of the time for fields a, b, and d, but 57 percent of the time for field c." These detailed interactions are scripted within VoiceXML and, from an architecture perspective, occur on the Web client side (and therefore do not generate the verbal equivalent of clickstreams). To transfer from one HTML page to another implies loading another document from a Web server, because only one HTML document is loaded at a time. However, a VoiceXML document can contain many dialogs, so transitions between dialogs do not necessarily imply round-trips to the server.

VoiceXML does not provide any explicit, standard mechanism for generating the voicestream equivalent of the HTML clickstream. Individual platform vendors may (and usually do) build in proprietary audit trail collection features.

The other option available is to implement the VUI so that VUI events can be inferred from server visits. The basic technique is to use Web-based URIs whenever fetching VoiceXML resources. This forces frequent interaction with the Web server, which the Web server logs. The same tools used to massage clickstream data can be used to massage voicestream data. See Table 10-3 for some techniques you can use to generate voicestream events.

Table 10-3. Techniques for Generating Voicestream Events

TECHNIQUE	CAPTURED EVENT	PRO	CON
Adopt a convention of coding one dialog per VoiceXML document.	Dialog transitions.	Simple and provides useful information about structuring dialogs.	Can't make use of document- level scoping.
Use recorded prompts.	Executing <audio> tag.	Provides fine-grained trace information. (For example, it can infer visits to individual event handlers.)	Doesn't work when TTS synthesis is required. Audio data can be massive and cause slowdownloads.
Use vendor-provided logging facilities in the voice platform.	Varies.	Can work without modifying application.	Proprietary.
Use external grammars and specify on-demand retrieval.	Loading documents, executing form items.	Can infer visits to individual fields (even if they don't have prerecorded prompts).	Makes VoiceXML code less readable, because expected responses are not visible inline.
Use external scripts.	Executing <script> tag.	Can use do-nothing scripts as trace points.	Makes VXML code less readable, because script is not visible inline.

Accessing the Voice Gateway

The VoiceXML interpreter is part of a voice gateway, which includes speech recognition and speech synthesis technology. All commercial voice systems contain more features than can be used through standard VoiceXML code.[1]

---

[1] As is to be expected with young standards driven by industry groups, to a certain extent the VoiceXML standard represents a "least common denominator" feature set that is agreeable to the participating vendors.

VoiceXML provides two principal means of getting at nonstandard features of the environment. VoiceXML properties are a mechanism to set configuration data in a standard fashion. The <object> tag is a mechanism to bridge the VoiceXML run-time environment and external services.

Using Properties

Platform properties are set using the <property> tag. Properties are scoped according to where the <property> specification appears. The platform uses the conventional hierarchical lookup from narrowest to broadest scope when determining what value of a property to use at a particular point in VoiceXML code. Curiously, VoiceXML properties may be set but not read.

VoiceXML defines a standard set of properties that must be supported by all platforms. Table A-7 in Appendix A lists the standard properties. (For further information, see the VoiceXML specification.) Several of the predefined properties have to do with tuning various time-out values that parameterize the voice recognizer. Others have to do with resource-fetching defaults and other platform characteristics. Platforms may implement additional, nonstandard properties as well.

In Listing 10-1, the first <property> tag sets the bargein property to false at document scope. Therefore, when the first prompt inside the form is executed, bargein is disabled. The default value for the property is inherited from document scope, because the property is not set at dialog scope. The second <property> tag sets the bargein property to true, but this time at field (anonymous) scope. The prompt for the field is therefore read with bargein enabled, because the (anonymous) scope overrides document scope.

Listing 10-1. Property Tags at Different Scopes

```
<vxml>
    <property name="bargein" value="false">
    <form>
        <!--bargein is disabled here-->
        <prompt>You cannot stop me!<prompt>
        <field name="test">
            <property name="bargein" value="true">
            <grammar> . . . </grammar>
            <!--bargein is enabled here-->
            <prompt> Go ahead and cut me off. <prompt>
        </field>
    </form>
</vxml>
```

The <object> Tag

The <object> tag can be used invoke platform-specific functionality from within VoiceXML. It is modeled on the HTML <object> tag, which is used to include an externally defined object on a page. Syntactically, <object> is a close relative of <subdialog> for the following reasons:

It is a form item that invokes other code and returns to the point of invocation.

It takes parameters through the <param> tag.

It returns results through an ECMAScript object.

The VoiceXML specification specifies the syntactic form of the <object> tag, but it does not specify any standard mappings to standard object invocation mechanisms such as DCOM, CORBA, or JavaBeans. This means that the set of extensions available for use in VoiceXML is defined solely by the platform vendor. As a developer, you can only write extensions to VoiceXML if your chosen platform provides you a way to do it.

Listing 10-2 shows an example of how the <object> tag might be used to invoke a (hypothetical) standard, platform-supplied dialog to elicit a person's social security number.

Listing 10-2. The <object> Tag

```
<form id="getSSN">
    <object name="SSN" classid="builtin://elicitSSN"
        data="../errorPrompts" />
        <prompt> Please say your security number as a sequence
                of nine digits, or key in the nine digits on your
                keypad." </prompt>
        <param name="requireResponse" expr="'false'"/>
    </object>
    <block>
        <prompt> Your social security number is: </prompt>
        <prompt><value expr="SSN.firstThree"/> dash </prompt>
        <prompt><value expr="SSN.middleTwo" /> dash </prompt>
        <prompt><value expr="SSN.lastFour"/> </prompt>
    </block>
</form>
```

In the example, the external object is identified by the classid attribute, which specifies a URI that is interpreted by the platform. The data attribute specifies the URI of data used by the invoked object—in this case, the location of recorded error prompts that can be used during the elicitation. The person's nine-digit social security number is returned in ECMAScript variable SSN, already neatly parsed into attributes firstThree, middleTwo, and lastFour.

The <object> tag accepts several more attributes, including standard form item attributes, codebase, resource-fetching attributes, and others. See the VoiceXML specification for more syntactical details, or see the documentation for your voice platform for details of how to invoke specific functions.

Advanced Event Handling

Due to the fact that speech recognition and synthesis must work in real time, event handling is an essential and core part of VoiceXML. To date, real-time applications have tended to be high-end software (as are voice platforms). Programming languages incorporate event handling in some form, but it's usually not in real time, and it's used by programmers. It will be interesting to see how VoiceXML's foray into mass-market, markup language–based event handling will fare.

The following sections delve into the details of how event handling works in the VoiceXML language and looks at some practical issues relating to the writing and maintenance of event-driven VoiceXML code.

"As If by Copy" Semantics

The VoiceXML specification contains the following paragraph (Section 11, Event Handling), which is easy to skip over:

> "An element inherits the catch elements ('as if by copy') from its ancestor elements, as needed. If a field, for example, does not contain a catch element for nomatch, but its form does, the form's nomatch element is used. In this way, common event handling behavior can be specified at any level, and it applies to all descendants."

While seemingly innocuous in its brevity, what this paragraph means is that the VoiceXML event handling model works quite differently from familiar, syntactically similar models in programming languages such as C++ and Java. Programming languages typically use the concept of *nested lexical scope*. Every data object or procedure is declared in a scope, which determines where the object can be referenced. A scope may contain other nested scopes, forming a hierarchy (see Figure 10-1). When an event is thrown in a nested scope, the "nearest" event handler in the hierarchy is invoked and the event propagates into the scope of the event handler. For example, if event *e* is thrown in Block D, the event handler in Block D is invoked. If event *e* is thrown in Block C (which has no event handler), the event propagates up the hierarchy to the event handler in the nearest containing scope—in this case, Procedure B. This model is called *lexical scoping*, because you can tell by reading the program in which scope an event handler is executed.

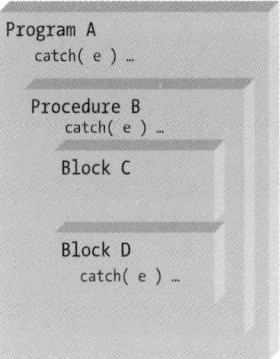

Figure 10-1. Lexical scoping

In the VoiceXML model, event handlers are declared in one scope but may execute in any contained scope. In other words, an event handler declared in the application scope may be executed in the scope of a particular form. For example, in Figure 10-2, when event *e* is thrown in Form C, the event handler from Document B is executed in C's scope. The behavior of the VoiceXML program is exactly the same as if the source code text of the <catch> element in Document B was copied into Form C. Thus, for example, any variable references in the event handler code would be resolved in Form C, not Document B.

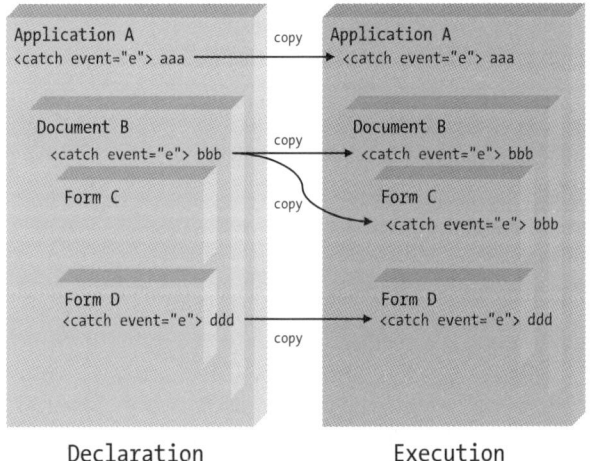

Figure 10-2. VoiceXML "as if by copy" scoping

"As if by copy" semantics makes it possible to define a single event handler that will handle all events of a certain type by declaring the event handler in application scope and nowhere else. The effect will be the same as if the one <catch> element were copied everyplace in the application where the event could be thrown. This seems to be what the specification means by "common event handling behavior." For example, Listing 10-3 and Listing 10-4 show a VoiceXML application that defines a complex group of interrelated event handlers and a simple form that "uses" them.

Listing 10-3. "As If by Copy" Sample Application

```xml
<?xml version="1.0"?>
<vxml version="1.0">
  <var name="tersePrompt" expr="'The terse prompt'" />
  <var name="helpPrompt1" expr="'First help prompt'" />
  <var name="helpPrompt2" expr="'Second help prompt'" />
  <nomatch count="1">
    <prompt>I didn't get that.</prompt>
  </nomatch>
  <noinput count="1">
    <prompt>
      <value expr="tersePrompt" />
    </prompt>
  </noinput>
  <catch event="nomatch noinput" count="2">
    <throw event="help" />
  </catch>
  <help count="1">
    <prompt>
      <value expr="helpPrompt1" />
    </prompt>
    <reprompt />
  </help>
  <help count="2">
    <prompt>
      <value expr="helpPrompt2" />
    </prompt>
    <reprompt />
  </help>
  <help count="3">
    <throw event="nomatch" />
  </help>
</vxml>
<?xml version="1.0"?>
```

Listing 10-4. "As If by Copy" Sample Form

```
<vxml version="1.0"
application="file:///H:/VoiceXML/SPIMApp/Tutorial/SmallExamples/
AsIfByCopyApplication.vxml">
  <form>
    <var name="mlname" expr="'VXML'" />
    <field name="hello">
    <grammar>hello</grammar>
    <prompt>Please say hello.</prompt>
    </field>

    <field name="goodbye">
    <grammar>good-bye</grammar>
    <prompt>Please say good-bye.</prompt>
    </field>

    <block>Good-bye to you!</block>
  </form>
</vxml>
```

When executing the form, Dialog 10-1 is valid.

Dialog 10-1. Application-wide Event Handling

C (computer): Please say hello.

P (person): Help.

C: First help prompt. Please say hello.

P: Help.

C: Second help prompt. Please say hello.

P: Hello.

C: Please say good-bye.

P: Help.

C: First help prompt. Please say good-bye.

P: Help.

C: Second help prompt. Please say good-bye.

P: Good-bye.

C: Good-bye to you!

Note that the same sequence of event handlers is invoked for both form fields, and that each field maintains its own event counters.

The bad news is that, in practice, event handlers associated with a field item usually perform field-specific prompting. In other words, instead of a generic "First help prompt," the prompt should say, "It's polite to say hello" for the first field and "Just say good-bye" for the second field. The "as if by copy" semantics hold out the promise that you could assign local variables to have the prompt strings defined on a field-by-field basis. However, <field> elements can't contain executable content, so you *can't* declare or assign a variable on a field-by-field basis. Therefore, there is no way to parameterize a single event handler so it works differently for different field items. The only option available is to use the <reprompt/> element in the common event handler, as shown in the example.

Techniques for Event Handling

As you saw in earlier examples, VoiceXML provides powerful but verbose event handling features. With these features, it is possible to construct VUIs that provide good prompt tapering and dialog structuring. However, the power comes at the cost of readability: If you look at Listing 10-3, it's hard to see the actual field prompting for the forest of event handlers. Furthermore, good design principles dictate that event handling should be consistent across fields and forms.

Subtleties of Subdialogs

It would be desirable to be able to factor out the event handling code from individual form fields and define it once. This would improve readability, improve software maintainability, and aid in consistency. A simplistic first approach is to look at what data changes between various uses of the event handlers and then create a subdialog with parameters for data specific to each use. In other words, the idea is to replace the field item shown in Listing 10-5 with a subdialog invocation like that in Listing 10-6.

Listing 10-5. Field with Verbose Event Handling

```
<field name="appointee" >
    <grammar src="/Step7/SimpleAppointment.gram#appointee" />
    <prompt count="1">Who are you meeting with?</prompt>
    <prompt count="2">Name?</prompt>
    <nomatch count="1">I didn't get that.<reprompt/></nomatch>
    <noinput count="1">
        <throw event="help" />
    </noinput>
    <catch event="nomatch noinput" count="2">
        <throw event="help" />
    </catch>
    <help count="1">
        <prompt>Say the name of a person.</prompt>
```

```
        </help>
      <help count="2">
          <prompt>
            You are adding an appointment.
                Say the name of the person you are making an appointment with.
          </prompt>
      </help>
  </field>
```

Listing 10-6. Static Subdialog Invocation

```
<subdialog name="appointeeHandler" src="staticFieldHandler">
  <param name="longPrompt" expr="'Who are you meeting with?'" />
  <param name="tersePrompt" expr="'With whom?'" />
  <param name="helpPrompt1" expr="'Say the name of a person.'" />
  <param name="helpPrompt2" expr="helpPrompt1" />
  <param name="theGrammar" value="'SimpleAppointment.gram#appointee'" />
  <filled>
    <assign name="appointee" expr="appointeeHandler.value" />
  </filled>
</subdialog>
```

The parameters to the subdialog are the information specific to each field. The implementation of the dialog would be a form with a single field like that in Listing 10-7. Unfortunately, when you try to actually code the subdialog, there is a roadblock because VoiceXML doesn't allow the grammar to be treated as a parameter passed to a <subdialog>. The value of the src attribute of a <grammar> tag must be a URI (and it can't be an expression that yields a URI). One possible approach is to turn off caching and point the <grammar> src attribute to a URI that dynamically generates the grammar. This approach is problematic because there is no way to inform the server of which field the grammar is for.

Listing 10-7. Hypothetical Reusable Static Subdialog

```
<form id="staticFieldHandler">
    <var name="theGrammar" />
    <var name="tersePrompt" />
    <var name="longPrompt" />
    <var name="helpPrompt1" />
    <var name="helpPrompt2" />
    <field name="theValue">
```

```
<!-- To achieve the effect of a reusable field-handling component,
        the grammar specified in the following line would need to contain
        the specific responses valid for the field being processed.
        However, there is no way in VoiceXML to parameterize the
        grammar being used. -->
<grammar src="????" />
<prompt>
  <value expr="longPrompt" />
</prompt>
...
  </form>
```

The solution is to dynamically generate the form with the grammar name (or the grammar itself) embedded in it. The grammar is identified in the `<subdialog>` invocation by a variable that is sent to the server. The modified invocation is shown in Listing 10-8, and the full text of the generated form is shown in Listing 10-9.

Listing 10-8. Invoking a Generated Subdialog for Event Handling

```
<var name="thisFieldsGrammar"
        value="'myGrammars//Step7/SimpleAppointment.gram#appointee'">
<subdialog name="appointeeHandler" src="/cgi-bin/generateFieldHandler"
        namelist="thisFieldsGrammar">
    <param name="longPrompt" expr="'Who are you meeting with?'" />
    <param name="tersePrompt" expr="'With whom?'" />
    <param name="helpPrompt1" expr="'Say the name of a person.'" />
    <param name="helpPrompt2" expr="helpPrompt1" />
    <param name="theGrammar" value="'SimpleAppointment.gram#appointee'" />
    <filled>
      <assign name="appointee" expr="appointeeHandler.value" />
    </filled>
  </subdialog>
```

Listing 10-9. Dynamically Generated Reusable Subdialog

```
<form id="dynamicFieldHandler">
    <var name="theGrammar" />
    <var name="tersePrompt" />
    <var name="longPrompt" />
    <var name="helpPrompt1" />
    <var name="helpPrompt2" />
    <field name="theValue">
```

```
<!-- The server generates the following reference to an external grammar
       based on the namelist variable passed in the subdialog call. -->
<grammar src="/Step7/SimpleAppointment.gram#appointee"
         type="application/x-jgsf"/>
<prompt>
  <value expr="longPrompt" />
</prompt>
<nomatch count="1">
  <prompt>I didn't get that.</prompt>
</nomatch>
<noinput count="1">
  <prompt>
    <value expr="tersePrompt" />
  </prompt>
</noinput>
<catch event="nomatch noinput" count="2">
  <throw event="help" />
</catch>
<help count="1">
  <prompt>
    <value expr="helpPrompt1" />
  </prompt>
</help>
<help count="2">
  <prompt>
    <value expr="helpPrompt2" />
  </prompt>
</help>
<help count="3">
  <throw event="nomatch" />
</help>
</field>
</form>
```

Style Sheet As Macro

Because VoiceXML is XML, you can bring some of the transformational capabilities of XML to bear on VoiceXML source code. Style sheets are a powerful technology for transforming one XML representation into another. Normally, style sheets come into play when dynamically generating presentation code (for example, HTML or VoiceXML) from an XML document. When using style sheets on source code, you're not generating code dynamically at run time—you're actually generating static code from handwritten code.

Listing 10-10, Listing 10-11, and Listing 10-12 show the transformation from an "XML-ized" version of the subdialog invocation to static VoiceXML using a style sheet (XSL). (This is a fragmentary example, and it does not produce a full VoiceXML document.)

Listing 10-10 shows a code fragment that uses the <reusableField> tag. This tag is not a VoiceXML tag, but it is used to generate a standard pattern of frequently used VoiceXML code. Listing 10-9 is the XSL style sheet that transforms <reusableField> elements into VoiceXML code. You'll look more closely at style sheets in later chapters. Without going into much detail, the trick to reading XSL style sheets is knowing that tags in the "xsl" namespace (that is, those that start with xsl:) are XSL processor instructions that will be replaced during transformation. Other tags are passed through to the output document. Listing 10-10 shows the result of the transformation.

Listing 10-10. Source Code with Embedded <reusableField> *Tags*

```
<?xml version="1.0"?>

<reusableField name="appointee">
    <inlineGrammar>alpha | bravo | charlie</inlineGrammar>
    <longPrompt value="Who are you meeting with?"/>
    <tersePrompt value="With whom?"/>
    <helpPrompt1 value="Say the name of a person."/>
    <helpPrompt2 value="Say the name of a person."/>
</reusableField>
```

In real life, this transformation would be performed at the time that the Web site is published into Web format (that is, deployment time). Notice that the input source code is concise, readable, and maintainable, but the style sheet is probably mysterious unless you work with style sheets a lot. This points to some tradeoffs here, based on experiences with using macro-based programming languages:

- Used sparingly and well, macros can help make source code more maintainable and consistent.

- Macros are themselves code that must be maintained by someone with specialized knowledge (in this case, knowledge of XSLT).

- Overuse of macros can lead to dense, unmaintainable code and can require a significant amount of training to use.

Listing 10-11. XSL Style Sheet That Expands <reusableField> *Tags*

```
<?xml version="1.0" encoding="UTF-8"?>
<xsl:stylesheet version="1.0" xmlns:xsl="http://www.w3.org/1999/XSL/Transform">
    <xsl:output method="xml" version="1.0" encoding="UTF-8" indent="yes"/>

    <xsl:template match="/">
    <xsl:apply-templates select="//reusableField"/>
    </xsl:template>

    <xsl:template match="//reusableField">
    <field name="{@name}">
    <grammar><xsl:value-of select="inlineGrammar"/></grammar>
      <prompt>
        <xsl:value-of select="longPrompt" />
      </prompt>
      <nomatch count="1">
        <prompt>I didn't get that.</prompt>
      </nomatch>
      <noinput count="1">
        <prompt>
          <xsl:value-of select="tersePrompt/@value" />
        </prompt>
      </noinput>
      <catch event="nomatch noinput" count="2">
        <throw event="help" />
      </catch>
      <help count="1">
        <prompt>
          <xsl:value-of select="helpPrompt1/@value" />
        </prompt>
      </help>
      <help count="2">
        <prompt>
          <xsl:value-of select="helpPrompt2/@value" />
        </prompt>
      </help>
      <help count="3">
        <throw event="nomatch" />
      </help>

    </field>
    </xsl:template>
</xsl:stylesheet>
```

Listing 10-12. Generated VXML Source Code (with Macros Expanded)

```xml
<?xml version="1.0" encoding="UTF-8"?>
<field name="appointee">
    <grammar>alpha | bravo | charlie</grammar>
    <prompt/>
    <nomatch count="1">
        <prompt>I didn't get that.</prompt>
    </nomatch>
    <noinput count="1">
        <prompt>With whom?</prompt>
    </noinput>
    <catch event="nomatch noinput" count="2">
        <throw event="help"/>
    </catch>
    <help count="1">
        <prompt>Say the name of a person.</prompt>
    </help>
    <help count="2">
        <prompt>Say the name of a person.</prompt>
    </help>
    <help count="3">
        <throw event="nomatch"/>
    </help>
</field>
```

Summary

In this chapter, you've looked at some advanced aspects of VoiceXML that are important in practice. These aspects become important when you broaden the scope from just programming the VoiceXML language to producing, deploying, and maintaining VoiceXML applications in the real world. Some features are already in the language (for example, resource caching, properties, and <object> tags) and will become "seasoned" as real VoiceXML applications mature. Some missing features (for example, audit trails and reusable dialogs) will be addressed in future releases of the language. Software engineering techniques and processes, such as the use of XSL macros for code reuse, will evolve as more and larger VoiceXML applications are developed.

Part 3
Incorporating Voice into the Web

IN THE PRECEDING PARTS, the focus has been on how to use VoiceXML to create voice interfaces. In this part, the camera dollies back for a look at the bigger picture of the overall architecture of Web applications incorporating GUIs, WUIs, and VUIs. In all likelihood, people will not build stand-alone Web applications for voice only. It's more likely that voice interfaces will be retrofitted to existing HTML-based Web sites, or that new Web sites will be built to incorporate multiple access modes from inception. Any successful Web application involves the interaction of many technologies, and to a large extent, VoiceXML will succeed or fail based on how well it cooperates with other technologies.

Chapter 11 provides a quick, general review of some the key technologies that VoiceXML will be used with. Chapter 12 explores the architectural issues that arise when incorporating voice into applications along with wireless and standard Web interfaces. Chapter 13 presents a prototype that pulls together the various technologies and demonstrates a transformational architecture. Detailed instructions are provided for installing the prototype from the companion CD, and the various components are dissected. Finally, Chapter 14 explores future directions for VoiceXML.

Overview of Related Web Technologies

THIS CHAPTER REVIEWS some technologies that interact to form a distributed Web application. The following technology briefings are intended as refreshers rather than primers. So many technologies are involved in a distributed Web application that no one can be master of them all. If you are already familiar with the technologies, feel free to skip any or all sections; if the concepts are brand new to you, check out some of the reference links for introductory material.

XML

A *markup* language is a language that tags the contents of a document with information about how to interpret the content. Markup is generally divided into two categories: pure content and presentation. *Pure content* markup annotates the content based on its meaning, without regard for how the content will be published or presented. *Presentation markup* interweaves instructions and hints about how to present the content in a particular medium.

Extensible Markup Language (XML) is a standardized syntax for a family of markup languages. A language in the family is defined by a document type definition (DTD) or an XML Schema. WML and VoiceXML are XML languages. HTML, although derived from SGML, does not comply completely with XML requirements, but its close cousin XHTML does. In addition, XML is being used to define the format of data interchanged between businesses, organizations, and computer systems.

Significant Features

- Text-based.

- Easily exchanged between platforms.

- Can be read by humans and edited in any text editor.

- Syntax is rigorously designed for machine parsing.

- New "dialects" can be defined without programming.

How It Is Used in Voice Enabling Web Sites

XML is used to express information from Web applications in a presentation-neutral format that can be shared among the XHTML, WML, and VoiceXML user interfaces.

Technical Overview

An XML document contains *elements, tags, attributes,* and free-form textual *content.* Elements have optional and required attributes. Elements can contain content and subelements. An element is a "noun" that identifies how to interpret its content. Attributes are "adjectives" that modify the element. Attribute values are always quoted. Elements are delimited by tags that appear in angle brackets.[1] An element can be delimited with a start tag and an end tag (that begins with /), or a single, bodiless tag that starts and ends in the same tag. The following example shows an element that contains content and two nested elements:

```
<myXMLElement name="Fred" extra="more stuff">
    this is free form content
    <myXMLSubElement>
        nested elements may also have content
    </myXMLSubElement>
    <bodylessTag extra="information"/>
</myXMLElement>
```

XML elements must nest hierarchically. In each XML document, a single root element contains all the other elements in the document. Therefore, an XML document can be thought of as a tree of branching nodes, where each node corresponds to a tag in the document.

A *DTD* or *XML Schema* defines the set of elements and attributes available in a particular XML language. The schema defines what order elements may appear

---

[1] To be hair-splittingly precise, *elements* are structural components of an XML language that are declared in the schema or DTD. *Tags* are the syntactic markers that are placed in XML document instances to delimit elements. In practice, however, the two terms are often used interchangeably, and I confess that I have not been rigorous in distinguishing the two throughout this book.

in, how the elements nest, and whether elements are optional or required. For each element, the schema defines required and optional attributes. The following XML Schema fragment could be the schema for the previous example:

```
<xsd:element name="myXMLElement">
    <xsd:attribute name="name" type="xsd:string" use="required"/>
    <xsd:attribute name="extra" type="xsd:string" use="optional"/>
    <xsd:sequence>
        <xsd:element name="myXMLSubElement" type="xsd:string"/>
        <xsd:element name="bodylessTag" type="xsd:string">
        <xsd:attribute name="extra" type="xsd:string" use="required"/>
        </xsd:element>
    <xsd:sequence>
</xsd:element>
```

An XML document is *well formed* if it can be parsed into a syntax tree representation by any XML parser. A document may have an associated schema. An XML document is *valid* if it conforms to its schema—that is, it is syntactically correct XML and it contains elements and attributes in the right relationships and order, as defined in the schema.

Where to Learn More

A wealth of information about XML is available on the Web. A good starting point is XML.org (http://www.xml.org/). *XML Bible,* by Elliotte Rusty Harold (http://www.ibiblio.org/xml/books/bible), is a comprehensive guide to XML.

XSL

XML Stylesheet Language (XSL) is an XML language that is used to transform a document from one XML dialect to another. The term "stylesheet" captures the original intent of XSL, which was to insert presentation markup into XML documents that provided content in a neutral format. A stylesheet written in XSL contains text templates and rules for how to merge the template text with content from an XML document. In practice, XSL is very powerful and has many more uses than just defining presentation styles.

Significant Features

- XSL is itself an XML language.

- Allows very powerful "tree-to-tree" transformations of documents.

- Can be read by humans and edited in any text editor.

- Stylesheets can be modified without changing application code.

- Declarative rather than procedural.

- Template-based.

How It Is Used in Voice Enabling Web Sites

XSLT is used to transform information from a presentation-neutral XML to XHTML, WML, and VoiceXML markup languages.

Technical Overview

XSL incorporates two distinct sublanguages: a formatting layout language and a template transformation language. The formatting layout language is concerned with placing text on a two-dimensional page (therefore, it isn't particularly relevant to VoiceXML, so I'll skip that part). The template transformation sublanguage (XSLT) is a general-purpose declarative language for rewriting documents.

An XSL document contains template rule definitions, XSLT directives for finding and inserting content from the input XML document, and uninterpreted text. To transform a document, the XSLT processor is invoked with an XSL document and an XML document as input. The XSLT processor parses the XML document and then executes the XSLT document. When the XSLT processor encounters text that is not an XSLT directive, it copies the text to the output file. When it encounters an XSLT directive, it processes it (see Figure 11-1).

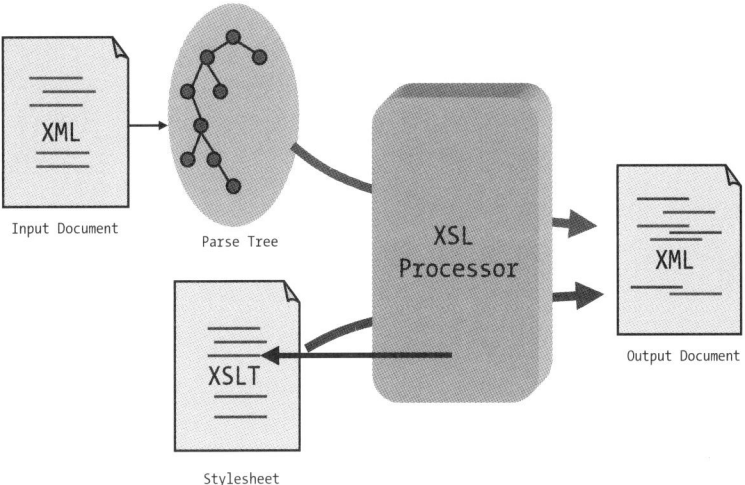

Figure 11-1. XSL transformation processing

XSL directives make use of XPath expressions. *XPath* is a complex syntax that is capable of designating any node, or set of nodes, in the parsed XML document. An absolute XPath expression might designate "the third node with element type myXMLElement" or "all myXMLElement nodes in the document with extra attribute value 'nothing'." A relative XPath expression refers to nodes relative to the node currently being processed—for example, "the last bodilessTag element descended from the current node" or "the node after the parent of the current node."

The workhorse XSL construct is the template (<xsl:template> element). A template has a pattern that specifies when the template is invoked. The pattern is expressed as a restricted XPath expression that is applied to a candidate node. If the pattern matches, the template is invoked with the candidate node as the current node. Output generated by the template is inserted in the output stream. The output may include raw text from the XSLT document and tag or content data from the input XML document.

Candidate nodes are generated by the <xsl:apply-templates> element. It specifies an XPath expression that generates zero, one, or many candidate nodes, which are then matched against all active templates.

Where to Learn More

Once again, a good starting point is XML.org (http://www.xml.org). Excerpts about XSL and XPath from *XML Bible,* by Elliotte Rusty Harold, are online at http://www.ibiblio.org/xml/books/bible/updates/14.html and http://www.ibiblio.org/xml/books/bible/updates/17.html.

Servlet

A servlet is a computer program that runs on the Web server. The servlet acts as a surrogate for a document. Instead of serving a file from the file system, the Web server invokes the servlet, which dynamically generates the text (or other content) for the document.

Significant Features

- Flexible and powerful—if you can code it, a servlet can do it.

- Requires programming.

- Designed to optimize multithreaded, multiuser usage.

- Awkward to maintain static text inside program source code.

- Template-based.

How It Is Used in Voice Enabling Web Sites

Servlets encapsulate code that can retrieve information from a variety of different sources, and then they generate a presentation-neutral XML version of that information.

Technical Overview

When a Web client requests a document from a URI that has been configured as a servlet address, the Web server invokes the servlet, passes it the HTTP request, and routes the output from the servlet back to the Web client. The servlet processes the request and writes text output to the output stream. Figure 11-2 illustrates the servlet processing model.

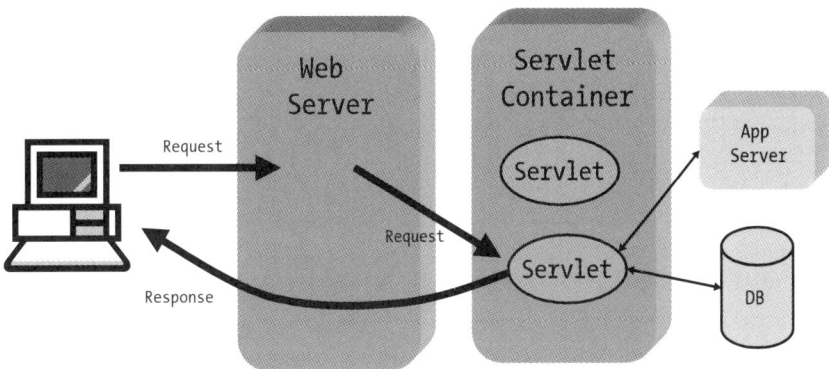

Figure 11-2. Servlet processing model

Servlets are components that are hosted in a servlet container. The servlet container is responsible for managing the lifecycle of servlet components and the resources they use. Typically, the servlet container is part of the Web server, but it may also be a separate add-on component.

Although servlets are commonly associated with dynamically generated HTML, the basic servlet model is a language-independent request/response protocol. Servlets can certainly be used to generate any XML language or any text output in general. The Java Servlets 2.2 specification (currently in final draft) has added the concept of filters, which can be used to incorporate stylesheet transformations into the servlet processing model.

Where to Learn More

Visit Sun's Java Servlet Technology site (`http://java.sun.com/products/servlet/`) for everything you need to know about servlets.

JavaServer Pages

A JavaServer Page (JSP) is a text document that contains interspersed static text, markup language, and programming language scripts. Conceptually, when a JSP is served, the page is processed as follows:

1. Static text is copied into the output stream.

2. JSP markup language directives are processed by the server.

3. Programming scripts are executed and their results are copied into the output stream.

The significance of these features is that they enable UI designers to edit markup tags and static content as text, without requiring programming intervention. Contrast this with servlets, where the markup and static text is embedded in Java code, which means that content changes require Java programmers to make program changes.

Significant Features

- Static text is maintained and edited as text in a file.

- Scripting requires programming.

- Custom tags can be defined to insulate JSP authors from script programming.

- Compatible with XML technologies.

- Procedural.

How It Is Used in Voice Enabling Web Sites

JSPs can be used to dynamically generate VoiceXML documents in the same way that they are used to generate HTML documents. The difference is that the static text embedded in the JSP consists of VoiceXML tags rather than HTML tags.

Technical Overview

Technically, a JSP is a species of servlet. When a Web client requests a JSP, the Web server invokes the "master" JSP servlet, passes it the HTTP request, and routes the output from the servlet back to the Web client. If the JSP has not been served recently, the master servlet compiles the JSP source code into Java source code, invokes the Java compiler to compile the resulting servlet, loads the servlet, and delegates the request to the servlet as described previously. If the JSP's companion servlet is already compiled, the Web server delegates requests to it just like any other servlet. Figure 11-3 illustrates this process.

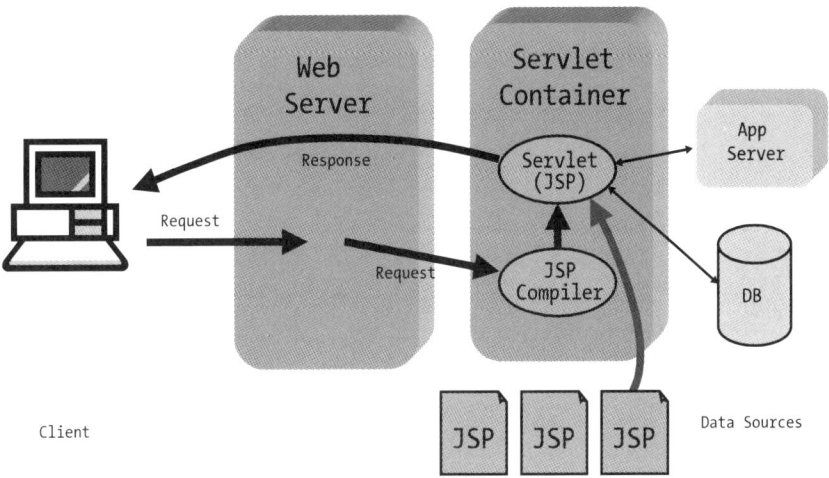

Figure 11-3. JSP processing model

The JSP specification defines a core set of XML elements that the JSP compiler recognizes. The set of markup tags available can be extended by importing a custom tag library. A custom tag library associates JSP markup elements with implementations written in Java. This enables JSP authors to invoke standard functions simply by coding XML markup tags into the JSP, rather than having to code the functions using scripting in Java.

The JSP processing model does not depend on Java as the scripting language (although the JSP specification does require Java to be supported as one of possibly many scripting languages). The concept of scripting can be generalized to incorporate other scripting languages, such as ECMAScript, Tcl, Perl, and so on, into JSPs.

> **NOTE**   *The scripting language required by JSP is Java (the programming language). The scripting language used in VoiceXML is ECMAScript, aka JavaScript. JavaScript and Java are not the same, and they are in many ways as different as they are alike.*

Where to Learn More

Visit Sun's JavaServer Pages site (http://java.sun.com/products/jsp/) for everything you need to know about JavaServer Pages.

XML Publishing

XML publishing is an infrastructure technology for the generation, publication, and processing of XML documents. All information is represented by documents, and the processing of information is achieved by repeated transformation of documents using stylesheets. Apache Cocoon is representative of this technology.

Cocoon is an open-source project sponsored by Apache. Apache has a number of XML-related projects underway. Cocoon closely integrates the servlet model of server-side processing with XML document processing. Cocoon processing is based on the concept of producing an XML document (pure content) in response to an HTTP request and then successively transforming the content markup into presentation markup using XSL transformations.

Cocoon is freely available and is easy to use with Web applications. However, because Cocoon is not a commercial product, it may not be appropriate for production applications. Production applications will likely use a commercial product that implements the same technology.

Significant Features

- All server-side processing works on XML documents. As a final step, a formatter may generate XML, HTML, or text for delivery to the client.

- Incorporates Java language scripting.

- While being processed, content is manipulated as parsed XML nodes, which avoids unnecessary reparsing.

- The Cocoon system is implemented as a J2EE servlet that will run in any J2EE-compliant servlet container.

- XSL transformation model combines template data with dynamic content.

How It Is Used in Voice Enabling Web Sites

XML publishing is used to implement a single application having multiple user interfaces. Information is obtained from business applications in XML format and then transformed into a presentation language appropriate to the user's means of access (Web browser, WAP phone, or voice phone call).

Technical Overview

When a Web client requests an XML document (file type .xml), the Web server invokes the Cocoon servlet, passes it the HTTP request, and routes the output from Cocoon back to the Web client. The Cocoon servlet orchestrates a series of transformations (see Figure 11-4). The first step is to invoke a *producer,* which materializes an XML document. A producer may be as simple as a Cocoon-provided program that reads and parses a static XML file. More typically, a producer is a program written in XML Servlet Processor (XSP), an Apache-defined language that intersperses template data with JavaScript. If the XSP producer has not been served recently, the Cocoon servlet compiles the XSP source code into Java source code, invokes the Java compiler to compile the resulting servlet, loads the servlet, and invokes the producer. The producer creates a parsed XML document. The parsed document is pipelined to zero or more *transformers,* which perform XSL transformations on the document. The resulting presentation markup is returned to the client.

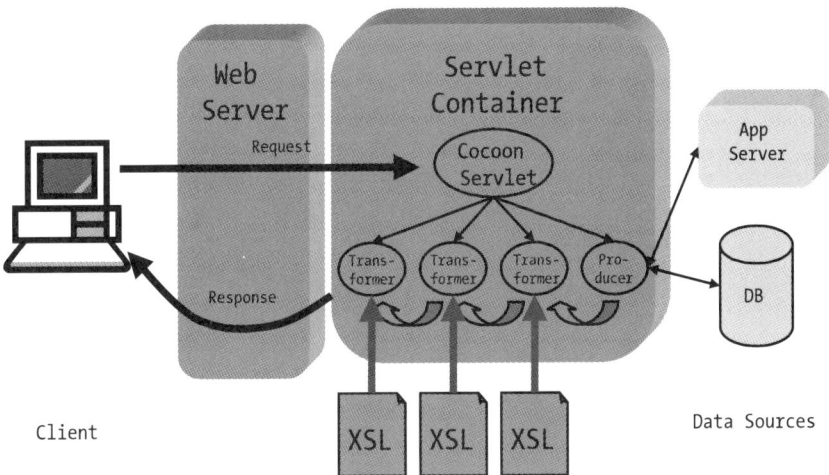

Figure 11-4. Cocoon processing model

Point by point, there are strong congruencies between the J2EE servlet/JSP processing model and the Cocoon model (see Table 11-1). The conceptually subtle, but very significant, difference between them is that the servlet/JSP model is based on processing text streams, while the Cocoon model is based on processing parsed XML documents. Because XML is far richer than plain text, this distinction makes Cocoon an elegant and powerful tool for serving XML documents.

Table 11-1. Servlet/JSP Features versus Cocoon Features

FEATURE	SERVLET/JSP	COCOON
Dynamic content generation	JSP language intersperses embedded tags, static content, and Java scripting; dynamically compiled into Java code	XSP language intersperses embedded tags, static content, and Java scripting; dynamically compiled into Java code
Processing model	Pipeline of chained servlets operating on a text stream	Pipeline of XSL transformations performed on a parsed XML document
Content transformation	Procedural, through JSP language	Declarative, through XSL stylesheets

There are a number of interrelated Apache XML projects underway, which brings quite an alphabet soup of technologies to bear in the Cocoon environment.

- *XSP:* A template language with Java scripting that is used to create XML documents dynamically

- *ESQL:* A set of XML tags that performs standard SQL queries and returns results as XML

- *Xerces:* An XML parser

- *Xalan:* An XSLT processor

Where to Learn More

Visit the Apache XML Project's site (`http://xml.apache.org/`) for everything you need to know about Cocoon and other Apache XML-related technologies.

Summary

In a real Web application, VoiceXML is just one of many powerful technologies that must interact and cooperate to do what the user wants. This chapter provided quick summaries of some selected fundamental technologies that are likely to be used in association with VoiceXML: XML, XSL, servlets, JavaServer Pages, and XML publishing. The next chapter looks at the overall architecture of Web applications and shows how these individual technologies work together. Not coincidentally, several of these technologies also appear in the Web prototype that will be dissected later in the book.

Adding VoiceXML to Web Applications

THIS CHAPTER EXPLORES some of the "programming in the large" issues that arise when designing large, new, voice-enabled Web applications or when retrofitting existing applications with voice. Some of the issues arise because of the special requirements of VoiceXML and voice; some of the issues are simply scaling issues that result from supporting another access mode, regardless of how it works.

One Application, Multiple User Interfaces

In the early days of the Web, it was clear what Web applications were about: delivering HTML to Web browsers. With the advent of wireless devices, it was necessary to shoehorn WML into the application. Because WML can be treated as a kind of "small scale" HTML, this presented tactical but not conceptual obstacles. Voice represents a fundamentally different access mode, and integrating VoiceXML into Web applications requires rethinking how the application is structured.

Rather than functioning as a monolithic control point for scripting interactions with a user, the Web application is evolving to resemble more of a "content clearinghouse" (see Figure 12-1) that collects content from a variety of sources and matches it to people in a variety of access modes. The process of matching content to a requesting user may involve format transformations, filtering, and generation of presentation code.

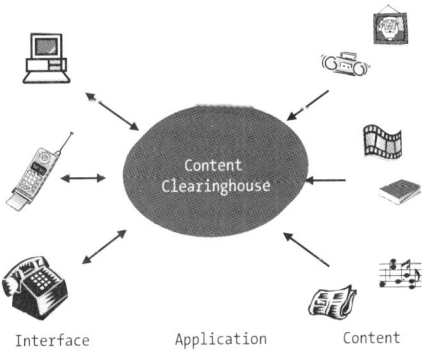

Figure 12-1. Application as clearinghouse

The Transformational Processing Model

The transformational processing model is illustrated in Figure 12-2. The arrows show how information flows through the Web application and is transformed along the way. The basic phases of transformation are as follows:

- *Produce:* Retrieve data from wherever it resides and transform it into a "presentation-neutral" format suitable for processing in the application.

- *Process:* Provide services of value to the end user by modifying the information and/or executing transactions based on information from the user and from data sources. In business applications, this is where business logic rules are enforced.

- *Format:* Filter and format the information content and structure so that it is suitable for rendering in a particular medium.

- *Render:* Interact with the user in the chosen interface medium (for example, speech or GUI).

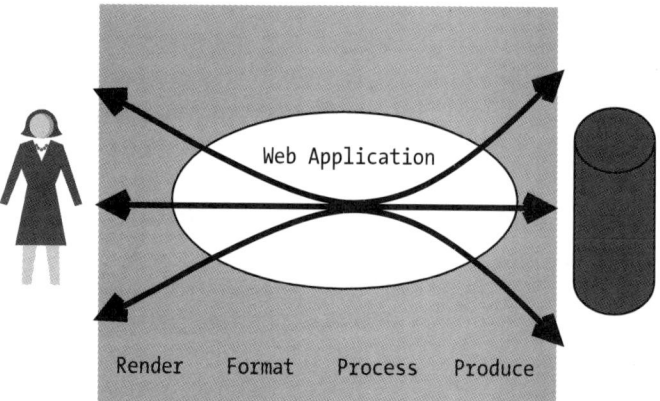

Figure 12-2. Transformational processing model

As Figure 12-2 implies, the goal is to work with multiple interaction media and multiple data sources, but implement the core processing only once. This is achieved by keeping each phase of the transformation separate and keeping presentation, processing, and persistent representation completely independent.

Special Needs of VXML

In terms of general system layout, VoiceXML and HTML work in the generic Web infrastructure. VoiceXML imposes some special twists described in the sections that follow.

Starting a Session

From a Web browser, a session is initiated by visiting the home page of the application, which is identified by a URL (for example, `http://www.voicexml.org/`). When initiating the session, the Web server may use cookies to identify the user or may require a user ID/password login sequence. Cookies are a reliable way to recognize a user, because they are stored locally on the computer that is running the Web browser. The duration of a session for an HTML browser is determined by the Web application (often by assigning inactivity timeouts to server-side session objects). Applications typically store cookies that contain session identifiers on user's PCs. A session may persist across multiple invocations of the HTML browser.

When using VoiceXML, the same session mechanism is at work. However, the VoiceXML browser runs on a gateway, not a local PC. The sessions are established between instances of the browser running on the gateway and the Web application server. A single VoiceXML browser instance handles one call. Therefore, VoiceXML sessions exist for the duration of a phone call to the gateway.

A VoiceXML session is initiated by phoning a VoiceXML gateway. There are several alternatives for how the call is connected to a VoiceXML browser instance.

There is one phone number for all applications hosted on the gateway. When calling the number, the person first identifies the desired application by voice and then is authenticated and connected to a browser instance.

There is a distinct phone number for each hosted application. The person is authenticated and connected to a browser instance.

There is a private phone number for each user. In this case, the call-in number can be used to identify the user and connect him or her directly to a VoiceXML browser instance.

Authentication Techniques

Four options that can be used to authenticate the user of a voice system are as follows:

- User speaks name and password

- User speaks or keys in user ID and keys in PIN

- User speaks name, system challenges, and user speaks response

- User speaks name and voice sample

The first option corresponds most directly to a conventional username and password login. This option is attractive because the voice interface uses existing user authentication information (that is, it is backward compatible with existing Web applications). It also works well in hands-free environments. Disadvantages with this option are that the password is spoken aloud and may be overheard (think of calling in from the airport), and it is subject to the normal foibles of voice recognition. For example, two people's names may sound very similar, causing recognition problems at login. In addition, a password should be unusual (to minimize the chances of being guessed), but that may make it difficult for the person to say it and/or for the computer to recognize it.

The second option is familiar to everyone who's used Interactive Voice Response (IVR) systems over the phone. The advantage of using the keypad is that keypad tones can be recognized unambiguously. The disadvantage is that requiring keypad usage is not conducive to hands-free use of the voice system.

The third option is a challenge/response style of authentication. Instead of specifying a single password, the user defines a set of challenges and responses. This can either be done explicitly (for example, the computer says "hello," the user says "goodbye"; the computer says "red," the user says "green"; and so on) or algorithmically (for example, the computer says "11," the user adds "43," and the user responds "54"). This approach overcomes the big drawback of the first option, because people can overhear only the response and not the challenge. As a practical matter, a drawback of this approach is that the challenge/response protocol is not widely used for logging in to computers, and hence people are not particularly familiar or comfortable with using it.

The last option is an interesting option that capitalizes on the use of voice. A person's voice can be used as a means of biometric authentication. In this situation, the person's voice is analyzed and matched against a predefined sample.

This approach is a slick and easy way to use voice technology. The major drawback is that authentication by voice analysis is not standardized, so application security must be built on proprietary technology.

Obviously, many variations and combinations of these techniques are possible. Currently, for example, you may perform financial transactions through a Web browser with password-based authentication. However, when you perform the same transactions over the phone (with a customer service representative), it is quite common to go through a challenge/response authentication process in which the customer service representative asks you two or three questions (for example, "What's your mother's maiden name?" and "What is your billing address and ZIP code?") to verify your identity. The questions are drawn from a pool of "personal facts" known about you, including your social security number, the amount of the last deposit you made, the amount of your last cleared check, and so on.

Dynamic Grammar Generation

Grammars perform the same function in VoiceXML that drop-down lists perform in GUIs: They encode and constrain the set of valid responses the user can give. I'll use the term "choice lists" to generically cover both concepts. Some choice lists are the same for all users—for example, navigational quick links to various points in a Web site. Some choice lists have a fixed set of choices, which may be enabled or disabled on a user-by-user basis. This is common for command lists, where the functions a user can perform are restricted by authorization level. Finally, some choice lists are unique to each user. For example, the list of all contacts in my address book is unique to me.

In the SPIM example, when the person wants to place a call, the computer will ask for the name of the person to call. Valid responses are defined by a grammar that contains the name of each known contact. The grammar is different for each user, and it changes as the address book is edited. The grammar, therefore, is generated dynamically out of the database on the server.

Grammars may be dynamically generated as either internal or external grammars. Internal grammars can be used when the VoiceXML interpreter loads a form that is generated on the server. This occurs when the interpreter executes a <submit next="uri"> element and uri identifies a generated document. In this case, the inline grammar is another piece of dynamic content that is derived from the database. External grammars can be generated when a <grammar src="uri"> element is loaded. In this case, uri identifies a generated document. Figure 12-3 illustrates dynamic grammar generation.

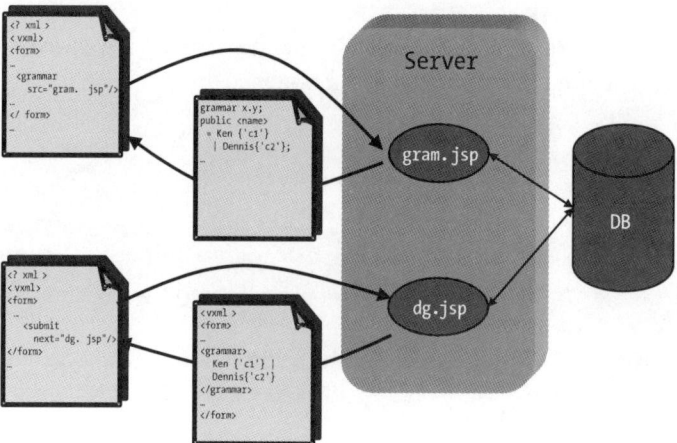

Figure 12-3. Dynamic grammar generation

Grammar tags may be used to specify the text that is returned to the VoiceXML interpreter when a phrase is recognized. For dynamic grammars, the tag can specify the database key value for the recognized item. For example:

```
<grammar type="application/x-jgsf">
    (Ken [Abbott]) {'C15467'} | (Dennis [McCarthy]) {'C23432'}
</grammar>
```

Using the database key as tag has the advantages of uniquely identifying the recognized item, despite potential variations in the exact phrasing, and enabling the database key to be passed back to the server on a subsequent <submit>. The server can perform a more efficient indexed key lookup from the database rather than a search on name.

Web Application Architectures

This section examines some of the architectural approaches for incorporating a GUI, WUI, and VUI into a single Web application. The focus will be on exploring the server-side technologies that can be applied to support all three kinds of interfaces.

Application Styles

To provide a frame of reference for categorizing various types of applications, I distinguish two dimensions: the processing style and the information style. As shown in Figure 12-4, processing styles range between *transactional* and

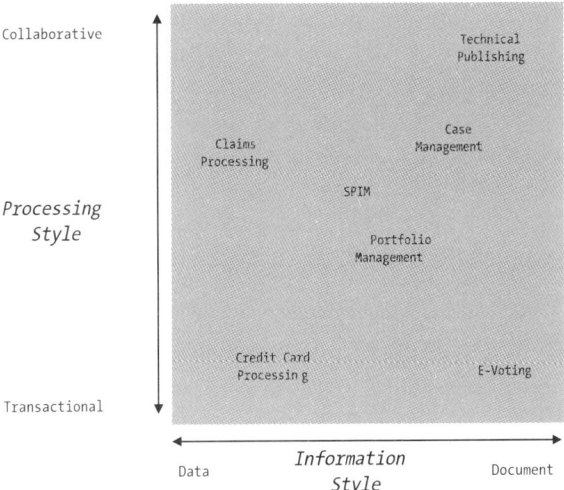

Collaborative

Technical
Publishing

Case
Management

Claims
Processing

SPIM

Processing
Style

Portfolio
Management

Credit Card
Processin g

E-Voting

Transactional

Data   *Information*   Document
                  Style

Figure 12-4. Application landscape

collaborative processing. Information styles range between *data* and *document*. These conceptual distinctions are useful to relate what the application does to the underlying technologies involved.

Data versus Documents

When I worked at Xerox in the late 1980s and early 1990s, a lot of effort was spent trying to pin down what it meant to be "The Document Company," and more specifically, what a "document" was. A definition in vogue back then (and still popular with me) was "A *document* is recorded information that is structured for human comprehension." By analogy, "*Data* is recorded information that is structured for machine interpretation." In other words, if the information is intended to be conveyed to a person, it's a document; if it's intended to be processed efficiently by a machine, it's data.

This definition captures the range of artifacts that people intuitively recognize as "documents." On one hand, there are utilitarian documents that are primarily a means of recording something—for example, a copy of the minutes of a meeting. On the other hand, there are documents that result from the creative work of people—for example, paintings, books, films, and so on. Documents that are the result of a creative or artistic process are specifically structured to produce a certain state of comprehension in a person and, by the way, are recorded so that they can be comprehended by many people. However, a row in a database, a file on disk or tape, a computer punch card, and so on are certainly data. Of course, there are fascinating gray areas: Is a printed bar code data or a document? What about an encrypted, compressed, JPEG-scanned image?

Translating between the two categories is not trivial. Consider what it takes to display the content of a row in a database on your computer screen (for instance, queries, data conversions, transactions, and so on). On the other hand, consider what's involved in converting a printed book into a machine-searchable electronic format (scanning, OCR, page recognition, and so on).

In a sense, markup languages represent an attempt to reconcile documents and data. Information recorded using markup language (XML in particular) is human readable, but it also can be interpreted by machines.

Transactional versus Collaborative Processing

This section introduces two contrasting styles of processing that involve computers. The point of this discussion is to develop a conceptual framework for distinguishing situations where a conventional, transactions-and-data style of processing is appropriate from situations where a collaborative, document-oriented style is appropriate.

Transactional Processing

Transactional processing occurs in the following steps:

1. Elicit the type of transaction the user wants to perform.

2. Gather all the information needed to process the transaction.

3. Submit the information and process the transaction.

4. Notify the user of the processing outcome (whether the process succeeded or failed).

5. Repeat all steps.

An example of transactional processing is when you buy stuff online. You implicitly state your desire to buy things (transaction type) by opening your shopping basket or adding the first item to it. As you browse, you add more items (gathering information about what you want to buy). When you check out, you provide personal billing information (still gathering). When you click the Submit button, all the information is submitted and the transaction is processed as a unit. The next page you see tells you whether the transaction succeeded or failed.

While buying and selling are the most obvious examples of transactions, other examples include applying for a service (for example, a credit card), performing various personal finance–related actions (for example, viewing your checking account balance), or submitting a bug report.

Database transactions, which are the heart and soul of most transaction processing applications, exhibit the ACID properties:

- *A*tomic: Transactions either happen or they don't—there's no middle ground.

- *C*onsistent: Transactions transform data from one consistent state to another.

- *I*solated (or *I*ndependent): A transaction produces the same result whether it is performed by itself or at the same time as others.

- *D*urable: Once performed, the results of a transaction persist until another transaction changes them.

Collaborative Processing

Collaborative processing embodies the following process for transforming information:

1. Someone initiates the process—for example, by submitting an application. A temporary case folder (or its ilk) is created, marked "in-process," and links to relevant information are placed inside.

2. The case folder is routed through a series of steps. At each step, the information is processed by a person or application, who may modify the information, link in more information, and/or change the status of the process (for example, from pending approval to approved).

3. After the process has passed through all the steps, the outcome of the overall process is assigned and the process stops. Final results of the process are archived and intermediate results may be purged or archived as needed.

Processing a mortgage application is a good example of collaborative processing. An applicant submits an application form, which starts a loan approval process. The folder is routed to various people, beginning with the loan processor, who assembles all the relevant documents (credit reports, appraisals, and so on). Some of the information is gathered by other people who are part of the process as well. Once the package is complete, it is routed to others—loan officers, underwriters, and so on—who review the package and approve or reject the loan application. Finally, approved applications move to the loan officers responsible for settlement.

The noteworthy characteristics of collaborative processing are as follows:

- Processing occurs in steps and completion of a step is signaled by changing the state of the process, usually by a person.

- Processing occurs in human time (minutes, hours, days, and so on) rather machine time (subsecond).

- Multiple people and applications are involved.

- Processing rules may be applied by people and not necessarily enforced by the computer system.

Multitiered Architectures

It is common practice now to implement Web applications using a multitiered architecture. In Figure 12-5, the tiers are overlaid on the transformational processing model. The image shows that the browser tier performs rendering, the Web tier performs formatting for various interaction media, and the application server handles processing and production of data provided by data source.

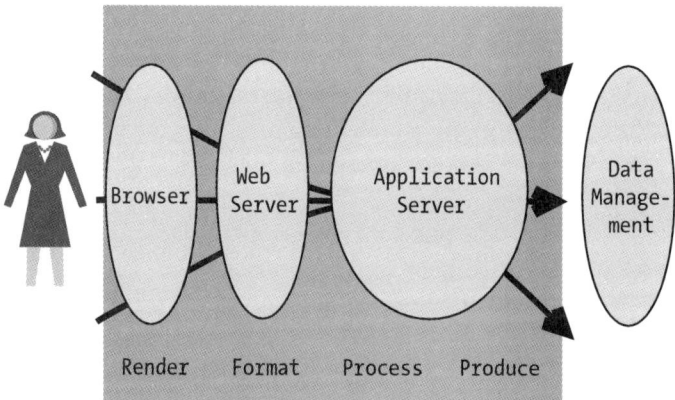

Figure 12-5. Multitiered Web architecture

The high-level architectural view in Figure 12-5 applies no matter what the underlying implementation technology. However, many choices and tradeoffs need to be made in designing and implementing the underlying technologies.

You'll see some examples of the alternatives in the following sections, and you'll investigate how the style of the application may influence the design and technologies chosen.

Servlet and Server Pages Architectures

Figure 12-6 shows a typical multitier architecture for an existing HTML-based Web site.

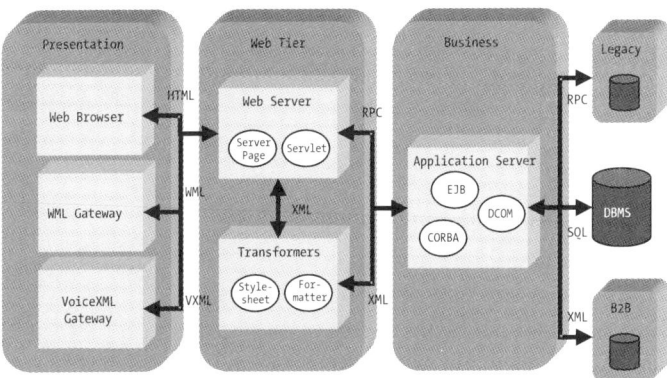

Figure 12-6. Current multitier Web architecture

The user interacts with an HTML browser running on a PC or workstation. The browser communicates with a Web server over the Internet using the HTTP protocol. The Web server is augmented with servlet and server page components to manage and publish content dynamically. The extension components communicate with an application server through an RPC protocol (such Java RMI, CORBA IIOP, or Microsoft COM+) over a secured network. In the application server, business object components implement business logic in a presentation-independent manner. Business objects may be persistent or nonpersistent and make use of "enterprise technologies" such as messaging, database management, and transactions.

This architecture has been proven successful in a number of e-business Web sites. The architecture is flexible, it can be deployed onto a variety of hardware and software configurations, and it provides independent scalability of Web response, business transaction processing, and data management.

In this architecture, servlets and server pages translate between two worlds. On the back end is the world of distributed, transactional processing: APIs, distributed computing services, legacy computer systems, and data stores. On the front end is the world of the Web: a network of hyperlinked documents that are structured for rendering to humans, unstructured interactivity, and so on.

XML Publishing Architecture

Figure 12-7 depicts an XML-centric architecture. In this document-oriented approach, information flows from point to point in the form of documents. Processing is structured on the workflow paradigm, in which documents are passed through a series of tasks that are performed by different people or programs. Documents are transformed from one schema to another as needed, and they are rendered as needed.

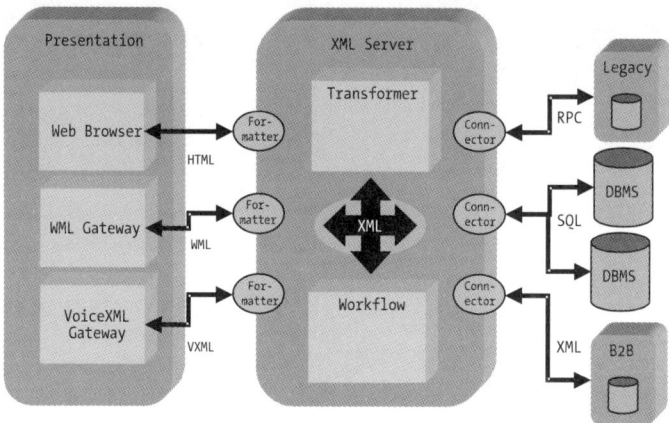

Figure 12-7. XML publishing architecture

Connectors are interfaces to sources and sinks of data. A connector abstracts access to a data source, such as a database, a legacy application, a peer document processing application, or a real-time data feed. Connectors convert the data between its native format and a *canonical* XML format, which is the lingua franca used within the XML server. The canonical XML schema is purely concerned with the logical structure of the information and is not oriented toward any particular presentation.

During processing, documents are routed to people and rendered for them. At the point when the document server is requested to render a document in a specific format, a *formatter* is invoked. Formatters abstract the process of rendering a document to a specific medium. A formatter transforms documents from their canonical form into an XML stream that is specifically tailored for presentation (for example, XHTML, WML, or VoiceXML).

Table 12-1 contrasts some of the key features of transactional and document processing architectures.

Table 12-1. Transactional versus Document Processing Architectures

	TRANSACTIONAL	**DOCUMENT PROCESSING**
Key Technologies	Servlets/server pages Distributed objects DBMS Transactions	Stylesheets XML documents Multimedia documents Workflow processing
"Sweet Spot" Applications	E-commerce Financial services Retail	Case management Application approval Collaborative design
Strengths/Weaknesses	+ Integration with legacy systems. + Underlying technologies are "experienced" with respect to scalability, reliability, and so on. + Cross-platform processing. - Complex.	+ Automation of multiperson business processes. + Document model is comprehensible to people. + Cross-platform information exchange. - Administrative tools/techniques not well developed.

Formatting: The Heart of the Matter

When retrofitting an existing Web application with voice, the hardest part is the formatting operation. In formatting, generic application data is structurally transformed into data structures that can be used by the user interface. For GUIs, these data structures include familiar elements such as pick lists, tables, menus, and so on. For VUIs, the data structures are dialogs, voice menus, and links and grammars. Because there is no cookbook translation between the data structures, good design is required. The following sections explore technical options for designing and implementing the formatting functions in a Web application.

JSP and XSL: Covert Cousins?

Because of the very different contexts in which they evolved, at first glance, JSPs and stylesheets seem more different than alike. However, they perform very similar functions: transforming information into a renderable document. In JSP, the input data is gathered through conventional computer processing: from databases, generated by programs, and so on. In this world, the underlying data is structured for machine processing. In XSL, the input data is documents, which are structured for human comprehension. In both cases, the outputs (of interest here) are text documents that can be rendered by some sort of browser.

The main difference between JSP and XSL as transformation languages is the scripting model: JSP supports a procedural style of scripting and XSL supports a declarative style of scripting. In the original JSP, script code was syntactically distinguished in enclosing <% and %>. The enclosed script is treated as Java source code. Because of this syntax, JSPs were not well-formed XML documents. As of JSP 1.2, JSP containers are required to support an equivalent, XML-compliant syntax. Furthermore, explicit scripting can be eliminated from JSP source code by using custom tags.

Listing 12-1 through Listing 12-5 compare equivalent code fragments implementing different approaches to iterating through a collection of items and generating a line of text for each. In the JSP examples, the bean "DoQuery" is a component that performs a query and returns a Java collection containing the results. In the XSL examples, the input document is an XML document that contains an <item> element for each item in the result set.

Listing 12-1. JSP/XSL Comparison: JSP with Embedded Script

```
<jsp:usebean id="results" class="DoQuery" scope="session" />
<%
  for(Iterator i=results.iterator(); i.hasNext();)
  { %>
    this is item <%= i.next(); %>
<% } %>
. . .
```

Listing 12-2. JSP/XSL Comparison: JSP in XML Syntax

```
<jsp:root . . . >
<jsp:usebean id="results" class="DoQuery" scope="session" />
<jsp:scriptlet>
  for(Iterator i=results.iterator(); i.hasNext();)
  { </jsp:scriptlet>
```

```
    this is item <jsp:expression> i.next(); </jsp:expression>
<jsp:scriptlet>
 } </jsp:scriptlet>
...
</jsp:root>
```

Listing 12-3. JSP/XSL Comparison: JSP Custom Tag[1]

```
<jsp:root ... >
<jsp:usebean id="results" class="DoQuery" scope="session" />
<customTag:forEach group="<%= results %>" item="i" >
    this is item <jsp:expression> i </jsp:expression>
</customTag:forEach>
...
</jsp:root>
```

Listing 12-4. JSP/XSL Comparison: XSL for-each *Tag*

```
<xsl:stylesheet ...>
<xsl:template match="/">
<xsl:for-each select="//item">
    this is item <xsl:value-of select="." />
<xsl:for-each>
...
</xsl:template>
</xsl:stylesheet>
```

Listing 12-5. JSP/XSL Comparison: XSL Template Rule

```
<xsl:stylesheet ...>
<xsl:template match="/">
<xsl:apply-templates select="//item" mode="showItems">
</xsl:template>
...
<xsl:template match="item" mode="showItems">
    this is item <xsl:value-of select="." />
```

---

[1] Based on Allaire Corporation's freely available JRun 3.0 Tag Library
   (http://www.allaire.com/documents/objects/Whitepaper/jruntaglib_syntax_1.pdf).

```
</xsl:template>
. . .
</xsl:stylesheet>
```

The bottom line is that JSP and XSL are similar in power and inscrutability. There is no killer technical reason for favoring one over the other. Personally, I give an edge to XSL because its recursive, template-based approach is somewhat easier to use for complex "tree-to-tree" transformations. On the other hand, the procedural style and Java-related syntax of JSPs are probably more accessible to existing software developers and Web designers.

Using JSPs and XML Together

JavaSoft seems aware of the potential redundancy between JSPs and XML stylesheet–based transformations. Over time, the two technologies will become more integrated. Already, evidence of this direction is visible in the upcoming release of the Java Servlet API 2.2 and JavaServer Pages 1.2. These and other upcoming releases increase the interoperability of XML and Java technologies (see `http://www.javasoft.com/xml/?frontpage-spotlight` for more information):

- The Servlet 2.2 specification includes the ability to specify a "processing pipeline" that allows stylesheet transformations on both the input to and the output from a servlet.

- The JSP 1.2 specification requires JSP containers support the XML-compliant syntax for JSPs.

- Java API for XML Processing (JAXP 1.1) defines a standard Java API for parsing and generating XML.

- The Java Architecture for XML Binding (under development) will enable translation of XML Schemas into Java classes.

In a white paper titled "Developing XML Solutions with JavaServer Pages Technology" (`http://java.sun.com/products/jsp/pdf/JSPXML.pdf`), several architectural options for using JSPs with XML are presented. Of particular interest to us is the section "Generating Markup Languages Using JSP Pages," which presents three approaches to generating multiple markup language presentations from a common XML data source. The three approaches are summarized in this section.

Single Pipeline

In the single pipeline approach (see Figure 12-8), the XML data is parsed under the control of the JSP. The output of the JSP is an XML document that contains the union of all information required for any of the possible presentations. For each presentation medium, an XSLT stylesheet transforms from the common XML to the markup language for the medium.

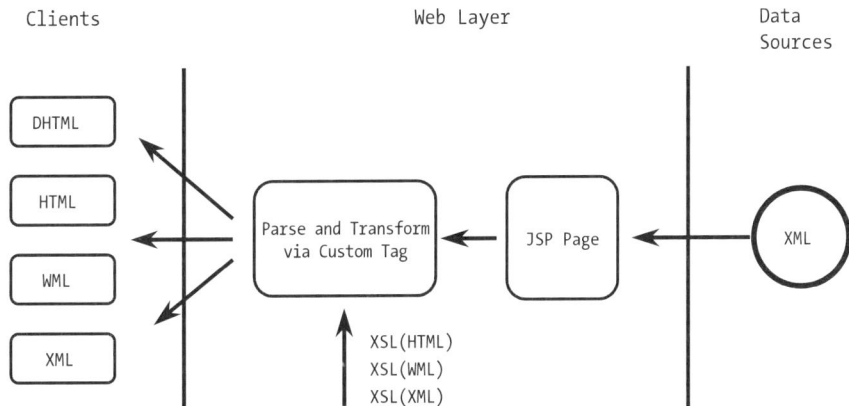

Figure 12-8. Single pipeline generating multiple markup languages (diagram courtesy of Sun Microsystems)

This approach is conceptually clean. Run-time costs include parsing the XML data, parsing the stylesheet, and applying the stylesheet. Given that the presentation media may be quite different and require radically different presentation flows (for example, consider the difference between presenting a table of data in HTML versus VXML), the transformations from the common format may be quite complex. This means that a lot of the UI design and implementation logic is implicitly coded into the stylesheet.

Multiple Pipeline

In the multiple pipeline approach shown in Figure 12-9, a different JSP is associated with each presentation medium. The JSP pages contain the static (template) data for each presentation markup language, and dynamic data is inserted by using custom tags and/or bean properties.

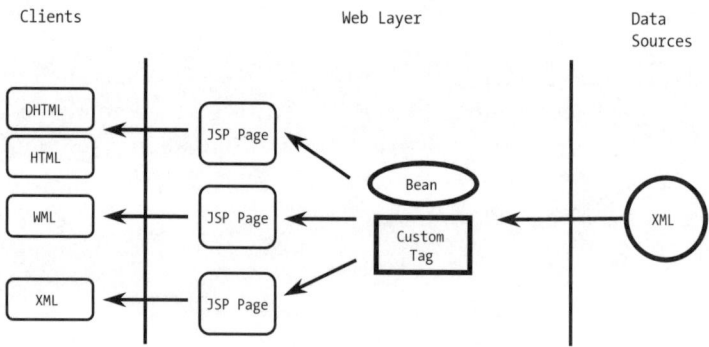

Figure 12-9. Multiple pipelines generating multiple markup languages (diagram courtesy of Sun Microsystems)

This approach uses JSP pages the way they were intended to be used. Page developers code presentation JSPs targeted for a particular presentation medium, and Java developers code beans and custom tags that encapsulate the application's data model. The main drawback to this approach is that it doesn't take advantage of XML. The source data is parsed and represented as objects, and the output of the JSPs is generated as text streams (that happen to contain XML).

Combined Approach

The single and multiple pipeline approaches can be mixed and matched by applying stylesheet transformations to the output of JSPs (see Figure 12-10). JSPs are used to handle the transition between object representation and XML representations specific to each presentation technology. XSLT stylesheets handle the XML-to-XML "style" transformations between similar XML dialects. Conceptually, this seems like an appropriate use of JSP and XSLT technologies. Pragmatically, it's not clear that using two transformation techniques rather than one is a win, given the additional costs of developing and maintaining in two technologies.

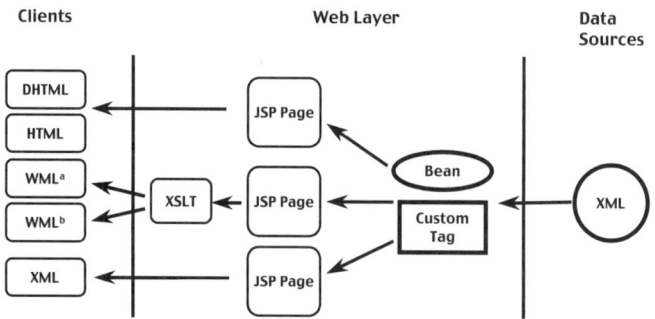

Figure 12-10. Combination pipeline generating multiple markup languages (diagram courtesy of Sun Microsystems)

NOTE *The diagrams from the JavaSoft white paper depict the data sources as monolithic "XML," which obscures one of the major advantages of the multiple pipeline approach. If you are retrofitting an existing Web application to support more presentation media, presumably there is an existing implementation of the application's object model. The multiple pipeline approach ties neatly into the existing application infrastructure, which may or may not involve XML. On the other hand, if the data sources are all nicely behaved XML producers and consumers already, what's the benefit of parsing it all, representing the information as objects, processing JSPs, and then generating XML again? In this case, an XML-based approach makes more sense.*

Summary

With the addition of voice as an interface medium, it is now becoming necessary to think of Web applications as switchboxes for connecting people and content. The transformational processing model provides a conceptual framework for relating the key steps in accessing and displaying content in a variety of media. The steps are as follows: produce, process, format, and render. These steps are general enough that they can apply to applications with HTML, WML, or VoiceXML interfaces.

In looking at Web application architectures, it can be helpful to categorize their "information style" and "processing style." Some applications manipulate data, which is generated and consumed by computers. Other applications manipulate documents, which are information packaged for human consumption. Transactional processing involves gathering all the information to perform a particular transaction, and then performing the transaction as a single, computer-controlled operation. Collaborative processing involves interaction of multiple people and applications over a "human" time scale.

Two multitiered application architecture options were characterized and examined. The popular servlet and server pages architecture is widely used in Web applications today, and it can be extended to handle voice. The XML publishing architecture is not currently in wide production use, but it has some strong features that are compatible with the transformational model. Although presented as alternative options, there are a number of subtle similarities and dualities within the architectures. A number of techniques for mixing and matching architectural elements, especially XML, server pages, and stylesheets, are possible.

With the conceptual foundation from this chapter, in the next chapter you'll plunge into developing a working prototype of the SPIM application. The prototype is based on the transformational model and uses the Cocoon XML publishing framework to manage the transformation of XML documents.

CHAPTER 13

The Web Application Prototype

IN THIS CHAPTER, you'll put together all the technology elements covered throughout this book to implement the Running Late function of the SPIM application. The result of this exercise will be a prototype voice-enabled Web application. The prototype will demonstrate the correct architectural relationships between the components, but the components were selected for ease of use, not for production (see Figure 13-1).

The purpose of the prototype is to demonstrate the feasibility of the architecture and provide a model for developing a "real" implementation. Try to keep the following two objectives in mind:

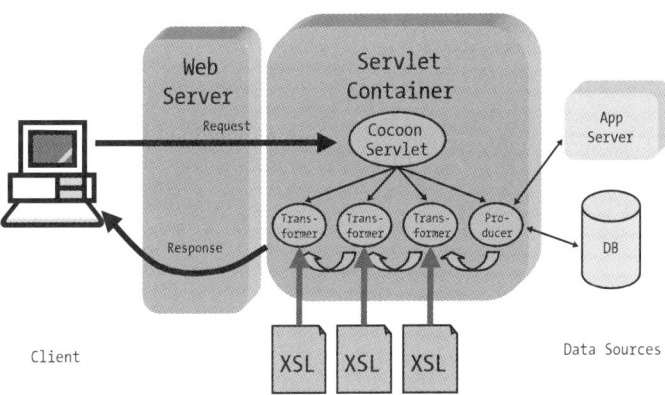

Figure 13-1. Architecture of the Cocoon-based prototype

- Leave the choice of production components and technologies open. Do not make the demonstrated architecture depend on proprietary aspects of a particular technology or component, unless you are already committed to use it in production or you know that the architecture permits the dependency to be removed.

- Don't get lost in the details. When integrating a multitiered distributed system such as this one, there are a multitude of fascinating technologies to be explored and a multitude of bugs and unimplemented features to frustrate. The purpose of the prototype is to validate the architecture *without* implementing a working system.

You can use the prototype and the information in the following sections as a concrete pedagogical example, or you can actually install the components and make it work on your computer. I have included some instructions to help you hands-on types install and run the prototype, but a complete, step-by-step tutorial is beyond the scope of this book. Therefore, I suggest you read through the following sections before jumping in and trying to install things. If you decide to run the prototype, be prepared for the fact that you will probably spend a lot of your time wrestling with installation, administration, and component integration issues, and relatively little time actually coding VoiceXML. Welcome to the modern world of component-based development at Web speed!

Prototype Setup and Installation

Here's what you need to do to prepare to run the prototype:

- Install the IBM WebSphere Voice Server SDK.

- Install and configure JRun 3.1. In the prototype, I use JRun as both the Web server and the servlet container for Cocoon. It is possible to use JRun as just a servlet container in tandem with another Web server, such as Tomcat or IIS.

- Deploy the SPIM Web application (including Cocoon 1.8.2) into JRun.

- Install an XML tool that supports editing and debugging of XML and XSL files. The prototype uses XML Spy. Other tool choices are possible, or you may use Emacs or the command line if you like.

- Set up an ODBC data source called "SPIMApplicationDb." The prototype includes a Microsoft Access database that can be configured as an ODBC data source.

Some of the software on the companion CD is evaluation software that will work for 30 days after installation. After this evaluation period, you will either need to buy the software or convince the manufacturer to extend your evaluation period.

> **TIP** *Wait until you're ready to experiment with the prototype before installing the evaluation software. This will maximize the time you have for experimentation.*

The installation instructions in the following sections are based on my experience installing software from the companion CD on my Windows 2000–equipped development machine. Depending on your operating system and the prior configuration of your machine, the installation procedures may vary.

> **TIP** *My machine is well equipped with RAM (384MB) and disk (more than 20GB), so I didn't hit any memory or disk limits. Although I have not performed an analysis to determine memory and disk requirements for this specific software configuration, based on prior experience I estimate that you should have at least 128MB of RAM (256MB is preferable) and 1GB of disk.*

Installing the IBM WebSphere Voice Server SDK 1.5

The IBM WebSphere Voice Server SDK supplies the voice platform and VoiceXML interpreter needed to run the prototype. Install it carefully and pay attention to any dialog boxes that pop up. For help, visit http://www-4.ibm.com/software/speech/enterprise/ep_11.html.

1. Execute IBM WebSphere\VoiceServerSDK\vssdkinstall_launcher.exe. Make sure there is plenty of space on the drive containing the temporary directory for unpacking. Dismiss the "The package has been delivered successfully" dialog box.

2. Execute IBM WebSphere\VoiceServerSDK\vssdkinstall_en.exe. Unpack it into same directory you used in Step 1. Dismiss the "The package has been delivered successfully" dialog box.

NOTE *This installs the U.S. English version (indicated by locale "_en") of the voice platform. You can install other languages by repeating Step 2 for the other available locales: "_de" (German), "_fr" (French), or "en_GB" (Great Britain).*

3. Go to C:\temp or whatever directory you specified.

4. If you do not have JRE1.3 installed, execute temp\install\jre13\ j2re1_3_0-win-i.exe.

5. Execute temp\setup.exe.

6. In Windows 2000, you will see the message shown in Figure 13-2 (ignore it, but be aware that the software is not officially supported on Windows 2000).

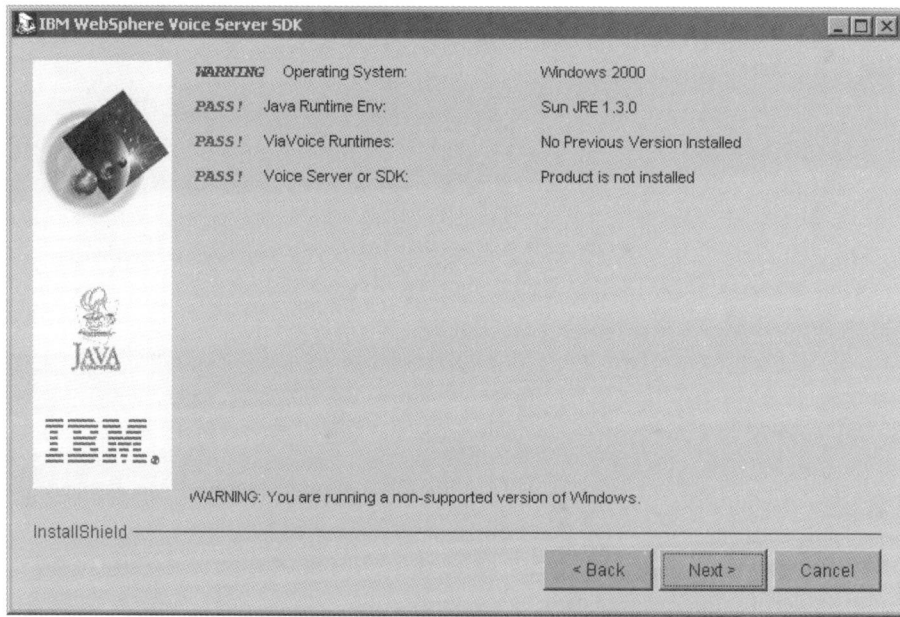

Figure 13-2. IBM WebSphere Voice Server SDK System Requirements dialog box (Windows 2000)

7. You'll be asked the usual questions about licenses and so on. Install to the directory of your choice. Click Next to install all features.

8. Reboot.

9. To install the upgrade to Version 1.5.1, execute IBM WebSphere\Voice-ServerSDKupdate.exe.

10. Reboot.

> **NOTE** *The Voice Server needs to set up your microphone and earphones before you use the voice browser. You can run the setup wizard from the Start menu (Start > Programs > IBM WebSphere Voice Server SDK > Audio Setup – US English). If you don't run it manually, the wizard will run automatically the first time you try to use the voice browser.*

Installing Allaire JRun 3.1

JRun 3.1 is an application server that includes a Web server, a servlet/JSP container, and an EJB container. The following installation procedure assumes that a JDK is already installed on your computer. For help, visit `http://www.allaire.com/products/jrun/index.cfm`.

1. Run jrun-31-win-us.exe.exe.

2. Do not enter a serial number. This will install a capacity-limited developer version. When you pick an installation directory, override the default and pick one with a short name (for example, D:\JRun[1]).

3. Select the full installation and click Next.

4. When prompted, do not install JRun services (uncheck the box).

5. Let the JRun Admin Server Port Number default to 8000.

---

[1] This sounds odd, but I encountered a pernicious bug caused by an internally generated CLASSPATH becoming too long and overrunning some string size somewhere (I don't know which component or OS was responsible). No error was reported, but evidently the classpath was silently truncated, causing JRun and Cocoon to start failing on obscure "Class not found" errors. Reinstalling JRun from \Program Files\Allaire\JRun to \jrun fixed the problem.

6. Enter a password and confirmation.

7. Answer questions about your desire to receive JRun product information.

8. Select "Start the JRun Management Console, I'll configure my web server later" and click Finish.

9. When the Management Console prompts you, log in as user admin, using the password you set in Step 6. (If your browser has trouble opening the Management Console page, wait a few seconds and click Refresh.)

Installing Altova XML Spy

XML Spy is an Interactive Development Environment (IDE) for XML. Within XML Spy you can edit and validate XML code, XML Schemas, and DTDs. You can also edit and run XSL stylesheets at the push of a button. For help, visit http://www.xmlspy.com/.

1. Run XMLSpy.exe.

2. Leave the key code blank for a 30-day evaluation.

3. Set the installation directory.

4. Choose the full installation.

5. Make XMLSpy the default editor for XML file types.

6. Click Yes in answer to the complicated question about XHTML.

7. Reboot.

Deploying the SPIM Application

I found installing and configuring Cocoon in its entirety to be tricky and very time-consuming. Because Cocoon is open-source software, there is no one responsible for supporting installation, so it's every person for him- or herself. To incorporate the tips and tricks I learned the hard way while installing Cocoon on my Windows 2000 system, I packaged the SPIM application, including Cocoon 1.8.2, as a J2EE WAR (Web ARchive) file. In theory, this application should be deployable into any J2EE-compliant servlet container. I have only tried it with JRun 3.1.

> **CAUTION** *The SPIM application installs Cocoon as its required run-time environment. The Cocoon environment has been configured specifically to make the SPIM application work properly. It is not intended to be a full-fledged, general-purpose Cocoon installation. If you are interested in using Cocoon without the SPIM application, I suggest you go to the Apache site (*http://www.apache.org/*) and start from there.*

To deploy the SPIM application, perform the following steps.

1. Stop the JRun admin and default servers.

2. Edit the jrun/lib/global.properties file. Replace this line:

```
java.classpath={jrun.classpath};{user.classpath};{ejb.classpath};
    {servlet.classpath}
```

with the following (all on one line):

```
java.classpath=
    {jrun.rootdir}/servers/default/spim-application/WEB-INF/lib;
    {jrun.classpath};{user.classpath};{ejb.classpath};
    {servlet.classpath}
```

3. Start the JRun Management Console (Start > Programs > JRun3.1 > Start Management Console). In the left pane, select and expand "JRun Default Server." Click the Web Applications link. In the right pane, select "Deploy a Web Application." Use the Browse button to find the file Prototype/spim-application.war on the companion CD. Fill out the forms as shown in Figure 13-3, and make sure the directory name is jrun/servers/default/spim-application. Click Deploy.

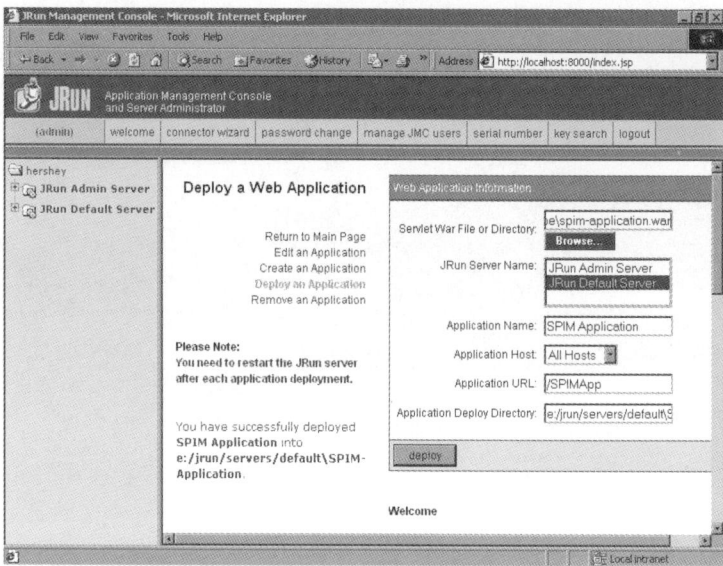

Figure 13-3. JRun Management Console (after deployment)

4. Stop the JRun Admin Server. Rename the following files (these are Java libraries that ship with JRun but are superseded by the versions that Cocoon requires):

```
/jrun /lib/ext/jaxp.jar -> /jrun/servers/lib/ext/jaxp.jar.BAK
/jrun /lib/ext/parser.jar -> /jrun/servers/lib/ext/parser.jar.BAK
```

5. Edit /jrun/servers/default/spim-application/WEB-INF/cocoon. properties. Search for the text string "SPIM Resource Protocol Workaround." The file protocols in the ten lines that follow should be edited to point to files in your JRun installation. For example, if you installed JRun in e:/jrun, the lines should read as follows (one line for each assignment):

```
processor.xsp.logicsheet.context.java  = file:///E:/jrun/servers\
    /default/spim-application/cocoon/resourcefiles/context.xsl
processor.xsp.logicsheet.cookie.java   = file:///E:/jrun/servers\
    /default/spim-application/cocoon/resourcefiles/cookie.xsl
processor.xsp.logicsheet.global.java   = file:///E:/jrun/servers\
    /default/spim-application/cocoon/resourcefiles/global.xsl
processor.xsp.logicsheet.request.java  = file:///E:/jrun/servers\
    /default/spim-application/cocoon/resourcefiles/request.xsl
processor.xsp.logicsheet.response.java = file:///E:/jrun/servers\
    /default/spim-application/cocoon/resourcefiles/response.xsl
processor.xsp.logicsheet.session.java  = file:///E:/jrun/servers\
```

```
    /default/spim-application/cocoon/resourcefiles/session.xsl
processor.xsp.logicsheet.util.java    = file:///E:/jrun/servers\
    /default/spim-application/cocoon/resourcefiles/util.xsl
processor.xsp.logicsheet.sql.java     = file:///E:/jrun/servers\
    /default/spim-application/cocoon/resourcefiles/sql.xsl
processor.xsp.logicsheet.esql.java    = file:///E:/jrun/servers\
    /default/spim-application/cocoon/resourcefiles/esql.xsl\
processor.xsp.logicsheet.fp.java      = file:///E:/jrun/servers\
    /default/spim-application/cocoon
```

6. Start the JRun Admin Server and the JRun default server. From a browser, enter the URL `http://localhost:8100/SPIMApp/VoiceSnoop.` Make the appropriate menu selections in your browser so that you are viewing the HTML source for the current page. You should see a VoiceXML implementation of the SnoopServlet, which echoes header and request information to the client. Or, run the IBM VoiceServer by entering the following command line:

    ```
    %IBMVS%\bin\vsaudio_en_us http://localhost:8100/SPIMApp/VoiceSnoop
    ```

Copying the SPIM Application

From the CD, copy the SPIMApp directory to a directory you create on your machine called "VoiceXML." When you're done, the VoiceXML directory contains a subdirectory called "SPIMApp."

Configuring the ODBC Data Source

The sample database for the SPIM prototype comes packaged as a Microsoft Access database. For generality, the prototype accesses the database using generic ODBC database drivers. The following procedure configures the Microsoft Access database as an ODBC data source. It is possible to configure the data source to use a different DBMS.

1. In Windows, bring up the Control Panel.

2. In Windows 2000, double-click Administrative Tools, and then double-click Data Sources. (On older versions of Windows, you may have to double-click the ODBC Administrator icon.)

3. Select the System DSN tab, and then click the Configure button.

4. Click the Select button, navigate to VoiceXML\SPIMapp\Db\spim.mdb, and click OK. You should now see the dialog box shown in Figure 13-4.

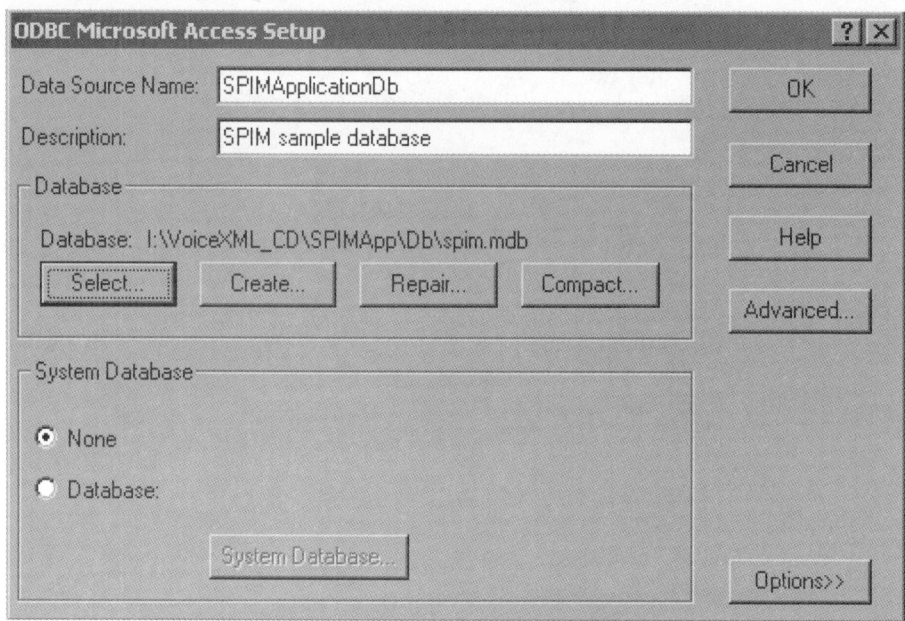

Figure 13-4. Microsoft Windows 2000 ODBC Setup dialog box

5. Click OK, exit the ODBC Administrator, and you're done.

Tips for Cocoon Enthusiasts

The following tips are included for those that want to try installing Cocoon and deploying the SPIM application themselves. This section can be skipped if you're not interested in tangling with Cocoon directly.

There are three important sources of information regarding installing Cocoon and configuring it to run with JRun.

- The Allaire article titled "JRun 3.0: Installing Cocoon Servlet" (http://www.allaire.com/Handlers/index.cfm?ID=17501&Method=Full) provides basic information on configuring Cocoon with JRun.

- The Installing Cocoon page (http://xml.apache.org/cocoon/install.html) on the Apache XML Project site provides information about installing Cocoon as well as some tips regarding JRun.

- The Cocoon mail archive (`http://xml.apache.org/cocoon/`
  `mail-archives.html`) offers a searchable source of support information for Cocoon.

To install Cocoon, follow the instructions on the Allaire site, plus the addendum at Cocoon site, plus the following undocumented hacks. Many of these require modifications to cocoon.properties.

- When defining the "Init Arguments" for the cocoon servlet mapping in JRun, use a relative URL. To set or view the URL, log in to the JRun Management Console. From the tree view on the left, click JRun Default Server/Web Applications/SPIM Application/Servlet Definitions. In the right-hand window, click the Edit button. The "Init Arguments" property is in the rightmost column of the table of servlet properties. For the servlet named "Cocoon," it should look like this:

`WEB-INF/cocoon.properties`

- To work around an apparent bug in how Cocoon resolves URIs with protocol type "resource:," unzip all the resource files (file type .xsl) from cocoon.jar into the new directory jrun/servers/default/cocoon-web-pub/WEB-INF/resources, and edit cocoon.properties to change the resource URLs to Web URLs. For example:

```
#processor.xsp.logicsheet.context.java  = \
#resource://org/apache/cocoon/processor/xsp/library/java/context.xsl
processor.xsp.logicsheet.context.java  = \
http://localhost:8100/cocoon-web-pub/WEB-INF/resources/context.xsl
```

- Add new formatter definitions to cocoon.properties as follows:

```
formatter.type.application/spim = org.apache.cocoon.formatter.XMLFormatter
formatter.type.text/vxml        = org.apache.cocoon.formatter.XMLFormatter

# SPIM
formatter.application/smil.doctype-system = \
        http://localhost:8100/cocoon/sql/spim.dtd
formatter.application/spim.MIME-type = application/spim

# VXML
formatter.text/vxml.doctype-system = \
        http://www.voicexml.org/voicexml1-0.dtd
formatter.text/vxml.MIME-type = application/x-vxml
```

- In cocoon.properties, replace the existing media type definitions (lines starting with `browser.`) with the following lines:

```
browser.0 = vxml=vxml
browser.1 = vxml=VoiceXML
browser.2 = html=MSIE
browser.3 = html=Mozilla
browser.4 = html=Netscape
```

To test that Cocoon is working properly with JRun, make sure that the JRun default server has been restarted and visit the URI `http://localhost:8100/SPIMApp/Cocoon.xml`. You should see the Cocoon status display.

Anatomy of the Prototype

This section provides a guided tour of the SPIM prototype. As you will see, there are various parts and pieces to the prototype. Each component is worthy of a detailed chapter of its own. In the spirit of architectural prototyping, I have tried to summarize the role of each component and give you the flavor of how it works. I leave the exploration of details to you.

The Database

The database has been modeled very simply. The schema is shown in Figure 13-5. A sample Microsoft Access database is located on the companion CD at VoiceXML\SPIMApp\Database\Db\spim.mdb[2]. There are two core tables corresponding to appointments and address book contacts. Each table has a generated primary key that uniquely identifies the entity. The Appointment table uses a Contact ID as a foreign key to the Contact table. (This models whom the appointment is with.) Auxiliary tables map integer-coded values for meeting locales and media to text strings.

---

[2] I also exported the tables into Comma-Separated Values (CSV) format, which is a text format that can be loaded into other databases and spreadsheets. The files are in the same directory as spim.mdb and have a .csv file type.

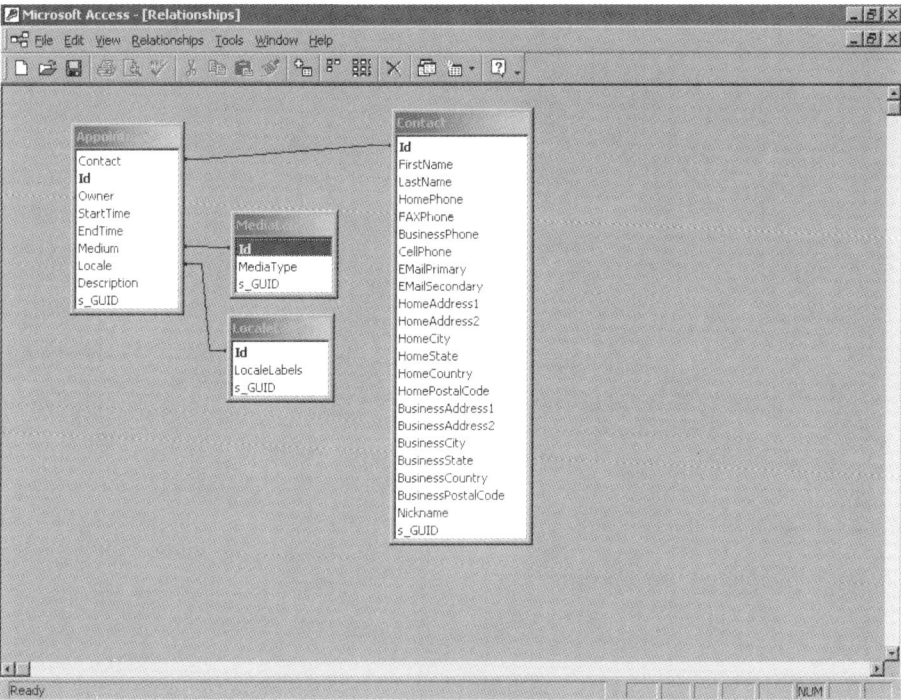

Figure 13-5. The SPIM prototype database schema

Refinements needed to flesh out this implementation include the following.

• Appointments are currently modeled with just two people: the Owner and the Contact. In reality, there would be one owner and a set of contacts.

• Appointments might be with people who are not registered contacts (that is, people who don't have an entry in the Contact table).

• The issue of how to model meeting times needs to be carefully thought through. The whole business of representing time in the database, being able to perform time-based queries, and appropriately representing time values as they are transformed between SQL representation, Java representation, and XML representation is a complicated, detail-rich process. For the purposes of the prototype, just store times as SQL timestamps and avert your eyes from problematic areas.

Producing Content Markup from the Database

When data is retrieved through a database query, the data is mapped into a single XML format. The XML format consists of a header (which identifies the SPIM user) and one or more Appointment elements followed by one or more Contact elements. Depending on the context for the query, the SPIM application determines how to interpret the relationships between Appointments and Contacts. For example, if the user is reviewing his or her calendar, there may be multiple appointments and multiple contacts (corresponding to the appointments within a given time period). For the Running Late function in the prototype, there will be at most one Appointment (scheduled for the current time) and one corresponding Contact. See Figure 13-6 for a pictorial view. File ..\SPIMApp\XML Samples\SPIM.xsd contains the XML Schema representation of the schema, while file `http://localhost:8100/cocoon/sql/Spim.dtd` contains the (nearly) equivalent DTD, which was generated from the XML Schema.

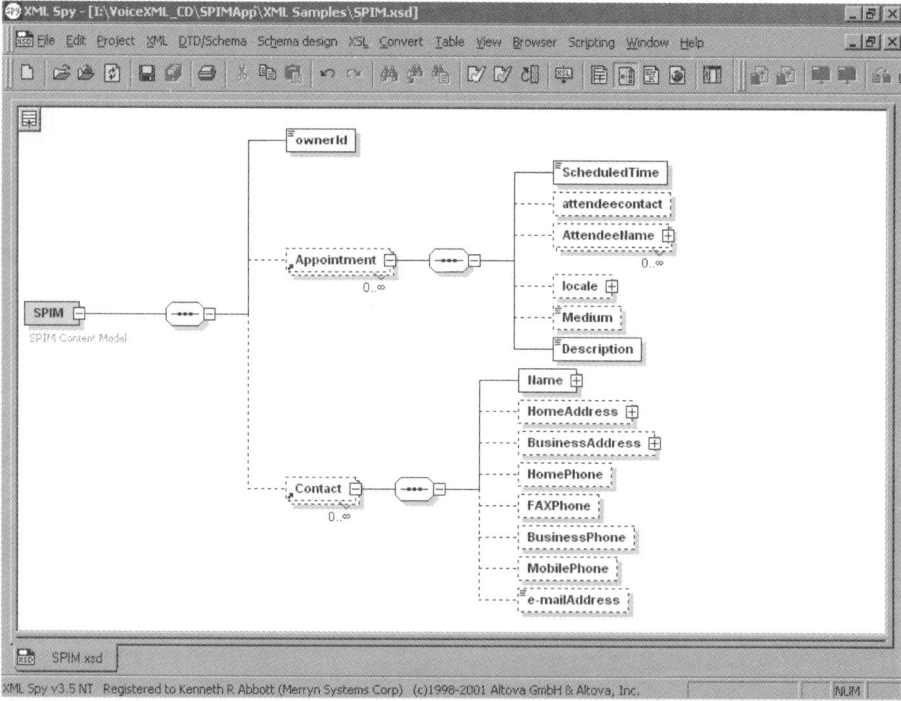

Figure 13-6. The SPIM XML Schema

Features of the Content Representation

The SPIM XML Schema uses some advanced features of the XML Schema language. Data types that appear in multiple contexts (such as people's names, phone numbers, and addresses) are modeled as complex types and simply referred to from elements that conform to the type. For example, the following code fragment declares the "address" data type. Elements Contact/HomeAddress and Contact/BusinessAddress are both of this type.

```
<xsd:complexType name="AddressType">
  <xsd:sequence>
    <xsd:sequence minOccurs="0">
        <xsd:element name="AddressLine1" type="xsd:string"/>
        <xsd:element name="AddressLine2" type="xsd:string" minOccurs="0"/>
    </xsd:sequence>
    <xsd:element name="City" type="xsd:string" minOccurs="0"/>
    <xsd:element name="State" type="xsd:string" minOccurs="0"/>
    <xsd:element name="Country" type="xsd:string" minOccurs="0"/>
    <xsd:element name="PostalCode" type="xsd:string" minOccurs="0"/>
  </xsd:sequence>
</xsd:complexType>
```

An address consists of an optional one- or two-line address followed by a city, state, country, and postal code (any or all of which can be omitted). Most elements are optional to allow for partial information being stored in the database. Furthermore, an integrity constraint (for example, there must be a city) probably should be enforced in the database, not the middle tier.

To associate Appointments and Contacts, XML ids are used. An *id* is an intradocument link that can be used to uniquely identify an XML element within a single document. The following schema fragment declares that each Contact element has an associated id attribute:

```
<xsd:element name="Contact">
    <xsd:complexType>
        <xsd:sequence>
            <xsd:element name="Name" type="PersonNameType"/>
            . . .
        <xsd:attribute name="id" type="xsd:ID" use="required"/>
        </xsd:complexType>
</xsd:element>
```

The following fragment shows that the id attribute of the Appointment/ attendeecontact element is a reference to another element in the same XML document.

```
<xsd:element name="Appointment">
    <xsd:complexType>
        <xsd:element name="attendeecontact" minOccurs="0">
```

```
    <xsd:complexType>
     <xsd:attribute name="id" type="xsd:IDREF" use="required"/>
     </xsd:complexType>
     </xsd:element>

     . . .
   </xsd:complexType>
 </xsd:element>
```

When a result set from a database query is mapped into your XML Schema, it is necessary to generate a unique id for each appointment and each schema. In the prototype, the generated ids are derived from the unique database keys as follows:

- For Appointments: "A" + <database_key> ("A12345678")

- For Contacts: "C" + <database_key> ("C987654")

This simple scheme is necessary because XML ids follow the same syntax as identifiers (and therefore can't start with a number).

> **NOTE** *Unfortunately, I was never able to get XML ids to work in Cocoon (despite lots of fruitless effort). I was able to verify that the XSL translators I tried handled XML ids correctly when invoked stand-alone (for example, from inside XML Spy), but not when invoked in the Cocoon environment. I don't know if this was a bug or a configuration problem.*

ESQL and the XSP Producer

As discussed previously, XSP is a Cocoon language for producing XML. The language contains special tags for intermixing template static text with Java language fragments. ESQL is an Apache XML technology for performing SQL queries from within an XSP logic sheet. In a nutshell, you can think of ESQL as implementing XML syntax for the JDBC query interface. To see a simple example of XSP and ESQL, visit `http://localhost:8100/cocoon/sql/RetrieveSPIMData.xml`. This example uses the ODBC/JDBC bridge to access the SPIM database and perform a query that returns the first and last names of all the Contacts in the SPIM database.[3] The basic concept is that XSP/ESQL provides a way to iterate through rows in a result set and embed the values of individual fields in XML markup.

---

[3] This is very useful to verify that the SPIM ODBC data source and ESQL database connection are working properly.

The actual producer used for the Running Late function is `http://localhost:8100/cocoon/sql/getCurrentAppointment.xml`. It produces XML like that captured in `http://localhost:8100/cocoon/sql/CurrentAppointment.xml`. This is the pure content markup from which the presentation markup will be derived (see the next section).

XSP is the Apache Cocoon approach to generating XML from any type of data source. Because XSP translates into Java, it is capable of generating XML from any data source accessible through Java, including file systems, databases, application servers, beans, legacy systems, messaging systems, and so on. ESQL specializes the XSP approach to SQL databases. However, there are other options for generating XML representations of relational result sets. In most approaches, the XML markup is derived directly from the database schema—each row is delineated by an element whose name is derived from the table or view name, and each contains subelements whose names are the same as database column names. This form of XML, direct from the database, can easily be transformed into middle-tier content markup through an XSL transformation.

Many databases vendors now supply *XML extenders,* which accept SQL in XML syntax and automatically format result sets into XML documents. The Oracle Technical Network also provides a free generic servlet that takes an SQL query as input and returns an XML document as the response (see `http://otn.oracle.com/software/tech/xml/xsql_servlet/software_index.htm`— registration is required). (Despite its source, the servlet is JDBC dependent but DBMS independent.)

Generating the Presentation

The previous section showed how to generate marked-up content from database data. This addressed the issue of how dynamically generated content gets into the Web application. The following sections look at how to generate the presentation code to send out to the client browser. Two cases are discussed separately: generating the presentation of dynamic content and generating the presentation of static content.

Transforming Content Markup into Presentation Markup

For dynamic content, the pure content XML produced is transformed into presentation markup by XSL transformations. The following processor instructions in the XSP producer specify that the output of the producer should be processed using one XSL stylesheet if the media type is "html" and a different sheet if the media type is "vxml."

```
<?cocoon-process type="xsp"?>
<?cocoon-process type="xslt"?>
<?xml-stylesheet type="text/xsl" href="RunningLateVXML.xsl" media="vxml"?>
<?cocoon-process type="xslt"?>
<?xml-stylesheet type="text/xsl" href="RunningLateHTML.xsl" media="html"?>
```

The media type is derived by Cocoon from the user-Agent field in the HTTP request header. The user-Agent field identifies the browser that submitted the request. In this case, you are only interested in distinguishing between HTML browsers and VXML browsers. The following section in cocoon.properties specifies the mappings between user-Agent values and media types[4]:

```
###########################################
# User Agents (Browsers)                 #
###########################################
# NOTE: numbers indicate the search order. This is VERY VERY IMPORTANT since
# some words may be found in more than one browser description. (MSIE is
# presented as "Mozilla/4.0 (Compatible; MSIE 4.01; ...")
#
# for example, the "explorer=MSIE" tag indicates that the XSL stylesheet
# associated to the media type "explorer" should be mapped to those browsers
# that have the string "MSIE" in their "user-Agent" HTTP header.
browser.0 = vxml=vxml
browser.1 = vxml=VoiceXML
browser.2 = html=MSIE
browser.3 = html=Mozilla
browser.4 = html=Netscape
```

When RunningLateHTML.xsl is applied to getCurrentAppointment.xml, the result is LateAppointment001.html. When RunningLateVXML.xsl is applied, the result is LateAppointment001.vxml. (The .xml and .xsl files are contained in the JRun deployment directory, JRun\servers\default\spim-application\ prototype. The .html and .vxml files are on the companion CD at VoiceXML\SPIMApp\Tutorial\Step10.) The transformation can be bench-tested in XML Spy by loading CurrentAppointment.xml, setting the project properties to specify which XSL transformation to use, and then running the XSL processor. Notice that the previously mentioned .xml files are snapshots of intermediate

---

[4] Notice that these are not the "default" Cocoon settings—they were set for the SPIM.

results that were captured for debugging and testing. In actual use, the .xml files would be transient files used during processing of a single Cocoon request.

Transforming Static Content into Presentation Markup

Although it is possible to dynamically generate all pages in a Web application, most applications contain at least some static content. For example, the basic menu structures of the SPIM application don't change, so it makes sense to treat them as static content. When Web applications only dealt with HTML source code, static content was handled by simply publishing HTML files into the Web server's directory tree and allowing the Web to serve the files directly without additional server-side processing.

With the addition of VXML (and WML), the situation becomes a little more complex. The issue is that even though the HTML and VXML presentations are different, the underlying static content is the same. If the corresponding HTML and VXML are stored in separate files, there will be a maintenance headache because the Webmaster will have to remember to manually synchronize changes to two files.

The SPIM prototype demonstrates an approach in which the static content is written in a content markup dialect that I'll refer to as "Web-Pidgin." Web-Pidgin is a "least common denominator" language that can be transformed into either HTML or VXML. It also allows pure HTML or pure VXML scripts to be inserted where needed. The advantage of using Web-Pidgin is that the static content is stored in one source file, which improves maintainability.

Overview of Web-Pidgin

The XML schema for Web-Pidgin is /jrun/servers/default/spim-application/ prototype/webcontent.xsd (see Figure 13-7 for a graphical representation). Root element <webcontent> contains subelements for menus, links, and forms. Each of these contains various attributes and subelements that capture all the information needed to generate HTML or VXML. In addition, the root element also contains the elements <html> and <vxml>. These elements "escape" to pure HTML or pure VXML, allowing arbitrary HTML and VXML documents to reside in the same file.

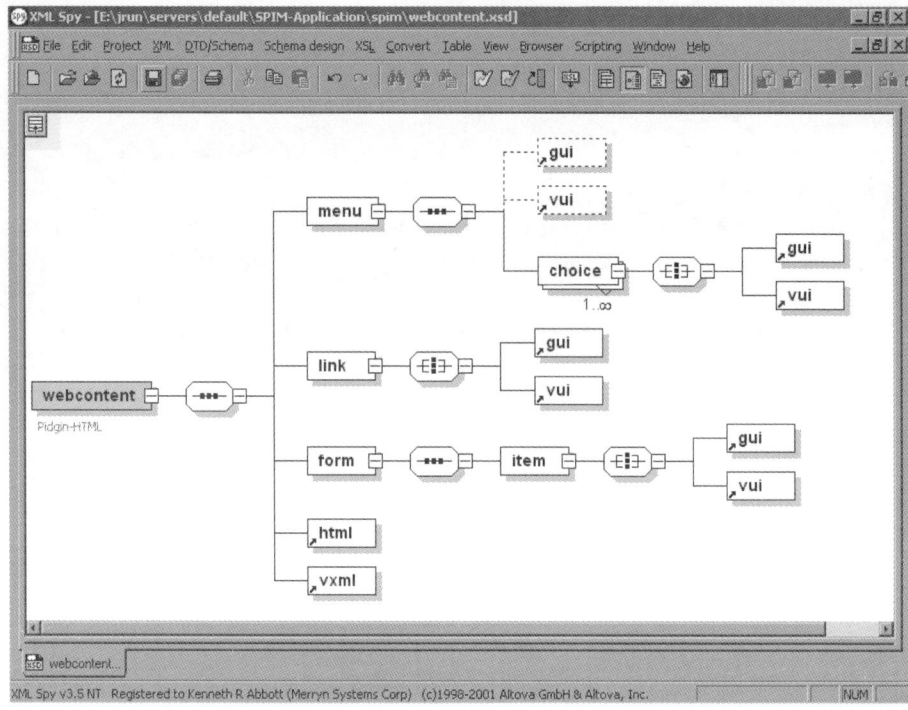

Figure 13-7. XML Schema for Web-Pidgin

When a Web-Pidgin file is served, it undergoes an XSL transformation. The transformation is determined by the media type of the requesting client, as described previously. There is one XSL stylesheet that transforms any Web-Pidgin document into HTML, and there is another stylesheet that transforms Web-Pidgin to VXML. These stylesheets determine how the shared Web-Pidgin constructs map to HTML and VXML language constructs. For example, in the prototype, a Web-Pidgin menu is transformed into an HTML page that contains a sequence of anchors (<A HREF=. . .> elements), one for each choice in the menu. In VXML, the Web-Pidgin menu appears as a VXML form with <choice> elements.

The SPIM main menu for the prototype is shown in Listing 13-1. To avoid confusion between Web-Pidgin elements and HTML or VXML elements, Web-Pidgin elements are all prefixed by the content: namespace identifier. Notice that some data items are common to both presentation styles (for example, the target URI of a menu choice is the same in HTML and VXML). In cases where different information is required for the different presentation media, the <content:vui> element captures prompt/response pairs for voice, while <content:gui> captures more verbose text for GUIs.

Listing 13-2 and Listing 13-3 show the result of transforming the content shown in Listing 13-1 into HTML and VXML, respectively. The stylesheet that transforms Web-Pidgin into HTML is shown in Listing 13-4. The stylesheet that transforms Web-Pidgin into VXML is shown in Listing 13-5.

Listing 13-1. The SPIM Main Menu (Web-Pidgin)

```
<?xml version="1.0" encoding="UTF-8"?>
<?cocoon-process type="xslt"?>
<?xml-stylesheet type="text/xsl" href="WebContentHTML.xsl" media="html"?>
<?cocoon-process type="xslt"?>
<?xml-stylesheet type="text/xsl" href="WebContentVXML.xsl" media="vxml"?>
<webcontent version="1.0"
    application="/SmallExamples/SPIMApplicationBasic.vxml"
    xmlns:content="H:\VoiceXML\SPIMApp\Prototype\webcontent.xsd">
    <content:menu title="SPIM Main Menu">
        <content:vui>
            <content:prompt>Your choices are: <enumerate/>
            </content:prompt>
        </content:vui>
        <content:gui>
            Please choose one of the following:
        </content:gui>
        <content:choice target="Calendar.xml">
            <content:vui>
                <content:prompt>Calendar</content:prompt>
            </content:vui>
            <content:gui>View Calendar</content:gui>
        </content:choice>
        <content:choice target="ToDo.xml">
            <content:vui>
                <content:prompt>To-Do</content:prompt>
            </content:vui>
            <content:gui>Review To-Do List</content:gui>
        </content:choice>
        <content:choice target="AddressBook.xml">
            <content:vui>
                <content:prompt>Address Book</content:prompt>
            </content:vui>
            <content:gui>Manage Address Book</content:gui>
```

```
            </content:choice>
        </content:menu>
        <content:link target="Late.xml">
            <content:gui>Running Late...</content:gui>
            <content:vui>
                <content:response>late | I'm late</content:response>
            </content:vui>
        </content:link>
</webcontent>
```

Listing 13-2. The SPIM Main Menu (HTML Presentation)

```
<?cocoon-format  type="text/html" ?>
<html>
    <head>
        <meta content="text/html; charset=utf-8"
            http-equiv="content-type">
        <title>SPIM Main Menu</title>
    </head>
    <h1>SPIM Main Menu</h1>
    <br>
    <hr>
    <em>Please choose one of the following:</em>
    <br>
    <br>
    <br>
    <a href="Calendar.xml">View Calendar</a>
    <br>
    <a href="ToDo.xml">Review To-Do List</a>
    <br>
    <a href="AddressBook.xml">Manage Address Book</a>
    <br>
    <a href="Late.xml">Running Late...</a>
</html>
```

Listing 13-3. The SPIM Main Menu (VMXL Presentation)

```
<?xml version="1.0" encoding="utf-8"?>
<?cocoon-format type="text/vxml" ?>
<vxml version="1.0">
```

```
    <menu>
        <prompt>Your choices are: <enumerate/>
        </prompt>
        <choice next="Calendar.xml">Calendar</choice>
        <choice next="ToDo.xml">To-Do</choice>
        <choice next="AddressBook.xml">Address Book</choice>
    </menu>
    <link next="Late.xml">
        <grammar>late | I'm late</grammar>
    </link>
</vxml>
```

Listing 13-4. Web-Pidgin to HTML Stylesheet

```
<?xml version="1.0" encoding="UTF-8"?>
<xsl:stylesheet version="1.0"
    xmlns:xsl="http://www.w3.org/1999/XSL/Transform"
    xmlns:content="H:\VoiceXML\SPIMApp\Prototype\webcontent.xsd"
    xmlns:fo="http://www.w3.org/1999/XSL/Format"
    exclude-result-prefixes="xsl content fo">
    <xsl:template match="/">
        <xsl:processing-instruction name="cocoon-format">
            type="text/html"
        </xsl:processing-instruction>
        <html>
            <xsl:apply-templates select="*"/>
        </html>
    </xsl:template>
    <xsl:template match="content:menu">
        <head>
            <title><xsl:value-of select="@title"/></title>
        </head>
        <h1><xsl:value-of select="@title"/></h1><br/>
        <hr/>
        <em>
            <xsl:apply-templates select="content:gui/node()"
                mode="passthrough"/>
        </em><br/><br/>
        <xsl:for-each select="content:choice">
            <br/>
            <a href="{@target}">
                <xsl:value-of select="content:gui"/>
```

```
            </a>
        </xsl:for-each>
    </xsl:template>
    <xsl:template match="content:link">
        <br/>
        <a href="{@target}">
            <xsl:value-of select="content:gui"/>
        </a>
        <xsl:apply-templates select="content:html"/>
    </xsl:template>
    <xsl:template match="content:form">
    <!-- form processing goes here -->
    </xsl:template>
    <xsl:template match="content:html">
        <xsl:apply-templates select="*|node()" mode="passthrough"/>
    </xsl:template>
    <xsl:template match="*|node()" mode="passthrough">
        <xsl:copy-of select="."/>
    </xsl:template>
    <xsl:template match="content:vxml"/>
</xsl:stylesheet>
```

Listing 13-5. Web-Pidgin to VXML Stylesheet

```
<?xml version="1.0" encoding="UTF-8"?>
<xsl:stylesheet version="1.0"
    xmlns:xsl="http://www.w3.org/1999/XSL/Transform"
    xmlns:content="H:\VoiceXML\SPIMApp\Prototype\webcontent.xsd"
    xmlns:fo="http://www.w3.org/1999/XSL/Format"
    exclude-result-prefixes="xsl content fo">
    <xsl:template match="/">
        <xsl:processing-instruction name="cocoon-format">
            type="text/vxml"
        </xsl:processing-instruction>
        <vxml version="1.0">
            <xsl:apply-templates select="*"/>
        </vxml>
    </xsl:template>
    <xsl:template match="content:menu">
        <menu>
            <prompt>
                <xsl:apply-templates
```

```
                    select="content:vui/content:prompt/node()"
                    mode="passthrough"/>
            </prompt>
            <xsl:for-each select="content:choice">
                <choice next="{@target}">
                    <xsl:value-of
                        select="content:vui/content:prompt"/>
                </choice>
            </xsl:for-each>
        </menu>
        <xsl:apply-templates select="following"/>
    </xsl:template>
    <xsl:template match="content:link">
        <link next="{@target}">
            <grammar>
                <xsl:value-of
                    select="content:vui/content:response"/>
            </grammar>
            <xsl:apply-templates select="content:vxml"/>
        </link>
    </xsl:template>
    <xsl:template match="content:form">
    <!-- form processing goes here -->
    </xsl:template>
    <xsl:template match="content:vxml">
        <xsl:apply-templates select="*|node()" mode="passthrough"/>
    </xsl:template>
    <xsl:template match="*|node()" mode="passthrough">
        <xsl:copy-of select="."/>
    </xsl:template>
    <xsl:template match="content:html"/>
</xsl:stylesheet>
```

Trying It Out

Now that everything is set perfectly, it's time to give it a try. Visit the
following URL from your Web browser or VoiceXML browser:
`http://localhost:8100/SPIMApp/prototype/SPIMMainMenu.xml`.
    You should see a window like the one shown in Figure 13-8.

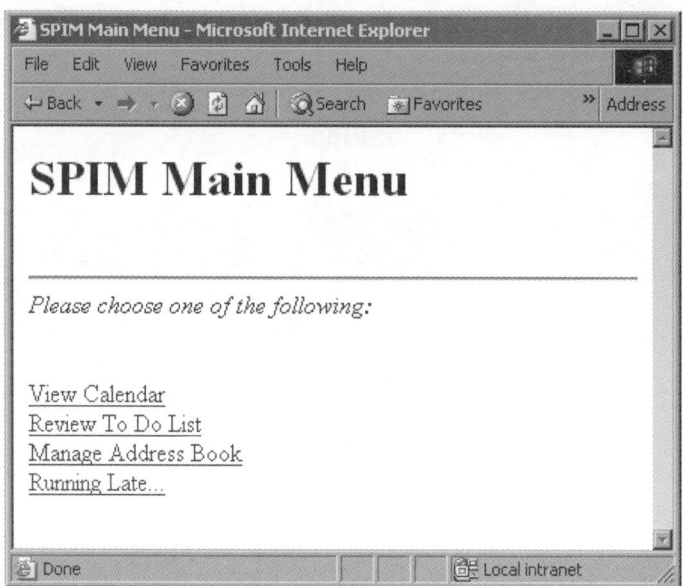

Figure 13-8. The SPIM main menu (HTML view)

If you're using the IBM WebSphere Voice Server SDK, type the following at a command-line prompt:

```
%IBMVS%\bin/vsaudio_en_US http://localhost:8100/SPIMApp/prototype/SPIMMainMenu.xml
```

You should hear the prompt in Dialog 13-1.

Dialog 13-1. The SPIM Main Menu VXML Prompt
C (computer): Your choices are Calendar, To-Do, Address Book.

In your chosen medium, you can browse through the menus. Most actions are not implemented, except for the Running Late link. Notice that in the HTML browser, Running Late appears like the three menu choices above it, because both menu choices and links are rendered as HTML links. However, VXML does distinguish between menu choices and links. VXML does not prompt for links, so it isn't mentioned in the prompt, but saying "I'm late" will activate the link.

In an HTML browser, the Running Late link will take you to the page shown in Figure 13-9. In a VoiceXML browser, the Running Late link will lead you to a dialog that starts with the prompt in Dialog 13-2.

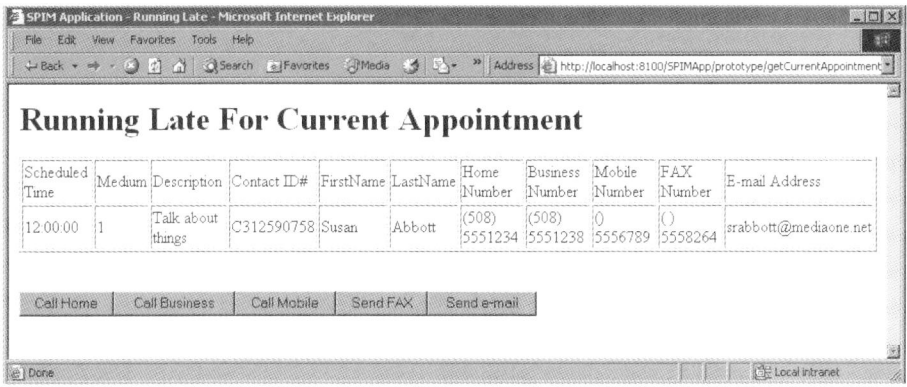

Figure 13-9. The Running Late page (HTML view)

Dialog 13-2. Running Late (VXML Prompt)

C (computer): You have a scheduled appointment with Susan Abbott at 12:00. Do you want to call home, call business, fax a message, or send an e-mail notice?

Tips for Dissecting the Prototype

To view generated VoiceXML in its text form from your Web browser, visit the following URL:
`http://localhost:8100/SPIMApp/prototype/SPIMMainMenu.xml?user-Agent=vxml`.
This overrides the value of the HTTP user-Agent header, so to the server it appears that the request comes from a VoiceXML browser. When the response is displayed, it may or may not look like much, depending on the XML capabilities of your browser (see Figure 13-10 for a partial listing of how Internet Explorer 5.0 displays the generated VoiceXML). You can view the generated VoiceXML code by selecting View Source (or equivalent) to display the text the browser is rendering. Selecting View Source from Internet Explorer 5.0 brings up a Notepad screen containing the unsightly, unreadable jumble of VoiceXML that was actually served (see Figure 13-11). I usually cut and paste the content from Notepad into a temporary VXML file in XML Spy. In XML Spy, switching to the grid view and back to the text view has the side effect of formatting the VoiceXML code so it can be examined more easily (see Figure 13-12).

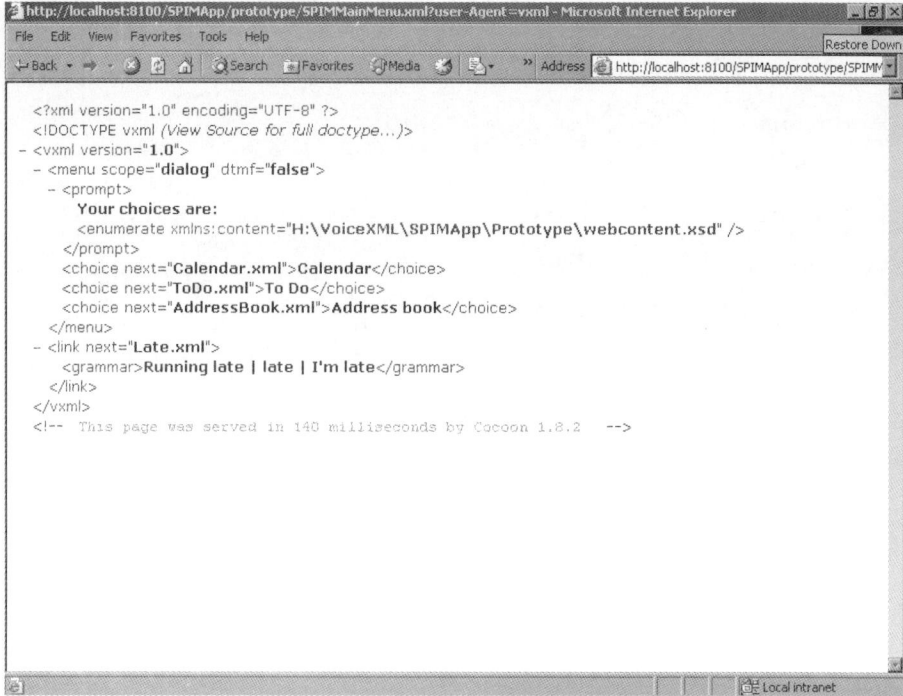

```
http://localhost:8100/SPIMApp/prototype/SPIMMainMenu.xml?user-Agent=vxml - Microsoft Internet Explorer
File   Edit   View   Favorites   Tools   Help                                                    Restore Down
 Back  ·  →  ·  ⊗  ⊠  ⌂  |  ⊘Search  ⊞Favorites  ⊛Media  ⊛  ⊠ ·   » Address  ⊠ http://localhost:8100/SPIMApp/prototype/SPIMM ▾

<?xml version="1.0" encoding="UTF-8" ?>
<!DOCTYPE vxml (View Source for full doctype...)>
- <vxml version="1.0">
 - <menu scope="dialog" dtmf="false">
  - <prompt>
      Your choices are:
      <enumerate xmlns:content="H:\VoiceXML\SPIMApp\Prototype\webcontent.xsd" />
    </prompt>
    <choice next="Calendar.xml">Calendar</choice>
    <choice next="ToDo.xml">To Do</choice>
    <choice next="AddressBook.xml">Address book</choice>
  </menu>
 - <link next="Late.xml">
     <grammar>Running late | late | I'm late</grammar>
   </link>
 </vxml>
<!--  This page was served in 140 milliseconds by Cocoon 1.8.2   -->
```

Figure 13-10. The Running Late function in VXML text

```
SPIMMainMenu[1] - Notepad
File   Edit   Format   Help
<?xml version="1.0" encoding="UTF-8"?>
<!DOCTYPE vxml SYSTEM "http://www.voicexml.org/voicexml1-0.dtd">
<vxml version="1.0">
        <menu><prompt>Your choices are: <enumerate
xmlns:content="H:\VoiceXML\SPIMApp\Prototype\webcontent.xsd"/>
                </prompt><choice next="Calendar.xml">Calendar</choice><choice
next="ToDo.xml">To Do</choice><choice next="AddressBook.xml">Address book</choice></menu>
        <link next="Late.xml"><grammar>Running late | late | I&apos;m late</grammar></link>
</vxml>
<!-- This page was served in 140 milliseconds by Cocoon 1.8.2 -->
```

Figure 13-11. The Running Late function in VXML in Notepad

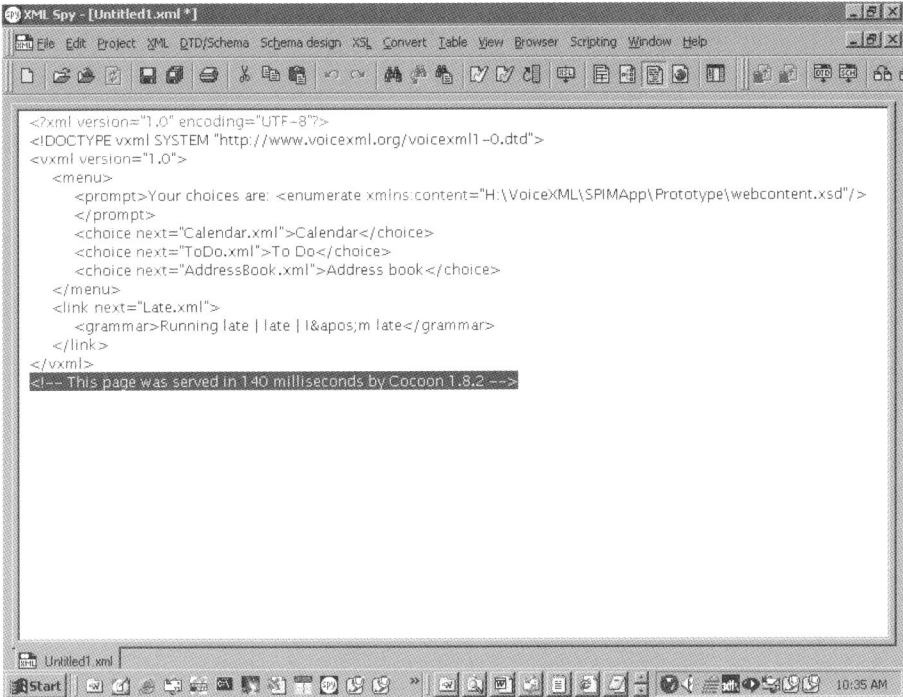

Figure 13-12. The Running Late function in VXML in XML Spy

All the "live" files used in the prototype are in directory jrun/servers/default/spim-application/prototype (see Table 13-1). The application works by visiting the XML files (.xml). The .xsl, .xsd, and .dtd files are used during Cocoon processing of the XML files. Schema files are in the "spim" subdirectory (see Table 13-2). The Samples subdirectory contains samples generated during development of the prototype (see Table 13-3).

Table 13-1. Index of Files in the Prototype Directory

FILE	DESCRIPTION
AddressBook.xml	Web-Pidgin for menu of the SPIM Address Book functions.
CurrentAppointment.xml	Sample of pure content markup generated from database by Cocoon XSP processor.
notImplemented.xml	Web-Pidgin file for unimplemented functions in the SPIM prototype.
Calendar.xml	Web-Pidgin for menu of the SPIM Calendar functions.
Late.xml	Web-Pidgin uses scripting to get the current time and pass it to server to process a late appointment (see getCurrentAppointment.xml).
getCurrentAppointment.xml	Server-side Cocoon XSP page that takes the current time and user name, performs an ESQL database query to get the current appointment, and generates pure content markup, which is then transformed by RunningLateVXML.xsl or RunningLateHTML.xsl.
SPIMMainMenu.xml	Web-Pidgin for the main menu of the SPIM prototype.
ToDo.xml	Web-Pidgin for menu of the SPIM To-Do List functions.
spim.xsl	XSL transforms the SPIM contact markup to HTML (used for viewing data from the database).
RunningLateVxml.xsl	XSL transforms pure content markup generated by "running late" database query to VXML.
RunningLateHTML.xsl	XSL transforms pure content markup generated by "running late" database query to HTML.
WebContentHTML.xsl	XSL transforms Web-Pidgin to HTML.
WebContentVXML.xsl	XSL transforms Web-Pidgin to VXML.

Table 13-2. Index of Files in the SPIM Subdirectory

FILE	DESCRIPTION
Spim.dtd	Data Type Descriptor for the SPIM pure content markup language (generated from SPIM.xsd)
webcontent.xsd	XML Schema for Web-Pidgin
SPIM.xsd	XML Schema for SPIM pure content markup
Address.xsd	XML Schema complex type definition for an address (used in SPIM.xsd)
PhoneNumber.xsd	XML Schema complex type definition for a phone number (used in SPIM.xsd)

Table 13-3. Index of Files in the Samples Directory

FILE	DESCRIPTION
LateAppointment001.html	Sample output derived by applying RunningLateVXML.xsl to CurrentAppointment.xml.
LateAppointment001.vxml	Sample output derived by applying RunningLateVXML.xsl to CurrentAppointment.xml.
CurrentAppointment.xml	Sample of pure content markup generated from database by Cocoon XSP processor.
RetrieveContactNames.xml	Test XSP processor used to verify SPIM database connection. It retrieves all people's names and displays them in an HTML table.
RunningLateRawVXMLOutput.vxml	Raw output from Cocoon processor that would be sent to VoiceXML browser.
names.xsl	XSL transforms list of names generated by RetrieveContactNames.xml into HTML.

Summary

If you've made it this far and you've successfully executed the SPIM Web application prototype, congratulations! As you've discovered, the hard work in prototyping is all the setup and configuration required to get all the components playing together. Problem diagnosis and resolution can be tremendously frustrating, because the hardest problems spring like weeds from the cracks between components, where there are no debugging tools. This is the "dark side" of component-based development: As an integrator, you spend most of your time on unglamorous administrative activities and very little time on the fun activity of writing code.

The SPIM Web prototype brings together representative technologies necessary to create a small-scale, multitier, working Web application. XML Spy is the XML IDE used to develop and bench-test XML, XSL, and schemas. The Web browser is up to you to choose (I used MSIE). The VoiceXML browser is the IBM ViaVoice SDK. JRun plays the part of Web server and servlet container. Microsoft Access, acting as a nonproprietary ODBC/JDBC data source, plays the role of database. Apache Cocoon provides the framework for generating and transforming XML in the Web server.

> **NOTE** *The set of components was selected based on capability and easy availability to developers. They may or may not be suitable for production. People who have seen the prototype often ask me anxiously about the "production worthiness" of Cocoon. There are several parts to my answer. First, open-source projects such as Cocoon are usually not about making "production grade" software. Second, the prototype uses version Cocoon 1.8.2, the latest "released" version, but Cocoon 2.0 is under way and has significant changes from 1.8.2. Last, Cocoon is not commercial software, and hence is not supported. However, Cocoon is not the only game in town: Many EAI vendors supply frameworks for XML processing, Oracle sells an XML processing framework, and upcoming Java standards are specifying increasing levels of XML support in standard J2EE environments. The bottom line is this: Don't confuse the prototype with production, and don't think that the expeditious choice of developer-friendly components for the prototype is an endorsement for use in production.*

With the prototype infrastructure in place, "coding" the SPIM application becomes an exercise in developing XML documents, writing XSL stylesheet transformations, and defining XML schemas to model the data at various steps in the transformational process. Samples of these various XML coding artifacts are available on the book's companion CD. Hopefully, these can serve as models for you to assemble your own application.

What's Next?

VOICEXML IS A NEW technology that has wide applicability and technical depth. As with any new technology, the current version is useful, but minimal. Over time, the standard will become richer in terms of functions and features incorporated into the VoiceXML standard itself, as well as its integration with other related standards.

In trying to understand the future directions of the VoiceXML specification, it is important to bear in mind an important pragmatic fact of life: Any approved standard is a cocktail of one part technology, one part politics, and one part expedience, shaken and stirred thoroughly. The fact of the matter is that technology standards are written by many people, often representing multiple businesses, who all have a vested interest in establishing a standard. However, everyone's interests are not the same. Vendors are interested in creating a standard because it establishes a market and decreases customers' risk in purchasing a product. However, each vendor also wants its product to be distinguished as the best. Therefore, sometimes there are things that obviously ought to be standardized from a technological standpoint but, as a pragmatic matter, can't get through the standards process.

The following sections examine some of the possible future directions for voice applications and the VoiceXML standard in particular.

Changes from VoiceXML 1.0 to VoiceXML 2.0

As this book is being written, the specification for VoiceXML 2.0 is being finalized and is nearly ready for public release. While the details of the specification are considered confidential by the W3C, certain general features of the new specification have been revealed publicly. Throughout the book, I've tried to call out areas which will be affected by known features of VoiceXML 2.0. Some of the new features are reviewed in this section. Notice that this information is tentative—not final—and this section is intended to show the direction that VoiceXML is moving.

Anticipated changes include:

- Incorporation of required support for the new W3C Speech Recognition Grammar Format and W3C Speech Synthesis Markup Language

- Improved, clarified mechanism for passing of tag data from the speech recognizer to VoiceXML interpreter

- Expanded, clarified features for controlling resource fetching and caching

- Expanded, improved features for telephony

From the perspective of a VoiceXML developer or user, VoiceXML 2.0 will probably be an evolutionary improvement on VoiceXML 1.0. Based on the scope of changes know at this time, VoiceXML 2.0 will offer no revolutionary new features or vastly expanded capabilities. This is not to say that VoiceXML 2.0 will not be a significant step forward. The development and incorporation of the standard grammar format and speech synthesis markup will dramatically increase the robustness, applicability, and portability of the whole W3C voice browser standards suite. VoiceXML 2.0 shores up the foundations of the entire language, which is important but not particularly glamorous or visible to everyone.

Grammar and Speech Synthesis Specification

The VoiceXML 1.0 specification is silent on the topic of how grammars are specified. It mentions JGSF and GSL as candidates, but requires neither and leaves the choice of grammar specification language open to the implementer of a VoiceXML interpreter. This approach was probably a political necessity in the standardization process given that the VoiceXML consortium consists of multiple vendors with existing products based on incompatible, proprietary grammar languages. However, it does leave a gaping hole in the portability of VoiceXML programs. Grammars are an essential part of a VoiceXML application, and the portability of grammars is as important to overall application portability as portability of the presentation markup code.

The W3C has released a draft standard grammar specification language called Speech Recognition Grammar Specification for the W3C Speech Interface Framework (`http://www.w3.org/TR/speech-grammar/`). The draft describes two syntaxes for the language: an Augmented Backus Naur Form (ABNF) syntax (familiar to language and compiler designers) and an equivalent XML-compliant syntax, which will be required by the next version of VoiceXML.

A snippet example of a grammar for saying the name of one of four cities is as follows:

```
<?xml version="1.0"?>
<grammar xml:lang="en" version="1.0">
  <rule id="city" scope="public">
    <one-of>
      <item> new york </item>
      <item> sydney </item>
      <item> boston </item>
      <item> berlin </item>
    </one-of>
  </rule>
</grammar>
```

As you can see, it looks more XMLy than the JGSF you have been using. For more information, read *VoiceXML Review*'s article titled "Introduction to the W3C Grammar Format" (`http://www.voicexml.org/Review/Apr2001/features/w3c-grammar1.html`).

The W3C has also released a draft specification of Speech Synthesis Markup Language (SSML) (`http://www.w3.org/TR/speech-synthesis`). This is an XML markup language for supporting synthesis of speech from text input. For a fuller description, read *VoiceXML Review*'s article titled "The Speech Synthesis Markup Language for the W3C VoiceXML Standard" (`http://www.voicexml.org/Review/Apr2001/features/ssml2.html`).

Reusable Dialog Components

VoiceXML defines the syntax for using a handful of built-in types (for example, `date`, `boolean`, and so on), but it does not specify the behavior of the types. For example, in VoiceXML you can specify that a field contains a `date`, but VoiceXML does not specify what utterances are recognized as dates.[1] Although the concept leads in the right direction, the data types as currently specified are not particularly useful. Because their behavior is not specified, they are not portable. Because no grammar language is specified, the VoiceXML specification is silent on the issue of how built-in types are accessed from custom grammars.

In the longer term, the goal should be to have a library of standard, portable dialog components that can be assembled to produce customized grammars and VoiceXML dialogs with a minimum of coding work. In addition to the general benefits of reusability, such a standard library would also be the foundation of localizable dialogs.

---

[1] For example, one voice platform might recognize "Tuesday next," "next Tuesday," and "January fourteen" as valid dates, while another might accept only utterances of the form "January fourteen two thousand and one."

The W3C has already begun work on this concept[2] and has produced a draft requirements specification for Reusable Dialog Components (`http://www.w3.org/TR/reusable-dialog-reqs`). Currently, the draft identifies the following dialog components:

- Yes/no

- Natural numbers

- Simple digit string

- Fully specified date

- Time

- Currency

- Menu

- Partially specified date

- Simple alpha string

- Simple alphanumeric string

- Simple error-recovery dialog

- Context-compensating date

- Telephone number

- Sectioned digit string

- Sectioned alphanumeric string

---

[2] Unfortunately, at the time of this writing, work on this standard was on hold in order to focus on getting the VoiceXML 2.0 standard out. There are some indications that while the concept of reusable dialog components is technically attractive to application developers, it may fall into an area where vendors agree to disagree for the purpose of distinguishing their products.

- Postal code

- Spelled name

- Spoken and spelled name

- Credit card information

- E-mail address

- Time range

- Duration

- URL

- Confirmation and correction dialog

- Browsable selection list

- Browsable action list

- Address

- Non-fixed alphanumeric string

Multimodal Interfaces

As currently conceived, HTML, WML, and VoiceXML are mutually exclusive. When you implement an interface, you pick one and that's it. Multimodal interfaces, which allow you to intermix elements of visual, voice, and even gestural behavior into a single interface, are a topic of study in research labs around the world. Surfing the Web using a multimodal interface, for example, could involve using a mouse or touch screen for graphical links and filling in forms by dictation (without requiring the keyboard). This mixed style of interaction is of particular interest for speakers of Asian languages, for whom the complexity of written language makes keyboards especially awkward to use.

Although the result may prove easy to use, development of multimodal interfaces is architecturally and technically complex. A multimodal interface must maintain real-time synchronization between the various modes of interaction. New interface paradigms and protocols will have to be developed to manage a single discourse that switches dynamically from one medium to another. So, expect to see multimodal interfaces in the future—but maybe not in the *near* future.

Architectural Issues

In their desire to agree on something and produce a useful result in a short amount of time, the codifiers of the VoiceXML specification were understandably forced to focus quite narrowly on defining the presentation language. Concerning bigger picture architectural issues, they were forced to collectively avert their eyes, because standardizing architecture is broader in scope, takes longer, and is harder to agree on. However, the problem with not addressing architectural issues is that fundamental properties of a real application, such as security, openness, and performance, cannot be handled in a standard way, which dilutes the usefulness of the standard.

Over time, if VoiceXML is successful, surrounding architectural issues are guaranteed to be addressed, but perhaps not by a standards or industry body. For example, no real application is going to be deployed without some sort of built-in security (even though security may have been considered out of scope of the VoiceXML language, the requirements must be met). Options for system-wide capabilities for security, performance management, administration, and reliability include the following:

- *Roll your own:* Build an application-specific capability.

- *Speech vendor supplied:* Use proprietary features of the underlying speech platform.

- *OS supplied:* Use proprietary features of the operating system (for example, Microsoft Windows).

- *Run-time environment supplied:* Use features of the run-time environment (for example, J2EE).

Most likely, applications will incorporate some combination of these options. With both the Microsoft community and the Java community apparently embracing XML as a core technology, I expect to see VoiceXML become another component technology that is assimilated into the competing frameworks from most platform vendors.

Integration with Enterprise Technologies

By "enterprise technologies," I am referring to the entire heavy-duty computing infrastructure that businesses rely on to make their applications scalable, robust, reliable, and available. Some of these commercial-grade technologies include the following:

- Database management systems

- Transaction monitors

- Concurrency control

- Messaging

- Performance and load managers

- Replication and failover

For the most part, these technologies have their roots in conventional, transactional styles of business processing. However, the increasing use of the Web for both e-commerce and customer service is driving integration of these middleware and back-room technologies with Web front ends. Software vendors are starting to provide these enterprise technologies in various middleware packages for use by Web applications: Application servers focus on hosting component functions in a robust environment; Enterprise Application Integration servers focus on providing easy, reliable connectivity to existing back-end applications; Enterprise Information Portals focus on transforming and moving content between producers and consumers.

As a Web presentation medium, VoiceXML will have to become firmly tied in with enterprise technologies. The prototype developed earlier used Cocoon as a framework, which was useful in illuminating the important points in the transformational architecture. However, Cocoon is primarily an XML publishing framework, and it currently adds no value in integration with enterprise technologies.

Addressing Security Concerns

Before VoiceXML can gain widespread acceptance, people will need to feel comfortable about the security of information exchanged using VoiceXML. Security is a complex and multilayered subject, on both technical and psychological levels. Curiously, the technical and psychological aspects don't necessarily reinforce one another in a strictly rational manner. In the psychological realm, "Perception is reality." Consider the following scenarios:

- You give your credit card to a stranger, who physically disappears with it for about 15 minutes, and then returns with a charge slip that you assume is the only imprint taken of your card.

- You call an 800 number, talk to an operator, place an order, and give your confidential credit card details to the operator over the public phone network.

- You visit an e-commerce site on the Internet, place an order, and upload your confidential credit card details to the vendor's computer using RSA encryption of transmitted and received information.

Which scenario is the riskiest? Obviously, there's no "correct" answer, but the third scenario certainly has sparked extensive popular attention and debate, while the first and second scenarios remain relatively unexamined (and hence, assumed "safe"). In fact, in the first scenario, the stranger (for example, a waiter) has ample opportunity to make multiple imprints of your card, and that person will have a physical copy of your signature. In the second scenario, the interaction takes place over the PSTN, which guarantees no security whatsoever. The third scenario is the only one in which any sort of technology is applied specifically for the purposes of security, and it's a high-powered technology at that. However, that doesn't affect the perception that buying things on the Internet is risky.

So, what's the verdict on VoiceXML? VoiceXML effectively combines the second and third scenarios. The connection between a human and a VoiceXML gateway is usually over the PSTN. The connection between the VoiceXML gateway and a Web site is (presumably) over an encrypted connection. One can argue that VoiceXML really doesn't add anything new to the mix, and therefore it shouldn't increase or decrease security concerns relative to existing procedures. On the other hand, from the perspective of computer security specialists, VoiceXML adds another way to access applications from outside. Computer security specialists may perceive this as a potential "hole in the firewall" and want to restrict public access. Restricting access runs counter to the promise of VoiceXML, which is to broaden and simplify access to applications.

Will people perceive a voice-enabled application as "just a phone call" where the other speaker happens to be a computer? Or will people perceive it as a potentially threatening interaction with a computer cleverly disguised as a phone call? Whatever the perception, there will probably be changes to the VoiceXML architecture and language to address such concerns.

Summary

VoiceXML is an important emerging technology. As the first release of a standard developed through the voluntary cooperation of competing vendors under time pressure, VoiceXML 1.0 is minimal and understandably has some warts. However, it draws strength from the experience gained from years of work on speech recognition, speech synthesis, and XML document processing. Because control of the VoiceXML standard was passed to the W3C, it has the potential to mature into a true foundation technology over time. The W3C is expected to release the VoiceXML 2.0 standard in late 2001. That release will begin a process of reinforcing the core VoiceXML language and integrating it with other W3C voice and Web technologies, as well as with Java Enterprise technologies.

Appendix A

A Quick Reference to VoiceXML 1.0 Syntax

Information in the following tables is excerpted from the VoiceXML 1.0 specification (`http://www.voicexml.org/specs/VoiceXML-100.pdf`). Page numbers in Table A-1 refer to page numbers in the VoiceXML 1.0 specification (PDF format).

Table A-1. VoiceXML 1.0 Tags and Attributes

TAG	PURPOSE	ATTRIBUTES	DESCRIPTION	PAGE
`<assign>`	Assign a variable a value.	name	The name of the variable being assigned to.	71
		expr	The new value of the variable.	
`<audio>`	Play an audio clip within a prompt.	src	The URI of the audio prompt. See Appendix E (of the VoiceXML specification) for suggested audio file formats.	46
		caching	See Table A-8.	
		fetchtimeout	See Table A-8.	
		fetchhint	See Table A-8.	
`<block>`	A container of (non-interactive) executable code.	name	The name of a form item variable used to track whether this block is eligible to execute; defaults to an inaccessible internal variable.	54
		expr	The initial value of the form item variable; default is ECMAScript undefined. If initialized to a value, then the form item will not be visited unless the form item variable is cleared.	
		cond	A boolean condition that must also evaluate to `true` in order for the form item to be visited.	

Table A-1. VoiceXML 1.0 Tags and Attributes (continued)

TAG	PURPOSE	ATTRIBUTES	DESCRIPTION	PAGE
`<break>`	JSML element to insert a pause in output.	msecs	The number of milliseconds to pause.	44
		size	A relative pause duration. Possible values are: none, small, medium, or large.	
`<catch>`	Catch an event.	event	The event or events to catch.	38
		count	The occurrence of the event (default is 1). The count allows you to handle different occurrences of the same event differently. Each form item and `<menu>` maintains a counter for each event that occurs while it is being visited; these counters are reset each time the `<menu>` or form item's `<form>` is re-entered.	
		cond	An optional condition to test to see if the event is caught by this element (as in `<catch>`). Defaults to true.	
`<choice>`	Define a menu item.	dtmf	The DTMF sequence for this choice.	28
		next	The URI of next dialog or document.	
		event	Specify an event to be thrown instead of specifying a next.	
		expr	Specify an expression to evaluate instead of specifying a next.	
		caching	See Table A-8.	
		fetchaudio	See Table A-8.	
		fetchhint	See Table A-8. This defaults to the documentfetchhint property.	
		fetchtimeout	See Table A-8.	
`<clear>`	Clear one or more form item variables.	namelist	The names of the form items to be reset. When not specified, all form items in the current form are cleared.	72
`<disconnect>`	Disconnect a session.	--	--	76
`<div>`	JSML element to classify a region of text as a particular type.	type	Possible values are sentence or paragraph.	44

Table A-1. VoiceXML 1.0 Tags and Attributes (continued)

TAG	PURPOSE	ATTRIBUTES	DESCRIPTION	PAGE
<dtmf>	Specify a touch-tone key grammar.	src	The URI specifying the location of the grammar, if it is external.	35
		scope	Either document, which makes the grammar active in all dialogs of the current document (and relevant application leaf docu-ments),or dialog, to make the grammar active throughout the current form. If omitted, the grammar scoping is resolved by looking at the parent element.	
		type	The MIME type of the grammar. If this is omitted, the interpreter context will attempt to determine the type dynamically.	
		caching	See Table A-8.	
		fetchhint	See Table A-8. This defaults to the grammarfetchhint property.	
		fetchtimeout	See Table A-8.	
<else>	Used in <if> elements.	--	--	72
<elseif>	Used in <if> elements.	--	--	72
<emp>	JSML element to change the emphasis of speech output.	level	Specifies the level of emphasis. Possible values are: strong, moderate (default), none or reduced.	44
<enumerate>	Shorthand for enumerat-ing the choices in a menu.	--	--	28
<error>	Catch an error event.	count cond	The event count (as in <catch>). An optional condition to test to see if the event is caught by this element (as in <catch>). Defaults to true.	39
<exit>	Exit a session.	expr	A return expression (e.g. "0", or "oops!").	75
		namelist	Variable names to be returned to interpreter context. The default is to return no variables; this means the interpreter context will receive an empty ECMAScript object.	

Table A-1. VoiceXML 1.0 Tags and Attributes (continued)

TAG	PURPOSE	ATTRIBUTES	DESCRIPTION	PAGE
<field>	Declares an input field in a form.	name	The field item variable in the dialog scope that will hold the result.	50
		expr	The initial value of the form item variable; default is ECMAScript undefined. If initialized to a value, then the form item will not be visited unless the form item variable is cleared.	
		cond	A boolean condition that must also evaluate to true in order for the form item to be visited.	
		type	The type of field (i.e., the name of an internal grammar). This name must be from a standard set supported by all conformant platforms. If not present, <grammar> and/or <dtmf> elements can be specified instead.	
		slot	The name of the grammar slot used to populate the variable (if it is absent, it defaults to the variable name). This attribute is useful in the case where the grammar format being used has a mechanism for returning sets of slot/value pairs and the slot names differ from the field item variable names. If the grammar returns only one slot, as do the built-in type grammars like boolean, then no matter what the slot's name, the field item variable gets the value of that slot.	
		modal	If this is false (the default) all active grammars are turned on while collecting this field. If this is true, then only the field's grammars are enabled: all others are temporarily disabled.	

Table A-1. VoiceXML 1.0 Tags and Attributes (continued)

TAG	PURPOSE	ATTRIBUTES	DESCRIPTION	PAGE
\<filled\>	An action executed when fields are filled.	mode	Either all (the default), or any. If any, this action is executed when any of the specified fields is filled by the last user input. If all, this action is executed when all of the mentioned fields are filled, and at least one has been filled by the last user input. A \<filled\> element in a field item cannot specify a mode.	64
		namelist	The fields to trigger on. For a \<filled\> in a form, namelist defaults to the names (explicit and implicit) of the form's field items. A \<filled\> element in a field item cannot specify a namelist; the namelist in this case is the field item name.	
\<form\>	A dialog for presenting information and collecting data.	id	The name of the form.	17
		scope	The default scope of the form's grammars. If it is dialog then the form grammars are active only in the form. If the scope is document, then the form grammars are active during any dialog in the same document. If the scope is document and the document is an application root document, then the form grammars are active during any dialog in any document of this application. A form grammar that has dialog scope is active only in its form.	
\<goto\>	Go to another dialog in the same or different document.	next	The URI to which to transition.	73
		expr	An ECMAScript expression that yields the URI.	
		nextitem	The name of the next form item to visit in the current form.	

Table A-1. VoiceXML 1.0 Tags and Attributes (continued)

TAG	PURPOSE	ATTRIBUTES	DESCRIPTION	PAGE
\<goto\> *(continued)*		expritem	An ECMAScript expression that yields the name of the next form-item to visit.	
		caching	See Table A-8.	
		fetchaudio	See Table A-8.	
		fetchhint	See Table A-8. This defaults to the documentfetchhint property.	
		fetchtimeout	See Table A-8.	
		Exactly one of next, expr, nextitem, or expritem must be specified.		
\<grammar\>	Specify a speech recognition grammar.	src	The URI specifying the location of the grammar, if it is external.	35
		scope	Either document, which makes the grammar active in all dialogs of the current document (and relevant application leaf documents), or dialog, to make the grammar active throughout the current form. If omitted, the grammar scoping is resolved by looking at the parent element.	
		type	The MIME type of the grammar. If this is omitted, the interpreter context will attempt to determine the type dynamically.	
		caching	See Table A-8.	
		fetchhint	See Table A-8. This defaults to the grammarfetchhint property.	
		fetchtimeout	See Table A-8.	
\<help\>	Catch a help event.	count	The event count (as in \<catch\>).	39
		cond	An optional condition to test to see if the event is caught by this element (as in \<catch\>). Defaults to true.	
\<if\>	Simple conditional logic.	cond	Condition to test.	72
\<initial\>	Declares initial logic upon entry into a (mixed-initiative) form.	name	The name of a form item variable used to track whether the \<initial\> is eligible to execute; defaults to an inaccessible internal variable.	55

Table A-1. VoiceXML 1.0 Tags and Attributes (continued)

TAG	PURPOSE	ATTRIBUTES	DESCRIPTION	PAGE
<initial> (continued)		expr	The initial value of the form item variable; default is ECMAScript undefined. If initialized to a value, then the form item will not be visited unless the form item variable is cleared.	
		cond	A boolean condition that must also evaluate to true in order for the form item to be visited.	
<link>	Specify a transition common to all dialogs in the link's scope.	next	The URI to go to. This URI is a document (perhaps with an anchor to specify the starting dialog), or a dialog in the current document (just a bare anchor).	30
		expr	Like next, except that the URI is dynamically determined by evaluating the given ECMAScript expression.	
		event	The event to throw when the user matches one of the link grammars. Note that only one of next, expr, or event may be specified.	
		caching	See Table A-8.	
		fetchaudio	See Table A-8.	
		fetchhint	See Table A-8. This defaults to the documentfetchhint property.	
		fetchtimeout	See Table A-8.	
<menu>	A dialog for choosing amongst alternative destinations.	id	The identifier of the menu. It allows the menu to be the target of a <goto> or a <submit>.	28
		scope	The menu's grammar scope. If it is dialog—the default—the menu's grammars are only active when the user transitions into the menu. If the scope is document, its grammars are active over the whole document (or if the menu is in the application root document, any loaded document in the application).	

Table A-1. VoiceXML 1.0 Tags and Attributes (continued)

TAG	PURPOSE	ATTRIBUTES	DESCRIPTION	PAGE
`<menu>` *(continued)*		dtmf	When set to true, any choices that do not have explicit DTMF elements are given the implicit ones "1," "2," etc.	
`<meta>`	Define a meta data item as a name/value pair.	name content http-equiv	The name of the meta-data property. The name of the meta-data property. The name of an HTTP response header. Either name or http-equiv must be specified, not both.	66
`<noinput>`	Catch a noinput event.	count cond	The event count (as in `<catch>`). An optional condition to test to see if the event is caught by this element (as in `<catch>`). Defaults to true.	39
`<nomatch>`	Catch a nomatch event.	count cond	The event count (as in `<catch>`). An optional condition to test to see if the event is caught by this element (as in `<catch>`). Defaults to true.	39
`<object>`	Interact with a custom extension.	name	When the object is evaluated, it sets this variable to an ECMAScript value whose type is defined by the object.	60
		expr	The initial value of the form item variable; default is ECMAScript undefined. If initialized to a value, then the form item will not be visited unless the form item variable is cleared.	
		cond	A boolean condition that must also evaluate to true in order for the form item to be visited.	
		classid	The URI specifying the location of the object's implementation. The URI conventions are platform-dependent.	
		codebase	The base path used to resolve relative URIs specified by classid, data, and archive. It defaults to the base URI of the current document.	

Table A-1. VoiceXML 1.0 Tags and Attributes (continued)

TAG	PURPOSE	ATTRIBUTES	DESCRIPTION	PAGE
`<object>` *(continued)*		codetype	The content type of data expected when downloading the object specified by `classid`. When absent it defaults to the value of the `type` attribute.	
		data	The URI specifying the location of the object's data. If it is a relative URI, it is interpreted relative to the `codebase` attribute.	
		type	The content type of the data specified by the `data` attribute.	
		archive	A space-separated list of URIs for archives containing resources relevant to the object, which may include the resources specified by the `classid` and `data` attributes. URIs which are relative are interpreted relative to the `codebase` attribute.	
		caching	See Table A-8.	
		fetchaudio	See Table A-8.	
		fetchhint	See Table A-8. This defaults to the `objectfetchhint` property.	
		fetchtimeout	See Table A-8.	
`<option>`	Specify an option in a `<field>`.	dtmf	The DTMF sequence for this option.	53
		value	The string to assign to the field item variable when a user selects this option, whether by speech or DTMF. The default value for this attribute is the CDATA content of the `<option>` element with leading and trailing white space removed.	
`<param>`	Parameter in `<object>` or `<subdialog>`.	name	The name to be associated with this parameter when the object or sub-dialog is invoked.	69
		expr	An expression that computes the value associated with `name`.	
		value	Associates a literal string value with `name`.	

Table A-1. VoiceXML 1.0 Tags and Attributes (continued)

TAG	PURPOSE	ATTRIBUTES	DESCRIPTION	PAGE
`<param>` *(continued)*		valuetype	One of data or ref, by default data; used to indicate to an object if the value associated with name is data or a URI (ref). This is not used for `<subdialog>`.	
		type	The MIME type of the result provided by a URI if the valuetype is ref; only relevant for uses of `<param>` in `<object>`.	
`<prompt>`	Queue TTS and audio output to the user.	bargein	Control whether a user can interrupt a prompt. Default is true.	44
		cond	An expression telling if the prompt should be spoken. Default is true.	66
		count	A number that allows you to emit different prompts if the user is doing something repeatedly. If omitted, it defaults to "1."	
		timeout	The timeout that will be used for the following user input. The default noinput timeout is platform-specific.	
`<property>`	Control implementation platform settings.	name	The name of the property to set. See Table A-7.	
		value	The value of the property.	
`<pros>`	JSML element to change the prosody of speech output.	rate	Specifies the speaking rate.	44
		vol	Specifies the output volume.	
		pitch	Specifies the pitch.	
		range	Specifies the pitch range.	
`<record>`	Record an audio sample.	name	The field item variable that will hold the recording.	61
		expr	The initial value of the form item variable; default is ECMAScript undefined. If initialized to a value, then the form item will not be visited unless the form item variable is cleared.	
		cond	A boolean condition that must also evaluate to true in order for the form item to be visited.	

Table A-1. VoiceXML 1.0 Tags and Attributes (continued)

TAG	PURPOSE	ATTRIBUTES	DESCRIPTION	PAGE
`<record>` *(continued)*		modal	If this is true (the default) all higher level speech and DTMF grammars are turned off while making the recording. If this is false, speech and DTMF grammars scoped to the form, document, application, and calling documents are listened for. Most implementations will not support simultaneous recognition and recording.	
		beep	If true, a tone is emitted just prior to recording. Defaults to false.	
		maxtime	The maximum duration to record.	
		finalsilence	The interval of silence that indicates end of speech.	
		dtmfterm	If true, a DTMF keypress terminates recording. Defaults to true. The DTMF tone is not part of the recording.	
		type	The MIME format of the resulting recording. Defaults to a platform-specific format.	
`<reprompt>`	Play a field prompt when a field is revisited after an event.	--	--	73
`<return>`	Return from a subdialog.	event namelist	Return, then throw this event. Variable names to be returned to calling dialog. The default is to return no variables; this means the caller will receive an empty ECMAScript object.	75
`<sayas>`	JSML element to modify how a word or phrase is spoken.	phon	The representation of the Unicode International Phonetic Alphabet (IPA)characters that are to be spoken instead of the contained text.	44
		sub	Defines substitute text to be spoken instead of the contained text.	
		class	Possible values are phone, date, digits, literal, currency, number and time. See Table A-9.	

Table A-1. VoiceXML 1.0 Tags and Attributes (continued)

TAG	PURPOSE	ATTRIBUTES	DESCRIPTION	PAGE
<script>	Specify a block of ECMAScript client-side scripting logic.	src	The URI specifying the location of the script, if it is external.	77
		charset	The character encoding of the script designated by src.	
		caching	See Table A-8.	
		fetchhint	See Table A-8. This defaults to the scriptfetchhint property.	
		fetchtimeout	See Table A-8.	
<subdialog>	Invoke another dialog as a subdialog of the current one.	name	The result returned from the sub-dialog, an ECMAScript object whose properties are the ones defined in the namelist attribute of the <return> element.	56
		expr	The initial value of the form item variable; default is ECMAScript undefined. If initialized to a value, then the form item will not be visited unless the form item variable is cleared.	
		cond	A boolean condition that must also evaluate to true in order for the form item to be visited.	
		modal	Controls which grammars are active during the subdialog. If true (the default) all grammars active in the calling dialog are disabled. If false, they remain active.	
		namelist	Same as namelist in <submit>, except that the default is to submit nothing. Only valid when fetching another document.	
		src	The URI of the <subdialog>.	
		method	The request method: get (the default) or post.	
		enctype	The MIME encoding type of the sub-mitted document. The default is application/x-www-form-urlencoded. Interpreters may support additional encoding types.	

Table A-1. VoiceXML 1.0 Tags and Attributes (continued)

TAG	PURPOSE	ATTRIBUTES	DESCRIPTION	PAGE
<subdialog> *(continued)*		caching	See Table A-8.	
		fetchaudio	See Table A-8.	
		fetchtimeout	See Table A-8.	
		fetchhint	See Table A-8.	
<submit>	Submit values to a document server.	next	The URI to which the query is submitted.	74
		expr	Like next, except that the URI is dynamically determined by evaluating the given ECMAScript expression. One of next or expr is required.	
		namelist	The list of variables to submit. By default, all the named field item variables are submitted. If a namelist is supplied, it may contain individual variable references which are submitted with the same qualification used in the namelist.	
		method	The request method: get (the default) or post.	
		enctype	The MIME encoding type of the submitted document. The default is application/x-www-form-urlencoded. Interpreters may support additional encoding types.	
		caching	See Table A-8.	
		fetchaudio	See Table A-8.	
		fetchhint	See Table A-8. This defaults to the documentfetchhint property.	
		fetchtimeout	See Table A-8.	
		If an ECMAScript object o is the target of a submit then all its (ECMAScript) fields f1, f2, . . . are submitted using the names o f1, o f2, etc.		
<throw>	Throw an event.	event	The event being thrown.	38

Table A-1. VoiceXML 1.0 Tags and Attributes (continued)

TAG	PURPOSE	ATTRIBUTES	DESCRIPTION	PAGE
<transfer>	Transfer the caller to another destination.	name	The outcome of the transfer attempt. (One of: busy, noanswer, network_busy, near_end_disconnect, far_end_disconnect, network_disconnect.)	63
		expr	The initial value of the form item variable; default is ECMAScript undefined. If initialized to a value, then the form item will not be visited unless the form item variable is cleared.	
		cond	A boolean condition that must also evaluate to true in order for the form item to be visited.	
		dest	The URI of the destination (phone, IP telephony address).	
		destexpr	An ECMAScript expression yielding the URI of the destination.	
		bridge	This attribute determines what to do once the call is connected. If bridge is true, document interpretation suspends until the transferred call terminates. If it is false, as soon as the call connects, the platform throws a telephone.disconnect.transfer.	
		connecttimeout	The time to wait while trying to connect the call before returning the noanswer condition. Default is platform-specific.	
		maxtime	The time that the call is allowed to last, or 0 if it can last arbitrarily long. Only applies if bridge is true. Default is 0.	
<value>	Insert the value of an expression in a prompt.	expr	The expression to render.	46
		class	The <sayas> class of the variable (e.g., phone, date, currency). The valid formats are the same as those supported in the <sayas> speech markup. See Table A-9.	

Table A-1. VoiceXML 1.0 Tags and Attributes (continued)

TAG	PURPOSE	ATTRIBUTES	DESCRIPTION	PAGE
`<value>` *(continued)*		mode	The type of rendering: `tts` (the default), or `recorded`.	
		recsrc	The URI of the audio files to be concatenated when mode is recorded.	
`<var>`	Declare a variable.	name	The name of the variable that will hold the result.	71
		expr	The initial value of the variable (optional). If there is no `expr` attribute, the variable retains its current value, if any. Variables start out with the ECMAScript value undefined if they are not given initial values.	
`<vxml>`	Top-level element in each VoiceXML document.	version	The version of VoiceXML of this document (required). The initial version number is 1.0.	14
		base	The base URI.	
		lang	The language and locale type for this document.	
		application	The URI of this document's application root document, if any.	

Table A-2. VoiceXML Variable Scopes

VARIABLE SCOPE	DESCRIPTION
session	These are read-only variables that pertain to an entire user session. They are declared and set by the interpreter context. New session variables cannot be declared by VoiceXML documents. See Table A-3.
application	These are declared with `<var>` elements that are children of the application root document's `<vxml>` element. They are initialized when the application root document is loaded. They exist while the application root document is loaded and are visible to the root document and any other loaded application leaf document.
document	These variables are declared with `<var>` elements that are children of the document's `<vxml>` element. They are initialized when the document is loaded. They exist while the document is loaded, and are visible only within that document.

Table A-2. VoiceXML Variable Scopes (continued)

VARIABLE SCOPE	DESCRIPTION
dialog	Each dialog (<form> or <menu>) has a dialog scope that exists while the user is visiting that dialog, and which is visible to the element of that dialog. Dialog variables are declared by <var> child elements of <form>, by <var> elements inside executable content (e.g., <block> content or catch element content), and by the various form item elements. The child <var> elements of <form> are initialized when the form is first visited. The <var> elements inside executable content are initialized when the executable content is executed. The form item variables are initialized when the form item is collected.
(anonymous)	Each <block>, <filled>, and catch element defines a new anonymous scope to contain variables declared in that element.

Table A-3. VoiceXML 1.0 Standard Session Variables

VARIABLE	DESCRIPTION
session.telephone.ani	*Automatic Number Identification.* This variable provides the result from the Automatic Number Identification service that provides the receiver of a telephone call with the number of the calling phone. This information is provided only if the service is supported, and is undefined otherwise.
session.telephone.dnis	*Dialed Number Identification Service.* This variable provides the result from the Dialed Number Identification Service that identifies for the receiver of a call the number that the caller dialed. This information is provided only if the service is supported, and is undefined otherwise.

Table A-3. VoiceXML 1.0 Standard Session Variables (continued)

VARIABLE	DESCRIPTION
session.telephone.iidigits	*Information Indicator Digit.* This variable provides information about the originating line (e.g., pay phone, cellular service, special operator handling, prison) of the caller. Telecordia publishes the complete list of II digits in Section 1 of each volume of the "Local Exchange Routing Guide". This information is provided only if the service is supported, and is undefined otherwise.
session.telephone.uui	*User to User Information.* This variable returns supplementary information provided as part of an ISDN call set-up from a calling party. This information is provided only if the service is supported, and is undefined otherwise.

Table A-4. VoiceXML 1.0 Predefined Events

EVENT	DESCRIPTION
cancel	The user has requested to cancel playing of the current prompt.
telephone.disconnect.hangup	The user has hung up.
telephone.disconnect.transfer	The user has been transferred unconditionally to another line and will not return.
exit	The user has asked to exit.
help	The user has asked for help.
noinput	The user has not responded within the timeout interval.
nomatch	The user input something, but it was not recognized.

Table A-5. VoiceXML 1.0 Predefined Errors

ERROR	DESCRIPTION
error.badfetch	A failed fetch. This may be the result, for example, of a missing document, a malformed URI, a communications error during the process of fetching the document, a timeout, a security violation, or a malformed document.
error.semantic	A run-time error was found in the VoiceXML document (e.g., a divide by 0, substring bounds error, or an undefined variable was referenced).
error.noauthorization	The user is not authorized to perform the operation requested (such as dialing an invalid telephone number, or one for which the user is not allowed to call).
error.unsupported.format	The requested resource has a format that is not supported by the platform (e.g., an unsupported grammar format, audio file format, object type, or MIME type).
error.unsupported.*element*	The platform does not support the given *element*. For instance, if a platform does not implement <record>, it must throw error.unsupported.record. This allows an author to use event handling to adapt to different platform capabilities.

Table A-6. VoiceXML 1.0 Built-in Types (Grammars)

BUILT-IN TYPE	DESCRIPTION
boolean	Inputs include affirmative and negative phrases appropriate to the current locale. DTMF 1 is yes and 2 is no. The result is ECMAScript true for "yes" or false for "no". The value will be submitted as the string "true" or the string "false". If the field value is subsequently used in a prompt, it will be spoken as an affirmative or negative phrase appropriate to the current locale.
date	Valid spoken inputs include phrases that specify a date, including a month, day, and year. DTMF inputs are: four digits for the year, followed by two digits for the month, and two digits for the day. The result is a fixed-length date string with format yyyymmdd (e.g., "20000704"). If the year is not specified, yyyy is returned as "????"; if the month is not specified mm is returned as "??"; and if the day is not specified dd is returned as "??".

Table A-6. VoiceXML 1.0 Built-in Types (Grammars)(continued)

BUILT-IN TYPE	DESCRIPTION
digits	Valid spoken or DTMF inputs include one or more digits, 0 through 9. The result is a string of digits. If the field value is subsequently used in a prompt, it will be spoken as a sequence of digits. A user can say for example "two one two seven", but not "twenty one hundred and twenty-seven".
currency	Valid spoken inputs include phrases that specify a currency amount. For DTMF input, the "*" key will act as the decimal point. The result is a string with the format UUUmm.nn, where UUU is the three-character currency indicator according to ISO standard 4217:1995 or null if not spoken by the user. If the field value is subsequently used in a prompt, it will be spoken as a currency amount appropriate to the current locale.
number	Valid spoken inputs include phrases that specify numbers, such as "one hundred twenty-three", or "five point three". Valid DTMF input includes positive numbers entered using digits and "*" to represent a decimal point. The result is a string of digits from 0 to 9 and may optionally include a decimal point (".") and/or a plus or minus sign.
phone	Valid spoken inputs include phrases that specify a phone number. DTMF asterisk "*" represents "x". The result is a string containing a telephone number consisting of a string of digits and optionally containing the character "x" to indicate a phone number with an extension. For North America, a result could be "8005551234x789".
time	Valid spoken inputs include phrases that specify a time, including hours and minutes. The result is a five-character string in the format hhmmx, where x is one of "a" for AM, "p" for PM, "h" to indicate a time specified using 24 hour clock, or "?" to indicate an ambiguous time. Input can be via DTMF. Because there is no DTMF convention for specifying AM/PM, in the case of DTMF input, the result will always end with "h" or "?". If the field value is subsequently used in a prompt, the value will be spoken as a time appropriate to the current locale.

Table A-7. VoiceXML 1.0 Predefined Properties

PROPERTY	DESCRIPTION
confidencelevel	The speech recognition confidence level, a float value in the range of 0.0 to 1.0. Results are rejected (a nomatch event is thrown) when the engine's confidence in its interpretation is below this threshold. A value of 0.0 means minimum confidence is needed for a recognition, and a value of 1.0 requires maximum confidence. The default value is 0.5.
sensitivity	Set the sensitivity level. A value of 1.0 means that it is highly sensitive to quiet input. A value of 0.0 means it is least sensitive to noise. The default value is 0.5.
speedvsaccuracy	A hint specifying the desired balance between speed vs. accuracy. A value of 0.0 means fastest recognition. A value of 1.0 means best accuracy. The default is value 0.5.
completetimeout	The speech timeout value to use when an active grammar is matched. The default is platform-dependent.
incompletetimeout	The speech timeout to use when no active grammar has been matched. The default is platform-dependent.
interdigittimeout	The inter-digit timeout value to use when recognizing DTMF input. The default is platform-dependent.
termtimeout	The terminating timeout to use when recognizing DTMF input. The default value is "0s".
termchar	The terminating DTMF character for DTMF input recognition. The default value is "#".
bargein	The bargein attribute to use for prompts. Setting this to true allows barge-in by default. Setting it to false disallows barge-in. The default value is "true".
timeout	The time after which a noinput event is thrown by the platform. The default value is platform-dependent.
caching	Either safe to never trust the cache when fetching, or fast to always trust the cache. The default value is fast.
audiofetchhint	This tells the platform whether or not it can attempt to optimize dialog interpretation by pre-fetching audio. The value is either safe to say that audio is only fetched when it is needed, never before; prefetch to permit, but not require the platform to pre-fetch the audio; or stream to allow it to stream the audio fetches. The default value is prefetch.

Table A-7. VoiceXML 1.0 Predefined Properties (continued)

PROPERTY	DESCRIPTION
documentfetchhint	Tells the platform whether or not documents may be pre-fetched. The value is either safe (the default), or prefetch.
grammarfetchhint	Tells the platform whether or not grammars may be pre-fetched. The value is either prefetch (the default), or safe.
objectfetchhint	Tells the platform whether the URI contents for <object> may be pre-fetched or not. The values are prefetch (the default), or safe.
scriptfetchhint	Tells whether scripts may be pre-fetched or not. The values are prefetch (the default), or safe.
fetchaudio	The URI of the audio to play while waiting for a document to be fetched. The default is not to play any audio. There are no fetchaudio properties for audio, grammars, objects, and scripts.
fetchtimeout	The timeout for fetches. The default value is platform-dependent.
inputmodes	The input modes to enable: dtmf and voice. On platforms that support both modes, inputmodes defaults to "dtmf voice". To disable speech recognition, set inputmodes to "dtmf". To disable DTMF, set it to "voice". One use for this would be to turn off speech recognition in noisy environments. Another would be to conserve speech recognition resources by turning them off where the input is always expected to be DTMF.

Table A-8. VoiceXML 1.0 Resource Fetching Properties

PROPERTY	DESCRIPTION
caching	Either safe to force a query to fetch the most recent copy of the content, or fast to use the cached copy of the content if it has not expired. If not specified, a value derived from the innermost caching property is used.
fetchtimeout	The interval to wait for the content to be returned before throwing an error.badfetch event. If not specified, a value derived from the innermost fetchtimeout property is used.
fetchhint	Defines when the interpreter context should retrieve content from the server. prefetch indicates a file may be downloaded when the page is loaded, whereas safe indicates a file that should only be downloaded when actually needed. In the case of a very large file (implying long download times) or a streaming audio source, stream indicates to the interpreter context to begin processing the content as it arrives and should not wait for full retrieval of the content. If not specified, a value derived from the innermost relevant *fetchhint property is used.

Table A-9. VoiceXML 1.0 Say-As Text Types

TEXT TYPE	DESCRIPTION
currency	The contained text is a currency amount. Leading and trailing currency symbols are ignored.
date	The contained text is a date.
digits	The contained text is a string of digits.
literal	The contained text is a string literal.
number	The contained text is a number.
phone	The contained text is a phone number.
time	The contained text is a time of day.

Index

apress™

License Agreement (Single-User Products)

THIS IS A LEGAL AGREEMENT BETWEEN YOU, THE END USER, AND APRESS. BY OPENING THE SEALED DISK PACKAGE, YOU ARE AGREEING TO BE BOUND BY THE TERMS OF THIS AGREEMENT. IF YOU DO NOT AGREE TO THE TERMS OF THIS AGREEMENT, PROMPTLY RETURN THE UNOPENED DISK PACKAGE AND THE ACCOMPANYING ITEMS (INCLUDING WRITTEN MATERIALS AND BINDERS AND OTHER CONTAINERS) TO THE PLACE YOU OBTAINED THEM FOR A FULL REFUND.

APRESS SOFTWARE LICENSE

1. GRANT OF LICENSE. Apress grants you the right to use one copy of this enclosed Apress software program (the "SOFTWARE") on a single terminal connected to a single computer (e.g., with a single CPU). You may not network the SOFTWARE or otherwise use it on more than one computer or computer terminal at the same time.

2. COPYRIGHT. The SOFTWARE copyright is owned by Apress and is protected by United States copyright laws and international treaty provisions. Therefore, you must treat the SOFTWARE like any other copyrighted material (e.g., a book or musical recording) except that you may either (a) make one copy of the SOFTWARE solely for backup or archival purposes, or (b) transfer the SOFTWARE to a single hard disk, provided you keep the original solely for backup or archival purposes. You may not copy the written material accompanying the SOFTWARE.

3. OTHER RESTRICTIONS. You may not rent or lease the SOFTWARE, but you may transfer the SOFTWARE and accompanying written materials on a permanent basis provided you retain no copies and the recipient agrees to the terms of this Agreement. You may not reverse engineer, decompile, or disassemble the SOFTWARE. If SOFTWARE is an update, any transfer must include the update and all prior versions.

4. By breaking the seal on the disc package, you agree to the terms and conditions printed in the Apress License Agreement. If you do not agree with the terms, simply return this book with the still-sealed CD package to the place of purchase for a refund.

DISCLAIMER OF WARRANTY

NO WARRANTIES. Apress disclaims all warranties, either express or implied, including, but not limited to, implied warranties of merchantability and fitness for a particular purpose, with respect to the SOFTWARE and the accompanying written materials. The software and any related documentation is provided "as is." You may have other rights, which vary from state to state.

NO LIABILITIES FOR CONSEQUENTIAL DAMAGES. In no event shall be liable for any damages whatsoever (including, without limitation, damages from loss of business profits, business interruption, loss of business information, or other pecuniary loss) arising out of the use or inability to use this Apress product, even if Apress has been advised of the possibility of such damages. Because some states do not allow the exclusion or limitation of liability for consequential or incidental damages, the above limitation may not apply to you.

U.S. GOVERNMENT RESTRICTED RIGHTS

The SOFTWARE and documentation are provided with RESTRICTED RIGHTS. Use, duplication, or disclosure by the Government is subject to restriction as set forth in subparagraph (c) (1) (ii) of The Rights in Technical Data and Computer Software clause at 52.227-7013. Contractor/manufacturer is Apress, 901 Grayson Street, Suite 204, Berkeley, California, 94710.

This Agreement is governed by the laws of the State of California.

Should you have any questions concerning this Agreement, or if you wish to contact Apress for any reason, please write to Apress, 901 Grayson Street, Suite 204, Berkeley, California, 94710.